PETER

Collected Poems

Oxford*Poets*

CARCANET

First published in 2002 by
Carcanet Press Limited
4th Floor, Conavon Court
12–16 Blackfriars Street
Manchester M3 5BQ

Acknowledgements
Grateful acknowledgement is made to Harry Chambers and
Phoenix Pamphlet Poets for poems from *The Small Containers*;
to Harry Chambers, E.J. Morten and Peterloo Poets for poems
from *The Snowing Globe*; and to Peter Jay and Anvil Press
for poems from *Night Watch*.

ISBN 1 903039 57 6 (trade paperback)
ISBN 1 903039 58 4 (library edition)
ISBN 1 903039 59 2 (limited edition)

The publisher acknowledges financial assistance
from the Arts Council of England

Set in Monotype Garamond by XL Publishing Services, Tiverton
Printed and bound in England by SRP Ltd, Exeter

Contents

Giles Scupham, 1962–2001

Our love is a dark lantern; your secrets keep
Under this driftwood tree, dark brick, stiff clay,
And all the foreground speaks of distances.
Caught in your indirection, we lose our way

To find you again, alone and undispersed,
Briefly at home in colour, line, the light
Echoed by patched water. Then cloud and leaf
Turn in the loose wind, follow you out of sight.

The Small Containers

Man on the Edge

Some people's faces fit central and dead;
His seems to skate off the sides of his head.
He leaves bits on his plate, the crusts from his bread.

He walks in the gutter and rides on the pavement,
Goes sightseeing in Woolworth's to feel different,
Hates being converted or told to repent.

He hunches or perches on a ledge or a rim,
Angling for corners where the light's pretty dim;
Has a horror of chairs folding great arms round him.

At the B Minor Mass or the May Queen's Coronation,
Amongst the Oh So Faces, his is the baffled one
Counting stripes on deck-chairs, chatting up a stone.

At night he and his darling make it nicely again,
But he ends up unsnuggled, watching the windowpane,
Resists the gemütlich caress of his Slumberdown.

He eats with his teeth and has no faith in glue,
Which won't stick with him, though it might with you,
And has lost more money than anyone thinks true.

He laughs much, with what could nearly be innocence,
Tickling himself with feathers of nonsense;
His words all lean sideways, blown by his eloquence.

He likes gappy-grin gargoyles, girls and cheap wine,
Pegs nodding like blue-tits on the washing-line,
Badly smashed-up people who are getting on fine.

He dislikes wasp-traps, pills and Education,
Considering blah blah what is good for the nation,
Lukewarm bathwater driptap conversation.

His favourite nightmare is of Lincoln Cathedral.
He's rigid on a plank in the tall transept angle,
Till the floor zooms up to break him and his fall.

When he shuts off and his face looks no more,
He's deploying escape routes from there to the door,
Wondering if he swallowed his heart cooked or raw.

When he's finally blown to Kingdoms Here and To Come,
With soft soap and music at a schmalzy crematorium,
He won't queue with the rest, he'll try and hitch home.

The Small Containers

Guilty, after a death, mourners conspire
To hide the evidence. The tumbled bric-à-brac
Burns, rots, is auctioned. Little survives
The rough dispersal. But this battered flock
Of small, obsequious containers
Will always come in handy. In our attics
Old cases slump, their black initials theme
For pure conjecture. Gorged with junk,
They dream of labelled journeys, destinations.
Scuffed box-files, trunks, and shaky cabinets
Accept the long confession of our lives.
Such confidants reserve their treachery
For when each cluttered room holds a last breath,
Marking our dissolution. Then, casually,
They spew us cleanly out; embrace our children.

Clean Sweep

Of late, he would recover the past, which slipped
Uneasily in and out his fingers. One object said
Skating on good black ice; another, climbs in the Highlands.

He had kept everything; annotated his life
With concert programmes, Cornish moss in an envelope,
Sepia dons immolated by Stearns, Photographers.

Reminder now of countless hurried breakfasts,
That faded correspondence; the monarchs' heads
Shifting their formal gaze, now left, now right.

These we chivvied into cardboard boxes:
Cards from German cousins, Museum papers,
Letters from ravaged France, passing the final censors.

In the study, Symonds' Renaissance, Jowett's Plato,
Refused to echo the applause some fifty summers old,
Dutifully given as Sanderson of Oundle presented them.

Order was reasserted. Some few weeks later
We destroyed casually the shots of his cherry tree
Discovered in the camera, three frames of film exposed.

Small Pets

Tipped from their carrier bags, they cannot hide
From creeping ambushes of stroke and pull.
Greedy and brief the love that these provide.
Quivering, nuzzling; eyes alert or dull,
They hover paws-in-air, edge nervous steps,
As much themselves as we can let them be.
We bait their timid breath with kitchen scraps
And gaze at eating as at wizardry.

No status here of clown or confidant.
They will not sleep on cushions, come to hand
Like those felicitous ones to whom we grant,
As favours, words they cannot understand.
Lacking such freedom and such privilege,
They feel our fondling fingers droop, grow cold.
Secure inside some makeshift hermitage,
Their meagre repertoire is quickly told.

Decrepit pensioners, in their shade allowed
To churr on wheels or crouch on dampened grass,
The guilt they offer hardens like a shroud.
We wait, impatient, for their cup to pass.
Then, when the draggled stiffness and the chill
Announce a death as vivid as a birth,
Our serious children make gay funeral,
Huddled upon the decorated earth.

Drawing Book

Their pictures mirror still
A country long denied us:
Her stable coloured houses,
His huge delightful birds,
The only family standing
Where the sun's yellow counter
Extends its innocent rays.
And all our trivial angers
Can draw no dark clouds over,
Or give an unjust ending
To their brief simple stories
Of once upon a time.

Hard are the paths which lead us
To reconciliation,
Despite the prayers we offer
For guiding and for guarding.
Now as they lie sleeping,
Softly deeply breathing
In close untidy darkness,
We gently move about them
And marvel at their faces,
Asking of these forgiveness,
Whose inexperienced fingers
Absolve us and renew.

Four Fish

Gay chalks and a blackboard. Watch Kate trace
Four fish. They hover softly in dark space,

Warming the kitchen by their tranquil glow,
Infallible, heraldic. Pictures flow

With casual extravagance, to live
Assured as flowers, and as fugitive.

These lack all claim or pretext; merely say:
Here is a world, and it behaves this way.

They mock our making by their candour; lift
Our hesitant, blunt senses; are true gift

For Rilke's Angels. Knowing our task is
To feed the invisible with our images,

We rub the blackboard clear: four fish allow
To swim in darker space more subtly now.

Wolves

It is cool October. Now the evening gathers
The garden into strangeness.
Leaves exchange unpleasing rumours;
Children's voices rise and fall.
'The wolves are coming! The wolves are coming!'
Taking substance from the smelly corner
Where the compost rots, their grey pelts
Shining with autumnal dews,
They huff the youngest with their chilly breath
To the safety of a lit kitchen.

Upstairs, a bedroom curtain flaps emptily.
'Shut the window.' His head lolls, reassured
By the firm love-words.
Outside, the night is troubled,
And Goat shivers, tethered in the zodiac.
While wolf-makers swap innocent glances,
Intent on a bedtime story,
The small child tosses. It is not easy
To have wolves wished upon you.
They wait patiently beside the bed.

Games

I

I spy with my little eye
The shift of leaves. In a thunderous sky
Birds with wooden faces fly.
Stiffly the wallflowers' dried blood
Curls on the grass. A cloud's hood
Covers the sun. Dark buds
Lean heavily over the crumbling wall
Where spiders work. Pervading all,
Something beginning with the Fall.

II

Growing warmer, growing colder,
Moving softly over deep carpet to
The numb gleam of silver,
Reflections in bevelled glass.
Lifting the velvet cloths,
Fingers in the lustre jug,
Growing warmer, growing colder.
Standing shaken, fingers
Scratching the books.
Dust in the air. Down the stair well
Eyes move, limbs move,
Traversing the space between
Bedroom, kitchen.
Growing warmer, colder. Colder.

College Reunion

Cool and black, cool and black,
The mourners cheat the almanack.

Trim on the consecrated lawn,
Their washed cars tremble in the sun.

'Nothing stirs behind, beyond,'
Say the heavy fish in the College pond.

'Your picklock name, your borrowed face,
The sprig of rosemary in your case,

Will not charm back that distant flock
Of gilded hours to the chapel clock.'

Now is the dumb warmth of stone,
A tourist, idle and alone.

But Genius Loci gestures where
An old room waits on an old stair.

Sherry at seven, dinner at eight:
After the Wake, the Lying in State.

As shadows gather in the hall
Where soft-foot waiters beck and call,

Minerva's minor deities
Adjust formalities and ties,

Their gowns and wrinkles hiding scars
Of wounds sustained in alien wars.

Calm portraits guard the long libation
Of Latin grace and slow oration.

Mnemosyne to the toast replies,
Rustling her withered images,

But candlelight and wine disguise
The pennies weighing on her eyes.

Time is gnawed down to the bone;
The mourners and the dead are one.

Outing for the Handicapped Children

The held boat rocks to the staithe. Cautious, absorbed,
The children coax their limbs to their intent.
Her crutch blinks in the sun. Cheated by absent muscles,
He sinks with dazed acceptance to the grass.
About them, nervous in the gentle air,
Hands hover and fuss; glad to be ignored.

The day swells, unfolds. Laughter, scattered talk.
We hoist through dripping locks, part the dry sedges,
Plotting a fluent course by trees and swans
While summer, soft and potent, blurs through the awning,
Soaking the varnished wood. Torpid as grounded bees,
Their dangled fingers comb the river's skin.

They manage, patient; share with buns and fruit
A shaming kindness. Tamed, drowsy, separate,
We offer them our slow unnatural smiles;
Tremble with intimations of their pain.
The day we gave, or stole, edges away;
The cool depths pull their faces from the light.

History Lesson

The air beats to the quickening tempo of their voices,
Who bob and scuffle; nonchalantly sustain
A sense of chaos; knot, unloose, assume
A communal identity.

Their records are unwritten, chronicled in his quick stutter,
Her withdrawal, locked unwillingly inside a magic circle.
Unhappiness sets apart, while the agreeable others
Relate; confident, anonymous.

How should they make secure a sense of time, whom Now,
Warm and imperative, suffices? Lively eyes
Gaze curiously down the grave, dead years.
It was all long ago.

Or sense of place, whose natural country is
The brief extension of their senses? A sunburnt room,
Its coughs and fidgets, dust and scattered books,
Seems, for the moment, home.

Obediently they stray through chequered centuries,
Where priest and king stand tonsured or austere;
Trace with a painful care each distant feature,
Heraldic, legendary.

This is correct. Her clumsy picture brings an image home;
His careless pages learn an awkward love.
The world, as they gossip seriously away,
Grows forty minutes older.

Un Peu d'Histoire: Dordogne

Freed from the cortex, axe and arrow-head
Lay out the cold millennia stone-dead.
Bastides bake on their grids. Historic crime
Demands we make a fairy tale of time.
The soft heart rots: a fossil carapace
Decks the dark hill-top, and each golden face
Smells of an ancient pox. The rough men hide.
We drink our sun and wine unfortified,
Sweating it out where giant glades of stone
Elide the cowl and hauberk into one.
Great Romanesque façades. Bleached timbers lean
By lime-washed naves, corruptible, sea-green.
In faded reds and blacks, the names rank where
The small brass badges tarnish. Triste, la guerre.
Fusillé. Asphyxié par le gaz. Towns burn;
A tufted pill-box haunts the river's turn.
In our worn house, the cat-ice floorboards crack.
Whose hands stretched suffering iron on the rack,
Made clocks from bombs – hands detonate lost hours –
Brackets from bayonets? The boar's head lours.
Sad wayside flowers and boards. In molten air,
A metal Poilu dies on every square.

Eye Clinic

Is Purgatory like this? The white dispassionate recorders
At their lecterns; those dark confessionals, greedy
To share our bodies' secrets? The curative process,
Compound of hope and fear, subdues; compels.
We sit humbly on scuffed benches, silent,
Each guarding warily his accustomed hurt,
Moving to names in the half-light. A child's cry
Tenses our separate selves. Incurious heads
Lift at a passing nurse, tracking her progress
Down the long aisles. Some, confused, wander
Like first-day schoolboys, clutching case-notes.

Here, all eyes are self-conscious, burdensome.
Neutered, drained of all elements which make for focus,
The backdrop lays no claim to our perception;
Colour would be too hostile. Dimly, pain
Silts up the ragged edges of our vision
From globes which swell above like giant eyeballs,
Distended, luminous. Walls ebb and flow like dreams.

Pain

Wanton, domestic,
My dear, I know your ways:

Profaning the temple,
Beating on the ear-drum,

Pounding a peasant dance,
Brutish, repetitive,

Teetering high-heeled
In the craters of dying teeth.

Driving carelessly,
You scrape on a long nerve,

Or pulling a knife on me,
Whittle a finger to screaming point.

These, your high feast days,
Almost too much to bear.

Cutting loose soon palls:
Back to the old routine,

Lying down naked,
Contrite, seductive.

When we make love, you know
I always come back for more,

Roused by your fancy bites,
Sweet nips and scratches.

I lie to the crook of your arm,
Sweating and shaken.

We know each other well.
Your absence terrifies.

They say you are a warning;
A warning to be gay.

No Cause

No cause, no cause. Adrift, he felt limbs tremble,
His tight skin burn, and the untidy room,
Stunned by such rough assault, crouch watchful back,
A frigid sun dappling the chequered floor.

Far worlds away, the children's careless voices
Tripped and fell. Only the clock drove on
Its balanced monotone. In that harsh pause
She stood as numb as ice, the tears in check.

And all was alien, lost: the cup she held,
The dumb cat shifting on the sill
And the green garden-light beyond the door.
How could there be for this no cause, no cause?

Waiting Room Fish

Are use, not ornament. Communicative dogs
Can bear a ruinous love; come back for more.
Who talks to fish? Yet the lit cage designs
To make us temperate, and its inmates move
Passive and cool receptacles for pain.

The filter softly gargles. Blubber mouths
Scavenge the glass. Eyes are bleak, incurious.

Thoughts too should steer at ease about their confines,
Skitter and twist, or balance fluently;
Learning from this prim hygiene to reject
The deviant nibbler of his neighbour's fins;
The wretch who palpitates in dark recesses.

Even in death didactic. How agreeable
To surface slowly: blank, inverted, ludicrous.

Arena

The puppets danced. And the child stared,
Serious and still. 'How do they work, Giles?'
'By magic.' Then, corrective, the quick codicil:
'By string.' Fluent Magic, ominous, delightful,
Presents himself in terrors, expectations,
Or six Red Admirals on the buddleia.
String, though somewhat lacking in éclat,
Is equally at home here; serves his term
Among Kate's schoolbooks, helps to patch a quarrel,
Or by a reasonable beneficence allays
Those sudden sobs which shake a darkening bedroom.

Let their hostility advance our interests,
Like oil and vinegar. We must admire
Magic's deft web, String's workaday solutions;
This dance of Retiarius and Secutor
In our arena. But, should the crunch come,
May any Emperor on hand to give his verdict
Turn his thumbs down for String.

The Snowing Globe

The Occasion

The cups and glasses started to unfold
Warm gestures against different sorts of cold.

The girl was dark and very luminous.
She was herself, and that, for sure, was precious.

The air was mild, the air was calm and tender:
Her bones were tricksy, and her wrist was slender.

The man read poems in a handsome way,
Their shapes now somewhat grave, now somewhat gay.

The lissom wife let fingers trip and stir
At her guitar. Softly, he looked at her;

Moved by the thoughtful stranger who lay hid
In that familiar sweet flesh and blood.

Smiles walked on tiptoe: bright or lazy birds
Which settled on the different sorts of words.

Some glasses brim so full of mortal light,
They make a Jack O'Lantern of the night.

Oh, strong amazements time is careless of.
Oh world, who spares her creatures little love.

The girl was dark; her hushed, observant eyes
Spun the room widdershins, back again clockwise.

She was a brilliant fluttering in a ring.
She was, he thought, a quick, precarious thing.

The curtains came down softly on this play
When glasses and guitar conspired to say:

Alone, on different sorts of roads, we go,
Through sheets of flowers and through sheets of snow.

The Snowing Globe

A trick of the fingers
And the world turns.
A drift of tiny snow.

The frosted reindeer,
Lost in a Christmas wood –
They will make room for us.

Thicker, colder the airs.
Softly, neatly,
You hurry to where I wait.

Your rough black coat
Brushes the sidling flakes.
They cling like burrs.

Under an ancient light,
Snow in your dark hair
Dissolves; glistens like tears.

Our eyes take fire.
We are preserved in amber
These fourteen crystal years.

Somewhere, our unborn children
Smile with your smile.
The snow is settling now.

Children Dancing

for Margaret

I

What shall we throw down
To image again the one theme,
Link our games to the one game?

The ache of print in stiff books,
The wrinkled vanities each day employs,
Our distances, our reservations.

What shall we piece together
To image again the one theme,
Link our games to the one game?

These fragile bones, built from dust,
A tinsel shade, a skein of music,
Our laughter, our serious eyes.

Now we accept all broken steps,
Provisional identities;
Wait on the eyes' absorption

Till patterns flow to the one pattern,
Delay Time's hatchet-men,
Her separations and habitual snows.

The elemental and undying children
Shift soft colours on a tolerant darkness.
We warm ourselves at their unwearying fires.

II

The cracks in an old floor
Crinkle across my eyes.
I feel threadbare.

How vulnerable she is:
I know her sweats, her tremors.
Admiration distresses me.

Having unlearnt such candour,
Must I become Prometheus,
Stealing fire from a skimpy body

Whose sweet, unsteady flesh,
Trailed hair, spaced fingers,
Are close and far as first love?

Supple in a damp leotard,
Her painted face beaten by light,
She is that Roman horn

Ever spilling, ever full.
Through her, our words and music
Assume strong presences.

A child moves towards death,
Shaping with each slight gesture
Ignorant benedictions.

III

Shadow and exhaustion overtake us.
After occasions of sunburst
All movement concurs toward silence.

Rigged frames, floods, battens,
Wear a shut, flimsy look,
Slewed to the blank flats.

Can I thread the dancers back
On to your voice of rough silver,
The sprung energies of music?

No. Laughing with linked peers,
They dismantle their borrowed faces,
Scatter our laborious archives.

We have our photographs:
Butterflies, slowly stiffening
In aromas of crushed laurel.

Rather, let memory play out
Her own ring dances and mandalas;
Compose cool, brilliant landscapes

Where we and the lost children can rehearse
Our affirmations, our secret codes,
Across the drifting years.

Mayday

Shall I enter into something like a conversation
With a world where old men, slow and faded,
Move quietly about the new green lanes?

Shall I walk where small suburban breezes
Scatter the light prams up and down the streets,
Lifting the mothers' nervous, fluttering dresses?

Shall I pat polished cars who keep their station
Under the pretty trees, their windows lowered
To free their friendly caves from an unwonted heat?

Today I will not offend you with my haunted face,
A forehead, as my children nicely put it,
Stamped map-like with symbolic marshland.

I shall lie quietly upon my double bed,
Which keeps your handsome impress still, my dear;
Calm, for a moment, like a cancer patient

Who knows that though his building stands condemned,
There are good days, when he can almost bear
To move about his chipped and tumbling rooms.

And all you birds, in soft unbroken voices,
Can tell me kindly, over and over and over,
How great are the idle pleasures of the feather-brained,

Allowing, perhaps, your clear draughts of spring water
To ease my solitary voice a little;
Set me croaking for love like a melodious frog.

World, today I do not dare to talk with you,
But I will listen while you spin your golden disc,
Your airs bright with the flowing shapes of girls.

Flesh

We are very close. I love you dearly.
Fondling my arms, I reassure you
Absent-mindedly, like the cat.

I tremble for you. In the unlit room,
I edge, wary of skull and genitals,
Wincing where darkness thickens.

My stomach thrills to the crisp snail
Wrecked on the path: that stir and froth
His painted egg has hatched.

The tangled car teaches me wisdom.
I would not have you threaded piecemeal
Through that crushed eye.

Such vulnerability is my concern.
Sick, yet healed like an old tyre,
I trust you to survive

Until I order them to burn you down,
Or pack you off where you may ease yourself
Most slowly from my valuable bones.

Early Summer

Small things get lost now;
There are intrusions,
Defeats in alien worlds.

This is the time to slide a foolish leaf
Under the flimsy legs that ruck
The pond's tight skin,

Or bury the grassed fledgeling,
Tender for the closed eyes, the ungainly head
On the lax grey neck.

The rambling bee, obtuse and hairy,
Unzips with his dull purr
The studious air.

He too will need us.
We hoist him to a window, smile
At his diminuendo horn.

Papery moths drift to the light,
Churr in a hand's cave,
Then out, out.

Later, much later, we shall assault the wasps,
Brewing them in our slow cauldrons
Of honey, vinegar.

At Home

Look, my garden bleeds.
It is a dereliction of faded shells
Whose soft inhabitants have moved away.

A small three-legged frog
Falls through water like a chipped pebble
To its own version of annihilation.

All this dark humus:
A soft compound of shared sufferings.
The earth is knit together with absences.

Oh cruel, cruel May,
Who lays her green and vicious icing on,
Sugaring our wickedness with birdsong.

I will have no more sunlight,
Where predatory, infected birds peck out
Profuse and twirling specks of idle life.

In my cool kitchen
I keep God's creatures packed in metal rinds,
Their simple natures conveniently crushed.

This ignorant sweet paste
Calls for a justice I can not perceive:
It mortifies my knowledgeable tongue.

Shaming the clotted sink,
An idle spider splays its loose dead legs.
Lifted, they hunch and droop, a closing flower.

Beyond my neat, dazed window,
Skinned bones offend the pleasantries of grass.
Look, my garden bleeds.

The Nondescript

I am plural. My intents are manifold:
I see through many eyes. I am fabulous.

I assimilate the suffering of monkeys:
Tiger and musk-ox are at my disposal.

My ritual is to swallow a pale meat
Prepared by my ignorant left hand.

It is my child's play to untie a frog,
Humble further the worm and dogfish.

When I comb the slow pond,
I shake out a scurf of tarnished silver;

When I steer the long ship to the stones,
A brown sickness laps at the cliff's foot.

Shreds of fur cling to my metalled roads,
Old plasters seeping a little blood.

I dress and powder the wide fields:
They undergo my purgatorial fires.

Come with me. I will shake the sky
And watch the ripe birds tumble.

It requires many deaths to ease
The deep cancer in my marrowbones.

I have prepared a stone inheritance.
It flourishes beneath my fertile tears.

A Wartime Childhood

Alert

I walked by ruins but I did not hear
The cold bone monks define the summer air
With Latin. Whether birds made marginal notes
Or wind riffled the leaves, I do not remember.
The long encyclicals of sound decline
To a gossip, a soft susurrus. Teased

By tremors and tumults powerless to stir
One ear of the buff cat placid by the fire,
I wait while an old night deepens, alert
To decode those messages my sleeping children
Will never understand, accustomed only
To her most friendly voices. First, I make sure

Rough, musty bags of sand hold off the garden.
Where yellow mesh gums to the window pane
A black sheet must permit no frond of light
To touch the flowing acres of the moon.
Warm and small, I explore with a dying torch
An under-the-table world in a guarded house.

Open to slow half-loops of thin sound,
Drawn to the ebb of a siren voice, I hunch
In my cockpit sheets. Night drones and bangs.
The Gods rain down for my most secret trading
Rough, dark-cored tokens from their thunderous world.
For me the morning streets are decked with silver.

The ghosts of sound recede, become merely
The soft coursing of blood. I make them swell,
Wave upon gathering wave. The night insists
On a tide of great planes, drumming, drumming,
Or a single stuttering drift, a cold absence.
I hunt softly along the edges of my nerves.

I walked by ruins but I did not hear
Their sinews twist and crack, their wooden hearts
Tumble and burn. Whether passing feet marked time
Or wallpaper caught the wind, I do not remember.
Slowly the pale sounds settle in my head,
Calmed to the traffic's breath, a gas-fire's whisper.

Range-finding

The rider fell. His obelisk
Marks the acceptance of a risk.

We feed it with our names, a penny
Slipped endwise down a cranny.

Off ploughland, the trees' region
Is home-ground for jay and pigeon,

Occasional fine bone or skull,
A sodden Ely Twelve-bore shell.

We move through to war's theatre:
An old quarry's white crater,

And hanging from a crumbled edge
Scatter chalk from lip to ledge.

We burrow for soft battered lead,
Rummage from their pocky bed

The blunt nose of Sten and Tommy,
The spent taper of 303.

Down range where mud is pressed
We rifle from an empty nest

Black clips, a spill of brass –
Blown eggs littered in the grass.

Clouds and sun stray out of mind.
Perfection is difficult to find:

That flawless cone whose polished case
Fits like a glove the milled base.

The skyline finger counts the hours;
Marks another's risk – and ours.

Toy Soldier

I sowed pence,
Teeth for armed men.

A lost sentry
Lies under my dreams,

His head secured
With matchstick, plasticine.

Cowled nasturtiums
Gave trailing cover.

Sweet militia:
Sweet war man.

In a deep ditch
He went to ground at last;

Worked his way
Under packed mould.

Stockades of stalks
Fostered new seasons;

Plastic wars
Litter an old terrain.

He stands at ease.
Pale roots evade him:

Lead for Saturn,
Infortuna Major,

Maintaining still
A token presence.

A kindly nodule
On which the skin slides.

Gas Mask

Oh, Mickey Mouse, you ruined man,
Your wrecked face bobs in the garden grass.
Who wrenched your flapping nose askew?

The projector hums. Through smoky light
You drive like mad in a baby car.
Fat wheels spin the wavering dust.

Your slippery flesh embraces mine.
I choke on a smell. You flubber and snore.
Elastic rucks my prickling hair.

My head contracts. I am tight shut.
My breath makes mist. I stare at time
Through deep-sea eyes with metal rims.

Unpicked

I am unpicked by every wandering thing:
That stormy girl, the impermanence of May,
The things birds tell me in the tunes they sing,
The tender tumult of my children's play.
All, all unpicks my bones, unpicks my bones;
I speak in dissonances, quarter tones.

I have flown thoughts and words so far down wind
No artifice will now decoy them home;
Hung out a heart for other hearts to find.
I am a man whom speech has driven dumb,
Crushed by the simple weight of being good.
I am a stone that brims with some dark blood.

I still have craft, and I can bandage you
The wounds of long-dead poets; in my car
These distant, careful hands know what to do.
I know small histories of beast and star.
I am the scattered pages of a book
Whose theme is lost. I wear an alien look.

I know the drowning fly, the shorn dark hair,
The soldier weeping on his iron bed
In some old hutment by a windy square.
I know the unhealing sutures in my head.
I am unpicked; I cannot face alone
The vigorous, careless damage I have done.

The soft bombs drumming on my childhood make
Their crazy thunder on my dreaming ear:
I know boys' savagery, and each mistake
That I accomplish draws me into fear.
I stand reproached and into danger where
The haunted faces of my friends lie bare.

There was a time I would have laughed to see
You bend and break under my wilful hand
In some wild contest, and your misery
Had fed those vanities I understand.
Such strength was worthless. A deep amnesty
Has called those weapons home that suited me.

I am unpicked, but if you need a way
Of making such destruction doubly sure,
A mocking word or glance in casual play
Will be sufficient. I shall still endure.
Rejection I have always understood:
Her enigmatic marble face, her hood.

You whom I chose, who seem to have a need
For what a scarecrow's pockets can supply,
Take what you want, if you have skill to feed
On simple food when other horns run dry.
I will keep little back. I hang my mail
In some museum on a withered nail.

I think of old-gold castles on French hills
And all those ancient slit and tippling towers,
Their deep-set, murderous, defensive skills
Open to soft invasions from the flowers.
Does each hurt bee die lacking power to sting?
I am unpicked by every wandering thing.

A Death: Cadouin

Evening. The strong light softens. Footbrake
Dipping our nose, we stumble, skirr and check,
Pulled to the green shade of a leaning hedge.
A white Citroën squats across the verge.
The sticky children fidget. A long pause,
Our engine idling to small village stirs.
Nearby, a man washes his car. Pipe lit,
Switch off. Out of the Citroën's tailgate
A stretcher eases. Trim and crisp as ice,
Those folds of blue and white. A yellow face,
Perched and prim, drinks at the fading sun.
A woman weeps. Her signal flowers burn,
Gay in their cluttered pots. Pain brims the air.
The corpse climbs stiffly up an awkward stair.
'Mon bébé, il est mort.' Shutters pull to.
A capable nurse reverses, lets us through
With an astringent smile. Auden in mind:
Icarus falls away from our concern.
Stiff water drums on tin. He swabs it down.
The sound of weeping stops at the next turn.
This was a dream, until the hay-cart horse,
That strong brown Papi, tugged an antique hearse
Clop-clop uphill, black mourners at his tail,
To marbles, immortelles, a new-dug hole.

Gouffre de Proumeyssac

How right, that suspension of disbelief, when amenably we agree
To offer an 'O Altitudo' to the sheer prodigality
Of Nature pulling her stops out. Voyeurs, we jostle to look
At the staggering vital statistics set down in her record book.
Our average craves a surplus. A holiday mood for us
Insists on a 'Look, no hands!', a sense of the marvellous.

Honour then all chasms and steeps: each grand unexpectedness
Whose Mirabile Dictu story stuns by a fine excess.
But in this towering theatre, this natural Headlong Hall,
Mr Milestone's question intrudes: by what name do we call
Such effects the second time round? When, galleried high, we throw
A glance at the Grand Tour traipsing and gaping away below,

Or above, to the Big Top darkness, where poised hangs La Meduse,
Watering a limestone garden with her tireless, fertile dews;
When we mark off the civilizations, dying by inches where
The tall stalks thicken and thin in the tranquil, cavernous air,
We are chastened, subdued by Gothic, by an ex-cathedra tone
In the voice of that primal trinity: time and water and stone.

Ah, whispering at our side then, that sly, subversive clown
Who lurks in the Holy of Holies, scales admirations down
With a sudden and Alice vision. In the dead hours of the night,
Alone with God and the limestone, the drip and the Disney light,
The crystals, the Dog, the Virgin, the glimmering souvenirs,
The Guide's gruff voice stomps on to the petrified, captive ears.

Moulin du Surrier

Genus Gerris,
Pond Skaters, Furneaux says, go
Sliding in long jerks. They do not confine
Themselves to the more sheltered nooks at the pond's edge,
But make peregrinations on the surface film,
Venturing well out into the open;
Allow the wind to drift them.
Children straggle;

Their loose limbs play
Scuttling games. With tiny shrieks
They twist on old tyres. They do not confine
Activity to where the tall green flags tack on
A ragged hem; caught in a boisterous progress,
Nowhere is out of bounds. Cool droplets skirl
As the light takes them. The heat
Stirs into life

Odonata.
Dragonflies, Furneaux says, are
Gorgeously coloured. The outer surface
Is highly polished. They cruise, large-eyed and slender.
The air thickens into reticulated wings.
They keep on course. There is no known way by
Which we can preserve these dyes.
Some touch down; light

On the grey sand,
Where, undressed to kill, idle
Girls cluster and sprawl. The outer surface
Is mostly brown. Gay in metallic blues and greens,
Abdomen and thorax attract collectors. Eyes
Wide, they watch the children bob and flurry.
The fragile Demoiselles sway
Where a reed stirs.

Museum Piece

Now, the adroit need to survive
Which weighed on you when slippery-handed Fulvia
Held you to running Roman water

No longer haunts you. Having made
A clean break with that nervous past,
Solicitously propped like an old granny,

You can deny that droll compulsion
To compete. Such heaps of Terra Sigillata
In the midden. No rat-race here.

And did you always know that you were special,
One whom the Lares and Penates favoured?
We must not drop old friends.

If Tacitus and Livy miss their cues,
You need no prompting; state unequivocally
That a full stomach is the primal good.

Though vocatives may seem inapposite,
Surely an O Pot is just recognition
Of long, if undistinguished service?

And even dirt, in time, grows venerable.
Removed beyond our washing, you are
As numinous as a philosopher's matted beard.

Mere food for thought, your pot-luck now.
No sense of strain, no chip upon your shoulder,
Your world is everything that is the case.

Vanity Fair

Come inside, please, come inside, inside.
Here is a chattering armful of wooden hoops.

If you can ring my heart, I give you prizes:
A dying goldfish, a green and monstrous vase.

Shake loose my blunt tin cars; watch me groan
To the butt and swing of their punched noses.

Make vicious circles on my dipping horses;
Admire their wrenched mouths, their staring eyes.

Climb my palisades of tangled steel:
Wrecked airships hung with wandering flies.

Rock back my coconut skull on its trembling neck,
Wing me with feathered darts, a flat sting of corks,

Or in my empty, empty spaces,
Loop your nirvanas in light wooden chairs.

Scream when I toss you my flossed hair,
Whose gummed threads sew your lips together;

Walk my crazy Munchkin house
Where warm winds hoo my skirts about your thighs

And rippling mirrors comb my flesh
Into extravagances of shimmering fat.

In those black and banshee passages
Behind my flailing battered doors,

Crouch and clutch in my rocking ghost train
As it clicks and slams over my crinkled rails,

Tickled by a trail of rats' tail string,
A swing of fraudulent dancing bones.

I make you free of this wild playground,
Its blue zickerings, electric rubber smells.

Oh, this is fun, this is amazing fun.
Come inside, please, come inside, inside.

Fats Waller

Ah, Mercy!

You beautiful dead man, still travelling through,
Racing along your wild and cool glissandos,

The Rhythm rocking, holding off, rocking:
Plucked thunders and floating winds. Sweet Thing!

The riffs go climbing through the blue-smoke airs
Of thirty years, of thirty missing years.

Pick us a tune, some old ridiculous song.
Shake it, break it, spin it edge-along,

Tack it up lightly to the trembling wires,
Swoop and clown astride its swinging bars,

Squeeze us your syruped stones through that
Most growly-gay deep voice, you big scat cat:

Hushed honey for sleepy people, a pulled-leg
For those whose aching feet are much too big,

All friendly milkmen and ain't misbehavers.
Croon your dark crotchets and your mocking quavers,

Give us your haunted popcorn yet again,
A crazy sugar that will keep us sane,

A hop-hop-hoppity of wandering chimes
To coax and tease us back to the good times.

Oh patty-cake, patty-cake baker man,
Spin us a perfect circle with each hand.

You died at thirty-nine. Old ivory bones,
You're weaving still those nets of tingling sound.

Ah, Mercy!

Good Morning

There it was, pounding and shaking at his ears again:
The inordinate chatter and posher of the world
Scouring the bedroom air like a wire broom.

The rites of Spring. Festoons of birds and lorries
Shrieked and hummed a new dawn chorus.
Even the milkman scampered with jigging bottles.

Perched behind breakfast toast and cornflakes lurked
The strange, enormous children. What casual seed
To flourish into flagpoles, hollyhocks.

They towered towards him, eyes as big as saucers;
Swept through the blitzed house all a-whirl,
Trailing sledgehammer limbs and alarming voices.

His wife's hair swirled and bobbed: smoky, turbulent.
Leaves pushed. Bloat goldfish gaped in a thick water,
Their mouths trembling with unrecorded exclamations.

He thought: the world is full of dogs and cars,
Woofing, smoking, molesting passing flesh.
Crossing rooms is hard as crossing roads.

He shrank like Alice; decided to fight backwards.
A warm gulf-stream of tea flooded his throat.
He swam desperately against the mounting tides

Pushing, pushing inside him, with him,
Awash with calendars and stupendous faces,
Bald heads, bold eyes and black-rimmed glasses.

Rice Krispies bounced and hissed. He cowered down,
Numbed by the Top Ten; prepared to let the hours
Detonate round his ears like mad bird-scarers.

Time to go, dear. He switched on his ignition,
Practised a bark or two, stormed up the hill.
The flowers catcalled him as he rode away.

Lessons in Survival

To stay good currency with your heart solvent,
Be a pink bus ticket used as a bookmark,
A maidenhair fern, pressed but eloquent.

Look for a hidey-hole, cosy or dark,
Where no peekaboo finger or eye can excite
A meddlesome bigwig to poke and remark.

Survival is mostly a matter of oversight.
Be an old pencil stub, a brass curtain ring.
Don't keep your lid screwed on too tight.

With luck, your neighbourhood fairy will string
You along as a glass bead, a silver key,
A saved blue feather from a jay's wing.

A person like you, a person like me,
Must contrive to find butter, but not too much jam;
Live happy and warm as a pick-a-back flea.

Don't be a new airport, the flag of Siam,
A battleship decked with bunting and trouble,
A three-volume novel, the Aswan High Dam,

To founder in foundries of smoke and pink rubble,
To swell and topple, absurd, indecent,
To puff and froth like an overblown bubble.

Be a bit too precious to throw away spent:
Be good for others or perhaps a lark.
Be a whispered name, not a granite monument.

Mandarin

The Game's Up!

He knew it, but sat playing Spillikins with Miss Austen,
Absorbed by two inches of ivory.
Her claws, he noticed, were exactly trimmed.

Come On Out Of There!

Was it Pope's Grotto, Plato's Cave?
He offered shy friendship to a quiet toad;
Politely ignored the jewelled tumour on its head.

I Can See What You're Doing!

This he doubted. He held a poem to the light,
Observed the smaller poem carved inside it;
Meditated anagrams of 'La Rochefoucauld'.

So You Won't Talk?

No. The alphabet had always wearied him:
That quite excessive ache of combinations.
He approved palatals – wished 'O' a trifle slimmer.

We're Coming To Get You!

Contact displeased him.
He wrote himself brief letters; even then
Could hardly bring himself to start them 'Dear'.

Bang! You're Dead!

Idly, he admired the delicate blood's
Recessive blue, adjusted the pleated shroud;
Buried himself in the manner to which he was accustomed.

Family Ties

Ah, they are martyrs to love.
See how it brims, how much the small house holds.
Sifting the pallid air, it settles like dust
On children, pets and flowers. A sweet infection
Drenches the double bed. Faces are drawn with the care
And strain. Love darkens the windows,
Lurks in the unwashed crocks and the pile of mending.
The family tremble like flies in a simmering web.

They lean to each other. As her words drift by,
Through the miasma small white faces peer.
The guarded children, gathered on the rug,
Play delicately together,
While stifling in its bonds, the baby whimpers.
Love guides the anxious glance, the probing finger,
The corrosive symptom which stabs him like angina

Or warms her to a comfortable ache;
Stirs in the patience of herbs, the sharp injection.
They carry it, bandaged and dosed,
In the car to the family cottage. How can they tame
This dangerous, gay sun which leaps at their eyes?

Lock, lock it out. Together, secure,
They clutch each other and founder,
The soft tongues licking, abased, the changing wounds.
Night swarms the bedrooms, restless, tropical.
Lapped in damp sheets the children twitch and sob,
While the defeated voices softly rising
Maroon them in the cruel tides of love.

Cancer

That fierce profusion shocked. Dark bric-à-brac
Squatted or crept. Tumbled on fading chairs
The yellow papers whispered mindless news.
Cards, violins and landscapes wound the walls
In brown lianas. Rank and order lost,
Objects reduced each other to mere signs,
Tokens of space possessed: to us, no more.

He shuffled, bent, about the loved detritus
Of many years, and clasped it tight,
A desperate salve for those unhealing wounds.
In, out, cells ramified. And when he died,
Locked in our love and admiration, we
Followed him to his burning. Still each room
Held his deep impress, like an unmade bed.

Hungry

I love you so much, my darling, that I could eat you.
Come closer, gingerbread lady: for such a morsel
    My mouth is eloquent to begin.

With a springing forest of hair, the keyboard toes,
A slice of warm tongue? I feel all-overish.
    I shall roughly encompass your skin.

After all, I have munched my way through a stolid farmyard
Of membra-disjecta. After a feast of small-fry,
    Shall I not swallow you whole?

No. I shall start with your smile, whose nice enigmas
Will chasten my clownish lips. I tremble to feel
    Your practical fingers mole

Deep into mine, your sinuous, rangy limbs
Stretch me and ease me. Such unusual grace!
    I grow sober, a little delicate,

And my metaphysic's astray. You deftly secure
My flyaway thoughts, and plait them neatly and sweetly
    Into suitable patterns. My intricate

Dear, you have straightened my nose. Your birdcage ribs
Arch with a freight of breasts: I tense to the strain,
    Preserve an unruffled front.

Can we settle each local difference? Agreed, our hearts,
Harmonious blacksmiths, measure their strokes as one.
    A stir in the loins? We won't

Dilate upon that. Man and wife are a single flesh.
Let us see through each other's eyes, each other's pretences;
    Our fancies tickled, delay

Your decision that this demand was a trifle excessive,
And that you must, with an absent-minded gesture,
    Slip out and saunter away.

Limbs

No, not the abandon, the threshing play
We take lying down.
Now the composure, the slack ease of feature;
We sink and drown,

The driving tools relaxed, the muscle and bone
That extend our will,
Forcing a tangible world of object and creature
To be active or still.

The curtains are drawn, though stirred by casual airs;
Love has been made.
Your hair, tossed back on a tumbled pillow
Lies dark, displayed.

And the limbs fall over; fluid, knowing their place,
Both yours and mine
Kiss and unkiss. Calm, in a state of grace,
They twine, untwine.

The sky will darken and grow again to light.
We move with the stars,
And our turning limbs will ride in the travelling night
With Venus, Mars.

Address Unknown

Who goes roaming at night through my bricks and mortar?
What tremors wander through my patchwork rafters?
Why do these small holes drip a slight buff powder?

I think of bulky mammals who roved here stolidly,
Munching and pulling at the ancient greenery.
A million years. I could sleep them away tonight.

My house is clipped lightly to an old hillside,
Held against cloud and shine by the wills of others,
Tacked up with sticky grit and threads of power.

Its teeth are set on edge by a guitar trembling;
Each thought unpeels a slim skin from the paintwork.
House, I have stuffed you with such lovely nonsense:

All these sweet things: Clare's Poems, Roman glassware,
A peacock's feather, a handful of weird children,
A second-hand cat with one pad missing, missing.

Where are you going, carrying us without spilling,
Sailing away, packed for a hero's funeral,
Freighted with love-gifts, all destined for strangers?

What is not there at all is what lasts longest,
The airs, the hill it seems that we have borrowed,
A hill itself settling to a new calm level.

Old tigers and stuff poke through my dirty windows.
At the door, Doctor Who swishes an antic mantle,
Commanding the bleeping future to throw me sideways.

I lie in bed; pack the house into my headroom.
Though bits hang out, it is safe from hags and urchins.
I shall put a bone round it, and a spell of closing

To keep away the Spoom, the Man in the Oke, the Succubi
Who shake small tremors through my patchwork body,
Rocking me awake with changeling, manic voices.

Painted Shells

Children pick painted shells to hear
Long tides come hushing on the ear;
Believe that in half-understood
And mortal rumours of their blood
Live groundswells of a deeper sea:
A language of Eternity.
Unmoved by flattery or command,
Our brutal hour-glass slips her sand
Where tides and tokens all concur
That child and dancer must defer
To Time, whose known inclemency
Will freeze the small bird from the tree,
And whose vindictive whiplash gives
No quarter to her fugitives.

Whatever cancers wait, we must
Confirm our hearts' instructions, trust
We are not only what we know
Our savagery and folly show:
Mere vacancies the dust assumes
To link dull cradles to dull tombs,
Sick children crying for a light
Where sweats and nightmares wind us tight
And no one comes – and if they did
The face they'd show had best be hid.
Our presences the more enhance
The linking figures in our dance
When what we say and do creates
A bonfire to amaze the fates.

My dear, by this charm repossess
Those airs and fires your ways express:
A candid smile to lift each heart,
Green-fingered talent in that art
Which shows how bravely souls are dressed
And how we may reveal them best.
Whatever luck the years advance,
May your five senses lead their dance
With that intensity and verve
The frayed edge gives the steady nerve;
And may you turn those trolls to stone
Who try to claim you for their own,
Whose doltish needs reduce each grace
To a shut look on a shut face.

May the old world that lets you through
Kindly incline her fruits to you,
Her metal landscapes part to make
Paths for your dancing steps to take.
Carry through wild or temperate air
The dark declensions of your hair;
Make all hobgoblins, all annoyers,
Imps, black vanities, destroyers,
That shocking crew whose yammering flocks
Fled poor Pandora's gaping box
Cower before you. May your feet
Keep measure with the Infinite,
Held in that intricate design
By far more potent runes than mine.

No amulet of words can stay
Our tender structures from decay,
Though buds unfrosted yet by Time
May flower precariously in rhyme.
We learn to recognize and bless
Whatever tames our wilderness:
Truant, sweet, divergent creatures,
Passions dancing in their features.
Though Nature's laws are obdurate,
Her sentence we can mitigate:
The artist's work is paradox,
A Chinese puzzle which unlocks
To show those gifts that he was made,
Their brightnesses transposed, repaid.

In Time and out of Time we move,
Inflicting pain, inflicting love,
Crusoes who salvage what we can
In our short, haunted, patchwork span;
And still in every fragile shell
Curl labyrinths whose echoes tell
The dancing words they must begin
To trace again our origin,
That distant and delaying flood
Which courses under mortal blood.
Where rivers ease into the sea
All musics mingle. We shall be
Rocked in those long tides at the ear
Children pick painted shells to hear.

Prehistories

West Country

1

The Grand Bard's wreaths and rituals decay,
Those sky-blue robes, archaic lexicons.

His old house bleaches among shoals of hay,
Voyaging nowhere all the summer long,

Worked by a dynamo of sentenced bees
Lodged in a cave under our bedroom sill.

As yet, their tongue needs no revivalist;
The walls thrum to a doomed plainsong.

We grieve upon their notice of eviction
Whose hive will congregate no sweetness.

All tenancies, save one, are held on lease.
We claim our native element's forbearance,

Yet stony seas leach out a dying tanker,
Languages founder, Lyonnesse goes down,

And the Bard lies under slate in Zennor churchyard
Whose fingers carved unsinkable trim ships.

2

Old night, I know you at this quiet fabling,
Your crickets sprinkling their light vocables.

Life goes barefoot on this stubbled garden:
A hidden sea is talking in its sleep.

Beyond the lackwit stones, the granite faces,
A sisterhood of cows makes cavalcade.

Badgers possess this place; they come for alms,
Noble antique beggars in grey fringes.

I smile for you, you small ones at my feet,
Tying soft webs of trill from stem to stem.

We make no shadows in this august starlight;
We rhyme softly, each out on his limb.

Jimp saltatoria, brown grass-dancers,
Little, they say, is known about your histories.

Male and female he created them. Sweet love.
The girls have ears. Only the boys can sing.

3

Sun sets here in a damp quarter,
Yet one is conscious of bones:

Snapped sticks, angularities of guttering,
The shaft and tines of a worn fork.

The apple tree's articulation gathers
A sage and silver lichen;

Beneath her branches, one sunk boulder
Heaves a mossed and buffalo flank.

Furred husks of bees lie drily tumbled
Under an entangled window.

Bracken whispers, her corrugations
Brittle and simple as old fossil fish,

And the ribbed water tank is bare;
She sings and tremors windily.

The blood's course falters at the foot:
We wither at our slow extremities.

Public Footpath To

Beyond the dented churns, the huddled farmyard,
Look, a green and lackadaisical finger
Reveals a hair-line fracture in the land.

Cold mud glints, beaten to a pale rivulet.
Button your coat against a change of season,
The sour attentions of a bramble frond.

Pause, lost, the thread absorbed by close-knit ploughland,
Stooping, unpick that crumpled fabric, palming
A broken tile, a freckled knob of bone.

Feel the chill rising: from damp skins of leaf-mould,
The swell of ground picked clean by flocking magpies,
The sodden beech wood clasping the dark hill.

Such slim capillaries, such seams and crinkles,
Overflown by clouds, nodded at by thistles,
Sealed by the impress of lost summer girls

And men whose ways were set by dawn and sunfall,
Offer a sense of flowers, endurances.
Time has stopped dead in their forbidden tracks

Where rank disordered trees and sniffling grasses
Huddle and fuss among the wind's rough twitchings,
Crumbling mouths yawn dimly at a hedge-foot.

Though a church tower makes her slight invitation,
Horizons alter as the bruised air thickens.
Let the past keep her right of way, while you

Are sensible, treading familiar ground again,
Of labouring barns, one self-sufficient tractor
Dragging the sullen landscape down to earth.

Ploughland

They drudged across the season's palimpsest,
The feathered horses, driven into rain;
Their dapples and attendant shades impressed
Upon the skies which pulled them up the lane.
    Light moves about the knotted ploughland, sown
    With undistinguished seeds of chalk and bone.

A sullen field, pegged out with brittle trees,
A water colour of the English School;
Her pawky hedgerows crumble to their knees,
The locked fires in her fractured flint lie cool.
    Old weathers broke her in, and we retrace
    The crows' feet etched on her dissolving face.

The lost teams and their leaders. All that care
Is mere commemoration by the wind.
A shower of bells freckles the cooling air;
Our booted feet drag with an awkward rind.
    Down in the levelled churchyard a few graves
    Remind the birds how well the past behaves,

Working along the bent flow of the land
With no more substance than our thought makes good:
A face limned on the air, a tenuous hand
To scribble in the margins of the wood.
    A rash of brickwork rubricates their claim:
    A foundered house, and a forgotten name.

The Home Farm lacked a tenant forty years,
Pigs littered grandly in the living room;
The rain is flighted with her children's tears,
A burnt tree's crater beckons to the tomb.
    One old man with his dog slows up the hill;
    A shooting party spaces out the chill

Where scatterings of green remind the day
Of beasts long cropped and felled: the molten dead
Still driving purpose through the common clay
In new returns of sacramental bread.
    The harnessed bells ride out upon their round,
    Tossing cold heads above the burdened ground.

Excavations

Time which antiquates Antiquities, and hath an art to make dust of all
things, hath yet spared these minor Monuments.

Sir Thomas Browne, *Hydriotaphia: Urn Burial*

1 *Holwell*

Monpazier relinquished a noble axe,
Lightly buried in an ochre pavement.

Holwell ruffled her ponds, lent an ammonite;
I tighten a mesolithic hand, follow a spiral,

Beat out the boundaries of withered oceans,
Quarry for silence under austere skies.

Land pulls down her unworked galleries,
Gathers her secret filaments.

There are gifts for the hacked acres;
Return is made, here where wind weeps ash,

The dump smoulders. Her stomach rises.
Fumes are exhaled from life's refusals.

A numinous machine in Monster Field
Chokes her gullet on a tip of spoil.

We annotate the scriptures of the hills,
And leaves close on half-burnt offerings.

2 *Taylor's Hill*

On home ground
We make frog garden:
Spades are trumps.

The skin strips
To a prickle of china,
Brick and slipware.

Earth recycles
Each old breakage.
Sixpence for the pudding.

Take her in the flank
With newsprint, sheeting,
Colonial fish.

Sun works hard.
Life breaks open
The surface tensions.

Under the lily pad
Old Leopard Spots
Crooks a long leg.

In autumn, drain her.
Frog's progeny peer
From high-rise flats.

3 Welwyn

A dual carriageway of chalk and mud
Betrays earth's tender hoardings.

Willow-herb, abundant on the site,
Seeds a vivid life on sufferance.

Yellow machines drone their defoliations:
Give me a lever, and I will move the world.

Exhausted aeons flare; life melts away
In a pother of bluish dust. The wind

Flutters a gay festoon of plastic pennons.
These towering inclines are defensible.

From half a bridge, a missed connection,
I consider this arterial surgery.

The land's bones lie in disarray;
Unreadable, her draughty palimpsest.

A new imperium holds, where scholars came
To grub for broken Rome with hasty fingers.

4 *Harston*

Rough chalk bowl,
The Sunday Army
Filled her full of lead.

She took it well,
Twisting their noses.
No more drill.

Just a bit older,
Scrub and sapling
Sweeten her neglect.

Her face dislimns,
Parting at the seams,
Molten in rain.

Leaf-moulds foster
New archaeologies:
Shell-case, punched can.

A silence of skulls
Where we once sat;
Felt air cleave

As wingtips kissed,
Pain touched down
From a canopy of sky.

5 *Sopwell*

A nunnery and mansion coinhere,
Enclose their orders in this tangled ground.
The site is intricate, and we must bare

Some Old Foundation nettle-rash implies.
The wild boys daily bring her to her knees,
Unlock the last bricks jigsawed to the sky.

The great reductions made, earth holds all close,
Shrinking her gums on Clio's wisdom teeth:
Height must be gauged from this impacted base.

We peel each layer through to yellow clay,
Build suppositions on that anchorage.
Hands ache with diagnosis. A hard case.

Slowly, the sun dries out the stones we skin;
Entrenchments deepen, and the shade extends.
We drink our tea and scour the shovels clean.

Salvation, if by works or faith, is toil.
A grace for the quiet dead, to work their bones
To pencilled lines: slight, yet more durable.

6 Cabinet

Each virtuoso displays
A Cabinet of Curiosities.

Earth gilds unguentaria,
Gives bronze patina,

Expending ichor
To bring Baraka.

She holds long leases,
Profits by losses.

Loving cups and rings
Make funerals weddings.

Like Doctor Hans Sloane,
Earth refuses none;

Hunts down her fauna
With Collector's mania.

Let Walpole chaffer
Over Strawberry Fair,

Or graver Browne
Cogitate on an Urne;

She yields without demur
Keepsake and souvenir,

Asks no security,
Proud of her memory.

Her price suits all means:
A few gift-wrapped bones.

No cabinet, no virtuoso,
Can put it all on show.

7 *Font de Gaume*

The ice has shifted, woods in equipoise
Weigh on the tumbled hillside. All's unchanged
Since the first savants of the limestone ways

Edged backward footsteps to where Font de Gaume
Lowers a cold hemline, inch by pleated inch,
And the slow zeros count the mileage gone.

The cavern breathes us in, and hushed we move
Towards our origin, a drift of children
About the two black nuns reserved by love.

We make obedience. The crisp words tell
Of shapes and limits scholarship has set
To counter sorcery with a shutting spell.

Fluent and grave, the ancient beasts release
Our loves and hatreds. High above our heads
The scarred rock sweats dull ochre, manganese;

Forms tremble and dissolve. We close to find
That heads are missing, horns become obscure.
Absolute zero: we begin and end.

8 Rouffignac

Rouffignac, Cave
Of a Hundred Mammoths.
C'est magnifique ...

But it is the station!
A little blue train
Pulls you up and down.

We sit there solemn,
Off to see the pictures.
Electrics hiss.

Earth did it by herself:
No detonations,
Broken pick-helves.

Masonic water,
The Grand Quarrymaster,
Undercuts us all.

Candled graffiti
Sprawl huge cages.
Kilroy was here,

Killing off mammoths,
Seven at a blow
On the nursery frieze.

9 Hauxton

Willow and osier take possession now
In a field of stones, dug out for victory.

I take the vanished cat-walk over the pits,
Feel the heavy belting slope towards me.

Black cycles of time: an endless drudge
And hoist of labouring iron. Recurrences.

A coarse rush of pebbles and water
Churns and stirs in the grilled cylinder.

I hear again that antique grind,
The flails threshing a cold harvest.

Perched on a conglomerate of rust,
I finger a belemnite's unthreaded needle

And the chaff flies. Where are the screens
To wash and filter these memorials?

The gravel throws its cataracts away;
The room shakes to these dislocations.

10 *Limeuil*

Chopped planes lower
To a dark mouth, rimmed
By a calcite frost.

At Limeuil, limestone,
The perfect rock,
Has golden opinions.

The eye remarks
A lizard, armorial
On his baked ledge.

Heat flutters the air.
Blues and Browns
Drift on their nerves;

Settle on spurges.
Hawk moth larvae
Ripen into their skins,

Their Joseph coats.
I feel the fret
Of their neat mandibles.

Declensions of sun.
The unshut mouth
Aches in drought.

11 Land's End

Our fertile soils wander ever downward.
Substance makes removal; the waters take her.

The ground is suffering. Quake and crater
Wrench out, reaching for equilibrium.

She contorts her memories. Her strata
Suffer displacement and oblivion,

Vertical and horizontal fold,
Thrust fault and overthrust.

Innumerable, the bedded points of life
Preserved by a light sift of detritus.

Fresh resin swells the mould; out of decay
We pick the inscription on the heart of stone.

Marcasite breaks out her iron nodules;
Her silver secrets crumble and rust.

Older and deeper still, those massive rocks,
Granites, whose only life is central fire.

Life and Letters

1

A father black-avised, takes the whip hand;
Hawthorn sways towards the scented dog-cart.

Chambers of maiden thought: annunciations.
A white sail, caught by wind and sun.

The noble folio is dragged guilty home
In fine exchange – a supper for a song.

Catullus breaks his old bones into flowers;
The staggering pagans bare each marbled nerve,

And one impossible She, with silly fingers,
Turns down his crisp and undefeated pages.

Released from Daedalus' restraining hand,
Icarus could spin the sun into the sea.

2

London deploys her iron labyrinth;
A Minotaur bites Ariadne's thread.

The work drives counter; cut across the grain,
Coarsens to acclamation or neglect.

A siren chorus at the Mermaid Tavern
Proclaims who's in, who's out: court news.

The new wounds ache, though harshly cauterized.
His old friends break like promises.

Nature steals back her dumb replenishings,
Easing regretful lyrics, anodyne.

Unreasonable tears. Each midnight shows
The scales at their dark equipoise.

3

The silences become remarkable;
His long walks dwindle to a turn.

Glad, now, to pause for music in the Abbey,
Caught faintly by the sloped woodlands.

Regret gathers for that long estrangement,
The one he could have shared all with,

Dead, exiled, or living unfrequented:
Some Chinese hermit with his scroll-work.

Time to arrange for the marmoreal fictions:
Truth some autumnal bonfire will consume.

A glacial and obsequious moonlight
Frosts out his hair, his favourite Cymbeline.

The Look

There was a quiet pressure in her face,
And when she raised her head, the stumbling look
Delayed upon the air: such alabaster
Closed up the crowded room like a dead book.
Her hair unwound its copper interlace.

A sketch of fingers working softly there
Unfolded a slow talk of cage and tower;
She overheard their private languages
And let each small, assuaging gesture flower.
She wore a silence that she would not share.

No matter now what the piano played.
Resolved antinomies of black and white
Lent a disguise of order to the hour.
The window spaces wept a morning light
Upon the trembling our assembly made.

He, ignorant of her white scrutiny,
Hoarded his brown and crumpled bones askance;
Hooded his mouth and eyes against the pulse
That beat inside the music or the glance,
Those looks that sent him wreaths for sympathy.

Then nothing which he had, and chose to give,
Weighed out an absence colder than a stone.
The grace-notes and the sunlight let them go.
Her fingers knew a way to live alone;
His dark, refusing eyes a way to live.

Birthday Triptych

1

Birth days: as of the spirit.
She cannot dissemble.
We break a fiery bread.

How should we navigate
The waves' coarse turmoil
Without appointed stars?

A luminary day, then.
Light of the first magnitude,
Confirm our chosen course.

Tides, in their slow recession,
Delay about your fingers
A light sweet freight of shells.

When fresh seas break,
May that beached miraculous wrack
Still hold its water lights.

On this your name day,
Under Janus, God of thresholds,
Past and future both become you.

2

The true gift claims us.
Look! The flowered paper
Spills and crinkles.

A drift of white tissue:
Snow wreaths in May
We missed last winter.

And the small sign disclosed
Says in a new voice:
I tell of love in the world

To steady and delight you.
A long draught fills our horn;
We cannot exhaust her.

We read a common language
Runed in each offered hand.
Here, riddles are their answers.

Eyes rehearse tender cues.
All images compose and celebrate
The selves we have become.

3

None can walk safely.
The roads are dark, unsigned,
The sky precariously blue.

We must endure
Flowers, the rain's refreshment,
Each beautiful absurdity:

Accept with clear laughter
The dissonance of white hair,
Pain at the source.

A tree shakes at your window
Her brilliance of leafwork,
Admiration heals us.

Our vulnerability preserves.
To counter such a strength
Time's tactics have no skill.

Love sustains. By this avowal
We cancel fear, whatever tremors
Approach us from the bowed horizon.

The Gift

Weights

There could be great weights leaning over
Pressing with a firm, indifferent power:

A sense of falling further than one knew
That there was any space to travel through.

There could be weeping: sourer fruit than tears,
A smothering fear that breeds all other fears,

A deep untying of the flesh and blood
No surgeon's wit has ever understood.

There could be other arms alert to share
To hold with a surprising, shaking care,

And no sufficient cause for that one thing:
The hands that could deny, held offering.

There could be armistice, a sense of proof,
New ways of dying into further life,

A strength more durable for its weaknesses,
Tender acceptance of responsibilities.

Conclusions

Would you try conclusions with me, whose racing tongue
Makes terminus to your most speaking silence,
Scenting the air with absence, a sift of tomb-dust?

In these wild chemistries, I must become a child;
Rehearse again, as once in tattered schoolrooms,
Distinctions of suspension and solution.

I remember how your cut flowers, sapped of comeliness,
Stood in a stiff perch, their own conclusions drawn:
A suspension to subdue the vase that held them.

Now, your bright gift-look, lost between light and shade,
Dissolves in the summery air's mild crucible:
A solution to subdue my dark insistencies

I would try conclusions with you, whose floated silences
Make terminus to my most faltering wordscape,
Scenting the air with presence, a sense of seed-time.

Where?

Where is it? In the silence,
Clinging like a moth to the crisp curtains.

Where is it? If a head droops,
It breaks: seven years' bad luck.

Where is it? Slipping from the cell
Made by your latticed finger-bars.

Where is it? A broken finger-nail
Crinkles it edgily into a slim wrist.

Where is it? Playing hunt the thimble,
Fluttering in a saucepan's metal skin.

Where is it? Drowning like a fly
In the cold embers of a coffee cup.

Where is it? The air drops it
As a slight key nibbles at a lock.

Where is it? A glum slur of feet:
It dies, ash fringing a spent match.

Demure

I am most taken by this demure mood, lady:
The gentle voice with which you ease the air.

Calmly you gather to yourself, float lightly
On your ridiculous gay cushion's crochet-work,

Geni-born through some dark Arab night,
Poised gravely in your own space and time.

The room darkens: lustre in your hair, your eyes.
Friends talk nothing in a language of ciphers,

Their words lent meaning by your meteor smiles:
Paradoxes of transparency and disguise.

I make small gestures to these formal ghosts,
My spirit bruised against your mysteries,

Caught and held centreless at your point of balance:
A woman's wisdom, a child's innocence of repose.

Landscapes

Twinned landscapes travelling under the one sky,
Valleys and hills chequered to the one cloudscape.

Green and incurable, our child looks,
Which tell each other simple, yet true, fables.

When shadow draws you, your pensive face
Drifting among that dear abundant hair,

I too am caught by night's grave transience,
A native of your element of darkness.

And when clear light breaks, we rejoice together,
Delighted dancers in each other's laughter.

Let the glass fall, to daunt fair-weather friendships;
We dare four winds. Unlock your balm and snow.

As If

As if the dying chapel in her grove,
With a most inward look, turned a blank face
To sunset and the lucencies of parting.
Then, briefly, let her golden surfaces
Enrich the air with generated light.

As if the clouds became the darkening sky,
And one wild bush, trembling upon the night,
Shifted the airs about and roundabout,
True author of the rain's diverse commotion.

As if such native sleight-of-hand is yours,
Performed, though, to an astonished daylight.
Some gifts confuse all reciprocity.

Park

My dear, how incautious of you
To set calm Sunday by the ears,
Ruffling the park's composure.
Have you no decorum,
Slamming the lake down flat?
It lies on its back, stunned,
Twitching to a nibble of fish,
And the hunched pavilion
Holds its breath, teetering
Into its shivering reflection.
Your careless hands
Beat the lawn's fitted carpet;
Your whirlwind smile
Sets a grey fountain swaying
And marble dancing-girls
Uncrooking their cold fingers.
Look, the pastel grannies
Scatter, a pale confetti,
Caught in your small storm,
And the huge trees gasp,
Wandering in the dust
Of their dark explosions,
While gaudy flowers leap up,
Naming you to the air
In smoky purples, yellows.
Come, dear, to the gate
And steal a backward look.
Slowly, the park is shaking you
Out of her long green hair,
Lulled to her old somnambulance.

Languages

Here is the mastery of many languages:
My heart defers to a great eloquence.

As she moves lightly, one most familiar
With wayward air in all its soft behaviours,

Her slender limbs speak with such fluency
They give names to the emptiest of spaces.

When her lips part, she sets her smoky runes
As patina upon her living silences.

In her hazel eyes, contained and tender,
I read a marriage between fire and water,

And when she greets me, her bright selfhood
Is a new Pentecost; Babel's resolution.

Quarries

Yes, I have my silent places too:
Serpentine quarries of linked words.

I cut each poem from a living rock,
Shaping it to your own dear likeness.

In that long no-time, I am alive with you,
Your presence palpable about my bones.

The sense of your small hands is terrible:
They work with me in secret, and I tremble.

You move about my splintered labyrinths,
Fingers trailing a kind white flower,

Haunting these lost and intricate dark blocks.
Pygmalion, I kiss you into life

And you hold out your longing arms to mine:
Your eyes blur to my own hot tears.

Can our tower fall, disperse to the four winds.
Whose one foundation stone is love, love?

Wind and Absence

Down wind, down wind, a soft sweep of hours
Trawling in time. My pulse races into darkness.

Adrift, I draw your absence close about me:
Take the small ghosts of your hands to mine.

Your voice, your smile: such Son et Lumière.
My nerves conduct you round my floodlit bones.

Certain salt-water fools pester my eyes:
I stub them out with rough, dumb fingers.

The wind rehearses idle punishments,
Shaking a crush of unrecorded leaves.

A long-dead singer clears his ashen throat:
You creep his old, cold music into life.

Poems bite on their pains. Dismayed, I know
The lines are scored in poker-work: black fire.

The haunted room trembles at your insistency.
Small ghostly hands, allay the air's distress

As wind gathers, menacing our naked spaces
In dead languages of distance and rejection.

Gifts

Giving is the gift of shadows: it is unbearable.
I have given you the essence of my darkness.

What else is there to give? You have my bent words,
The look that picks out ghosts from kindly air.

I have given a face dislimned, a body all but mastered
By pain, that molten flux soldering bone to bone.

I have given my familiars, those bleak, unwearied ones
Who will ride out time with me to the unguessed end.

I have prepared such gifts with night-time tears,
Secure in the sense that you would turn your face away.

And still you hold your strong, small hands to me,
Though my black gifts draw blinds about your eyes.

I shake like a stemmed leaf in a gale of love;
I poise in the storm, as clear and vulnerable as glass

Through which your vestal light steadies and purifies.
Snow in the wind enchants your most dear hair.

Summer Ghosts

We are the small ghosts of summer,
Eavesdroppers on the chit-chat of her clouds:

Our faces enigmatic as folded maps,
Our bodies a mere thickening of sunlight.

Butterfly hands, hovering, mating,
Smiles haunting the stiff green wheat.

Air smooths our voices into new textures;
Grass keeps no memento of our impress.

We procreate our deepest solitudes,
Scan the eyes' horizons for a sign.

Harvests intensify: a sense of gold.
How may two ghosts ripen into substance?

Divers

We knew infallibly: love marked the spot.
Oh, charted faces, time-worn and marine!

After a year tossed among waves of hair
Brimmed eyes and flotsam glances,

In a free fall we leave the surface play
And work of light; traverse the permeable deeps

That close about our origins. All births
Are dumbly recognized in these slow worlds

Where silence and the beautiful darknesses
Drift and brood above the spirit's dancing floor.

In echoing cadences of green slow-motion
We celebrate the ancient mysteries:

Combers for lost gold in a lodge of sand
Amazed discoverers of our buried selves.

Close

At the close of a long summer, slow green fires
Consume the wandering fly and the poppy's membrane.
Life dwindles to a vigorous wreckage of bleached grass.

Heavy shadows beat the lawns to a duller gold,
And children's voices at the cool rim of twilight
Break the horizon, sturdy as trees and spires.

Let our eyes disentangle, hands drift apart, my dear,
Tired with the careful weight they have long carried.
Our senses tremble at the season's change

To wake again, astonished by a russet harvest
Or the first sifting of a hushed snowfall.
We grow in darkness, groping for new light.

Vertigo

Weary of foundering in Victorian silence,
Where pale occasional lamps disperse the gloom,
We find the strength to make a slight transition
And pace the balcony beyond the room.

Hands on the elegant railing, we admire
The melancholic trees, the broken fence;
Below, the tussocks in the formal garden
Mourn for their topiaried lost innocence.

Then you, ingenuous, with cat-felicity,
Swing yourself lightly on the rocking bar,
Back to the lawns, your hands crossed negligently,
Conscious that certainty can lean so far.

I grip the rail, inconsequently know
The centres of our gravity misplaced,
While hands and hearts, in fair-ground convolutions,
Perform their ritual in measured haste.

The grasses hiss, and the lean wind displaces
Curled leaves that swiftly turn a madder brown.
I, stay-at-home, gaze where your body presses
The unrecalcitrant dark flotsam down.

But your inevitable fall delaying,
You tire, step delicately down, and stare
With mock solemnity, sly comprehension,
Through that deep emptiness of cheated air.

Annotations

Love's the plain text of all our lives – in fine,
She suffers annotation. Codes and bows
Make decorative stains, and summer spells
Charm lustred inks and waters high, then dry.
        We hoard a sideline wrack of cards and shells;
        The drawer spills over, and the album swells.

There's a brief eloquence; if yours or mine,
A kiss can rubricate her Book of Hours
Before a wicked gloss creeps round the page.
We blame our hearts on strangers when we find
        Her gutter margins crowd with lust and rage,
        Peeping and steepling through dark foliage.

Yet innocence persists, though we decline
To conjugate her single verb, to give.
One day, considering flowers' pillow-talk,
I found, pressed to the heart of some gilt book,
        A stiff and brittle silk. I took the stalk,
        And found the spectre of a rose could walk.

Signed, Sealed, Delivered

1 Signed

This Indenture made
Between Myself and Time
Witnesseth that

A chain of paper
Binds me lightly
To the gathered shades:

An Army Surgeon,
Publican, Spinster,
Clerk in Holy Orders.

I breathe their skins,
My passage contoured
By their footsteps.

They are engrossed
In ancient deeds,
A semblance of movement,

Their bounds delineated,
Drawn in the margin
Of these presents.

A brass clock ticks
In consideration of the sum
Of their dry gestures.

2 Sealed

A rustle of leaves.
Wax deploys
Her scarlet heraldries.

Poppy and balsam:
Weeds climb rampant
On a green silk ground.

In confirmation of tenure,
The evening snails
Etch in silverpoint.

Cats attest ownership
With a dawn sacrifice
Of entrails, feathers.

I move between
All ghosts and creatures
Who set here hands and seals,

Their parchment skins
Secured in the grave's
Diminutive tenement.

Love is the fee simple
Of these hereditaments,
Messuages, appurtenances.

3 Delivered

Who will give me
Receipts for the duty
I cannot pay?

What heirs, executors,
Unborn assigns,
Will own this burden?

Beneficial owner
Of a chancy sunlight,
A chestnut's shade,

I mark a trilling of wings,
Visitations of bees
In the unsown border.

Delivery comes.
Genius loci,
Your shrine topples.

Unborn machines
Ruminate on a sour rubble,
Doors lie open

To winds rising
And a rain descending:
To a foliage of clouds.

Talismans

1 *Christmas Lantern*

Such flim-flam: a hutch of crumbling card
And the light's composure. Still talisman,

I think of nights your lucencies beguiled,
While the house rocked to the soft blundering guns.

I set my heart upon your heraldries
Where snow lies faultless to a cobalt sky, ⌣

Counting your shaken stars, adrift on paths
Diminishing among your vivid pines.

Frail monstrance, with an old anticipation
I set you here above my sleeping children:

The branched reindeer at the huddled bridge,
⌐ The simple house, offering her candled windows.

For their eyes now, your most immaculate landscape
And all the coloured rituals of love.

2 *Village Minstrel*

There, boxed hugger-mugger,
A few sad fictions,
Lost grammars, dying bibles.

And Clare, in scuffed half-roan:
Blue tributary stains
Wandering the marbled boards.

'To Dr Darling, M.D.,
With the author's best respects
And most grateful remembrances.'

December, eighteen twenty-seven.
The rented Helpston acres,
A freehold tenement of words.

I hold his winter gift,
A light between each darkness.
Who list presume to Parnasse Hill?

I search the engraved eyes.
Who could wish him less
Than his own inscription?

On my reliquary shelf,
His undefeated gold
Takes to this latter sunlight.

3 Marbles

They lurk in unfrequented corners,
A milky Venus, banded Jupiter,

Their planetary motions and disguise
Adept at eluding Time's removals.

This cold and crystalline survivor
Invites a slight clairvoyance:

Cracked asphalt, warm to the hand,
A blur of birdsong and white flowers,

A summer child, making and breaking
His solitary, erratic ring.

Taw and Alley skip and tinkle;
An old blood-brotherhood re-forms

Where all the lost and pretty dancers
Play the light music of the spheres.

Emblem and scene: indissoluble.
A twist of sunlight at the core.

Behind the Figures

O hours of childhood,
hours when behind the figures there was more
than the mere past, and when what lay before us
was not the future!

Rilke

1 Earth

Loam is friable:
A crumpled darkness
Lit by flowers

Whose candid petals
Dress with white
The lawn's hem.

A mower draws out
Ribbons of light;
Throws a green waterfall.

Baize table land.
The iron rollers
Grind her down.

Worms cast out
Their whorled pyramids:
Dumb signatures.

The bed glistens
To slug trails,
Porcelain shells.

She tells a secret:
A ripening chrysalis
Tickles the palm,

Works her sharp tip.
An imago shut
In a twist of shade.

2 Air

January night
Unfolds the slow
Particulars of frost.

The witch fingers
Of webbed icicles
Catch her breath;

She lays bare
A dog shout,
A branching nerve.

Scratch fronded glass:
The summerhouse
Is thatched with light.

Engrossed by cold,
A child perches
On skimble bones.

A retinal scar's
Familiar hieroglyph
Slides over

A new fretwork,
A chalk sky
Seeded with birds.

To powdered asphalt
Some will come
For stone ground bread.

3 Fire

Salamander days.
Rising sun
Burns off the dew.

Tight raspberries break
A sweet meat
From bobbled flesh;

Embryo life
Pales and curls
At the molten core.

Gold bruises out
Sharp loganberries
To finger stains.

Windows exchange
A summer heliograph
Of light messages.

A burning glass
On a hand's back:
The ellipse tightens,

Kindles a dance
Of smoke veils,
A pale flame.

A black hole
Through which a world
Slips, and falls.

4 *Water*

A stone bird-bath:
Fluttering wings
Fuss brackish water.

The old butt swells
Her iron ribs'
Cool breeding ground

Into the scum
Unshipped oars
Crawl and founder,

The grass legs,
Translucent wings,
Faltering where

Striated larvae
Pause and hang;
Filaments tingle.

A shadow play
Of green and amber
Lowers and fades.

The light takes
These gauze deaths,
Silk entanglements.

Loose gnats drift
Where their children
Sink and rise.

The Secret

The wagtail's semaphore in black and white,
A diadem spider, tense on corded dew,
Globular clusters of slow snails, clambering
At the wall's foot:
The daylight, filled with speaking likenesses.

Yet the dusk found him clenched, all lost for words;
The landing clock, hummocked by shadow, knew it.
Then a blue print frock, loose and talkative,
Spilled, interposed.
The conversation hung by a friendly thread.

She turned. 'Is anything the matter?' 'No.'
Only the fluttering secret a child must keep
Safe for the cold white acreage of sheets,
The moon's barred face:
Cows in the dusk, floating their clouded tongues.

Rain, sibilant on grass, came troubling on.
At night, while the old house cracked its joints
Or shivered its dusty timbers, the fledgeling secret
Broke out its wings.
When morning sun glanced in, his bird was flown.

Convulsion

Dragged brutally from sleep by a long, alien cry,
We tense, give startled glances. Something pleads
With bleak demands to be assuaged or beaten down.

She trembles, sweats. Her round and vagrant eyes
Lack sight. We must control this random violence;
Oppose with helpless words this gift of tongues.

So strange an absence loosens every part
Of our close world. In the unfriendly light,
Doll, cupboard, chair stare blankly back at us.

Ice, not love, eases. Hands recall gentler skills;
Our voices falter. Calmed by her dull sobbing
We sit, stiffly. At the night's cold margin

Our house resumes its usual tentative posture.
Someone we know is back. Something has left us.
We realize how great a strength went with him.

Home Again

Propelled through time and space,
We make re-entry here;
Breathe a known atmosphere.

Nothing is out of place,
And yet we find it all
Alien, inscrutable.

It seems we must accept
The shape things draw on air
Merely by being there:

The faded walls, adept
At letting criss-cross books
Paper over the cracks,

The stolid easy chair
That sags like a stone sill
Or worn memorial.

Since with this world we share
An old complicity –
We brought it to be,

Why is the look so strange
On mine, or my child's face,
Caught in a looking glass?

What base yet out of range
Can send instructions now
How to make contact, how?

Prehistories

1

Adrowse, my pen trailed on, and a voice spoke:
'Now, you must read us "Belknap".' My book was open.

I saw their faces; there were three of them,
Each with a certain brightness in her eyes.

I would read 'Belknap'. Then a gardener's shears
Snipped fatefully my running thread of discourse.

And in my indices, no poem upon which
I could confer this honorary title.

Foundering in dictionaries and gazetteers,
I came there: Belas Knap, a chambered tomb.

The lips are closed upon that withered barrow:
A dummy portal, a slant lintel hung

Beneath a scalp of ruinous grass, her walls
A packed mosaic of blurred syllables.

2

Entering is a deployment of small silences,
Frail collusions and participations.

A scrape of some sad traffic on the ear,
Bird song at her old insouciance,

I pull these down into an underworld
Of images alive in their dark shelter.

Such corridors are tacitly inscribed:
Do not abandon hope here, but desire.

When old men's voices stumble down the lane,
They too must be my dry accompaniment.

There is a shrinking in each new encounter,
A heaviness attendant on the work.

The vanished bone sings in her shallow alcove,
Making a sacred and astounding music.

Ghosts are a poet's working capital.
They hold their hands out from the further shore.

3

The spirit leans her bleak peninsulas:
Our granite words loosen towards the sea,

Or hold, by some wild artifice, at Land's End.
The Merry Maidens dance their come ye all,

Keeping time to the piper's cold slow-motion,
Their arms linked against the lichenous Sabbath.

And a menhir, sharp-set, walled about
By a dirt-farm, a shuffle of lean cows,

Accepts, as of right, our casual veneration,
All fertile ceremonies of birth and death.

I see you standing, the new life quick in you,
Poised on Chun Quoit into the flying sky.

There, in that grave the wind has harrowed clean,
Our children crouch, clenched in a fist of stone.

The Hinterland

David

Arcadian, the scrolled trees lean
Over the head of the youngest son.

He plays for Saul and Jonathan,
For the curled flock, and for Absalom.

His elegiac pipe the organ
Strengthens into diapason;

The bells' brotherhood gives tongue
Where sallies leap to lin lan lone,

Spheres and Angels turn their song
To the propped harp's fingering.

Whatever is done, undone, done,
The gathering musics run as one.

Under the Words

Under the words, the word. There, for a moment,
Suffusions of slow light welled up and broke
Against unsettled surfaces.

Cadence against cadence. In their cut sheaf
Perdita's daffodils felt each torn spathe
Darken and cool as a deflected shaft
Broke head from stem. Wind set about
The resilient garden with a skirr of snow.
A globe of water on the sill inverted,
Subdued, then held these tiny languages:
Transposed scales of the Camera Obscura,
Aeolian harps, the unforced elements at play.

And now the white page, crowded to the margin –
So little space to write between the lines,
To place, against that weight and density,
The flying stance of wind or daffodil.
Under the footnotes, mesh and ply of tongues:
At windows, babel of obscuring snow.

The Piece

The straighter edges grow, dislimn and falter,
A light hand pausing at the wavering hem,
Placing the boundaries of sky and water,
Establishing the ground-rules of the game:
    The browns and greys from which it must ascend,
    The blues and greys from which it must depend.

Between the lines, a tumble and collusion
Of shades which cancel out to monochrome:
Fingers coax local colour from confusion,
Sprawled leopards on the shield, an onion dome,
    A coach's crusty gold, twinned horses' heads,
    Blocked hollyhocks afloat on airy beds.

They move as islands, distant yet related,
While patient clouds unscumble, and the wood
Fills out with leaf-work. Now, the celebrated
Ride stiffly through a patchwork multitude.
    Untroubled mountains fill with white: the place
    Is seen quite clearly as a crooked space

For that one piece whose blank sin of omission
Has failed the leaning sails, the smiling queen,
And put the heralds out of their commission.
What now can prop the swiftly falling scene,
    Come from some dust world back into its own,
    The ungiven line, the key, the cornerstone?

The Sledge Teams

History is polar,
A texture of webbed silences.

Her violent carnival,
Paraded tongues and costumes,

Bequeath a legacy:
White cerements, a shrouded rigour.

Our eyes ache.
The Blizzard Empires keep their secrets.

Fleshed in crystal,
A few old sledge teams and their leaders

Work each to his crevasse.
Black punctuations of ice,

Snow-blind, undeflected
By our lips freezing as they call.

Museum

Past Nature's nerveless limbs and pinions,
Hooked into dull parodies of motion,
Comes History, with another object lesson.

Here, Clio's rambling bargain basement offers
Brocades and truncheons. They make submission
To the bleak dictates of monologues, monographs.

Those played-out toys our children must not hold,
This polished cradle, obstinately lack
The casual context of a nursery world,

And sealed by glass, each skull and arrowhead
Delays, then slips our psychometric stare,
Who lack a means to focus on the dead.

Such flotsam teases by its air of statement.
Better the ruined bird, whose image spans
The blue dimensions of the firmament.

Topology of Ruins

It seems the nature of these forms to grow
Continuous as trees; their roots must ramify
And further pillars, arches, walls extend
In a more stable element than air.
Worn stairs climb easily, demonstrate for us
The ever-hopeful nature of ascent.
Knowledge that Heaven is unattainable
Relies on no more evidence than this.
Doorways accept the facts of exit, entrance,
But make no crude assertion which is which,
Nor even indicate here is not there.
Windows admit all modes of looking-through;
Columns at their springboard stance could throw
From each to each some absent mass of stone,
Yet bear instead the full weight of the sky.
From these infer the flawed, the tentative,
Are the most fitting gestures to assume?
Rather, lying at ease on the shaved grass, ⟶
Accept release from the burden of believing
So didactic, so complete a statement.

Dry Grass

A toss of dry wind sways the feathery husks
Where Burnet moths ripen their folded silks.
Roads nod and shimmer at their scumbled edges,
Busy with bright studs of flies. Nothing here
But silver conversations in the hedge –
Rumours of light freight lightly borne, let fly –
And a gauze clock relinquishing her segments
To bent horizons whitening beyond
The cancelled footings of an old hutment:
A scuffed exposure where the pale blades turn
Over and over in a ceaseless light.
On Eastern dunes marram wires out the sky
And blown volumes of small sand slew distance
Against distance. Air cleans her trackless fathoms;
The churchyard bleaches, darkens, to the death
And resurrection of this coarse tide hauled
Across the pleated grave-clothes, the dimmed brass.

Pompeii: Plaster Casts

It seemed to Pliny, stationed at Misenum,
A trembling pine stood from the distant peak.
When Vulcan beat new armour out for Rome

The vines that healed the landscape told green lies,
Skeined cupids hooded their toy bacchanals
And sparkling Venus dimmed her tesserae.

Those who in tremor fled the glinting pall
By an Ovidian sleight-of-hand renew
The loves and foliage of the littoral;

But here, where ashen faces tell the tale,
Cold anchorites pressed from retaining cells
Still fend off skies that neither pass nor fall.

Under the cockled ruins and stubbed columns
Glass coffins sequestrate a finer dust;
A long girl bares her lips against your kisses.

Conspiring years blurred out her skeleton;
Earth took the contours of her cooling flesh,
Saving a few stained teeth, a cranial bone,

And to that last of gestures – 'I must die',
Some dark enclosure kept a secret faith.
Annealed to shredded togas, sandal ties,

She and her fellows lie composed in fury,
Haunting the vault, their own substantial ghosts.
Air twists in pain, thickens to effigy.

Minsden

The chapel bears this press of trees,
Leading old windows, topping out
Some roof above the fallen roof,
Bustling their heavy green about
The shrouded flint. A pallid breeze
Picks at the twigs and faded stuff,
Fussing the tangled floor: dust blurs
Lost village and lost villagers.

Life here without her facing stones
To rule and quarter out the sky.
Only the pleated crunch, a spill
Of light poured off rough drapery
As blacks and whites and ochre tones
Work shifts about the curtain wall.
Ground shakes to sun: the rough infill
Glimmers about the nave and chancel

Where history, historian lie,
Recorder and recorded dead;
His granite flake split, slewed across,
Dark table for a sunburnt head
Of votive flowers: the twist and tie
Of camomile, corn, scabious.
Black flint secretes a fuller shade:
Cool gold strikes out across the glade.

Cumae: The Sybil

1

An ilex for Diana's hair,
A city solid as the air.

The stiff sails of Aeneas curl,
Find a temple stunned with gold.

Green leaves cannot hold their tongues,
Tablets are cut to Virgil's song.

The still sea goes hush-a-hush
Whose fish refuse Palinurus.

The price is high, her books are nine:
A murex robe spins for Tarquin.

2

Mourning Daedalus hoods his eyes,
Lizards thread the sunken maze.

His fingers will not limn his loss,
The bay wears blue for Icarus.

Chambered echoes are thrown, held;
The quarried glades of rock feel cold.

Aeneas calls the God by name,
His men break flint out into flame.

Three books burn: a sacrifice.
Proud flesh rises at Lucrece.

3

The wells are dry: rings of stone
Marry earth-flesh to earth-bone.

Furred and dumb, the Acropolis
Hangs its weight upon Aeneas.

Dark and bright speak volumes where
Cut blocks guide and thin the air.

Torn windows flay the light bare,
Misenus crackles on his pyre.

Three books burn. On the Capitol
The heads of Tarquin's poppies fall.

4

The sun tricks out a bough with gold,
But all the forests are long felled.

Aeneas leaves his men behind,
A marble torso props the wind.

The birdless lake is brimmed with shade
The solitudes are all betrayed.

A shipwreck of great masonry:
Rome is ash, the last books die.

His sword knows Tarquin cannot read.
The world's rivers run with blood.

Marginalia

1 *Leaf from a French Bible* circa *1270*
Villeneuve-les-Avignons

A single leaf. Deuteronomy.
The untrimmed vellum keeps its pinholes;
Guide-lines rest uncancelled.

Under the Uncials' lantern capitals,
Whose gentler reds and blues are hung
On vines of gossamer,

The blocked ink scorches on the page.
Textus quadratus: bent feet hook
The linked chains of the Word.

A slant-cut nib works on; the skin
Takes texture. God is woven close –
The figure in the carpet.

And at the margin, crabbed, contracted,
Lies evidence the page was read. No more.
A commentary on silence.

Wind in the cloister's lost mandala;
Cold hands re-cut the blunted quill.
Somewhere, the child Dante

Sees Folco Portinari's quiet daughter,
And all the formal rose of heaven opens
On the one slender stem.

2 *Jeremy Taylor:*
The Rule and Exercise of Holy Dying, 1663

— Grey flowers in their pleated urns,
The frozen spray, the flying skull,
And the dark words' processional.

Thomas Langley Purcell. His book.
About the Doctor's text extends
A glossolalia of hands.

Where the Baroque moves into night
These light and active fingers thrive,
Cuffs frilled, the mood indicative.

And one small coffin, monogrammed,
Nibbed out with nail-heads. Nota Bene.
The period of human glory.

The sepia glitters and grows pale,
Memorial of a heart at school;
Praeceptor, student, work there still.

'You can go no whither but
You tread upon a dead man's bones.'
I read you still between the lines.

A shut book – as a church door closed
On congregations known, unknown,
On tireless monitors of stone.

3 *Rider's British Merlin, 1778*

The almanac's green vellum skin is rubbed
To duckpond water. There, stub fingers felt
For the cold patina of a broken clasp.

Under the stitching and the rough-cut ties
The 'Useful Verities fitting all Capacities
In the Islands of Great Britain's Monarchy'

Hold their rusticities of red and black,
Pragmatic as all northern frost and mud.
Look to your Sheep. Eat no gross Meats. Sow Pease.

The rightful owner still some revenant
From foundered England, scrawling his Receits,
Juggling his Honny, Daffy Elixir, Terpedine,

For the Rumatis, the Coff, For Nervious Complaints.
'Jesus Jesus Jesus My teeth doth ake
And Jesus said Take Up thy Cross and Follow me.'

No name. And yet by sleight of charm and simple,
In language stripped by dumb hedge-carpentry,
Some churchyard clay turned Goodfellow survives

The Bale-fires leaping out at Coalbrookdale,
The long-defeated children, all the sparrows
God seemed to have no eyes for when they fell.

Answers to Correspondents

Girls' Own, 1881

Queen of Trifles, we must consider your question
    Puerile and foolish in the last degree,
And May Bird, while we thank her for the letter,
    Must be less extravagant with the letter 't'.
Hester, imagine the sum required for investment
    If all could claim a pension who were born at sea.

Paquerelle, we fall back on the language of the Aesthetics:
    Your composition is quite too utterly too too;
Joanna, ask the cook. Gertrude, we are uncertain –
    What do you mean by 'will my writing do?'
Do what? Walk, talk or laugh? Maud, we believe and hope
    The liberties taken were not encouraged by you.

Constant Reader, if, as you hint, they are improper,
    We still do not see how to alter your cat's eyes;
Marinella, your efforts to remove tattoo-marks
    Are wasted. Wear longer sleeves. We do not advise
Cutting or burning. Smut, we could never think it
    A waste of time to make you better, and wise.

Tiny, the rage for old china is somewhat abated;
    Sunbeam, we are ignorant how you could impart
Bad habits to a goldfish. Inquisitive Mouse,
    Your spelling is a wretched example of the art.
Little Wych Hazel, we know no way but washing;
    Rusticus, may God's grace fill your heart.

Tonjours Gai, your moulting canary needs a tonic;
    Xerxes, write poetry if you wish, but only read prose.
Cambridge Senior, we should not really have imagined
    It would require much penetration to disclose
That such answers as we supply have been elicited
    By genuine letters. You are impertinent, Rose.

Dissolution

Recall now, treading the cloister garth's clipped grass,
That time the Commissioners urged their sweating horses
About the uneasy land. Under huge gates they paced,

Ironically savouring that final confrontation,
The long concessions leading to surrender.
Houghton, Whiting: some took martyrdom. To fresh vocations

Most adjusted, leaving the cool painted house
Of prayer, and all its various furniture,
Each known and local contour of a dwelling place.

Lead bubbled, wood-smoke ascended. Rough secular hands
Fluttered both text and commentary, levelled well-set courses
Of cut stone for manor, mansion. God made no visible amends.

A spectacular pleasure, some. Bolton to the suave Wharfe leans
Her vacant choir. From Crowland's screen, decaying features
Gaze severely at the unlettered town.

Such emblems landscape bears as sands bear shells:
Twinned tokens, disciplines where life declines.
In an attentive ear, the same far rumour swells.

Rule

Freshets of rain: in such a glister
Decay speaks with her Roman tone;
God's City lies in scattered chapters,
The warm bread broken into stone.
> Eve passes with her basket; was
> Learned deeply here in bells and grass.

On features limned by Towne or Crome,
The ivy wanders à la mode:
An Early English style, appointed
To recollect us to our God.
> Light, where the foliaged waters run,
> And cattle lodged on gleams of sun.

The County History trails its blazons,
Bound in the tenantry's cowed skin;
Armorial in dissolution,
The Western sky looks full, yet thin.
> Sir Priest, in Tennysonian bands,
> Lies chancelled into folded hands.

Amen. The loose leaf of a Psalter
Glosses in gold our primal sin,
The ways we went through fire and water.
Those reds and blues embroidered in
> The hammered uncials lose their threads,
> A tangled harness for beast heads.

The power is stated, spent, retained:
Old Lear, Victorian with bright eyes,
Is bearded in his den with flowers.
John Gilbert's rough calligraphies
> Work out new crowns of thorn, entwine
> Cordelia as Columbine.

The Rector's horse is beautiful;
The Curate's jade is picturesque.
A disenfranchised demon wears
His runnelled face in sour grotesque,
> A conduit for the tumbling skies.
> We feel the water-table rise,

Staining the vellum signatures,
Parting the mason's greening seam;
The arks of our lost covenant
Beach out on Ararats of dream
    In rain which congregates the night
    Across such breadth, and from such height.

Atlantic

There's loss in the Atlantic sky
Smoking her course from sea to sea,
Whitening an absence, till the eye
Aches dazed above the mainmast tree.
    The fuchsia shakes her lanterns out;
    The stiffening winds must go about.

Green breakers pile across the moor
Whose frayed horizons ebb and flow;
Grass hisses where the garden floor
Pulls to a wicked undertow.
    A ragged Admiral of the Red
    Beats up and down the flowerbed.

Granite, unmoving and unmoved,
Rides rough-shod our peninsula
Where curlews wait to be reproved
And petals of a hedge-rose star
    The beaten path. Uncoloured rain
    Rattles her shrouds upon the pane.

Beyond the ledges of the foam
A dog seal sways an oilskin head;
The Carracks worked old luggers home,
Black rock commemorates the dead.
    The sea shouts nothing, and the shores
    Break to a tumult of applause.

But mildewed on the parlour wall,
The Thomas Coutts, East Indiaman,
Enters Bombay. Her mainsail haul
Swells to the light. A rajah sun
    Accepts her flying ribbon still,
    Though bracken darkens on the hill.

A peg-leg cricket limps the floor.
See, China Poll and Jack link hands.
Blown long ago on a lee-shore,
His hour-glass run on to the sands,
    He bids her wipe her eye, for soft,
    A cherub watches from aloft

Who knows our hulk is anchored fast,
Though timbers fret in their decline.
The cattle heads are overcast;
The gutter shakes her glittering line.
    Rage at the door. Winds twist and drown.
    We founder as the glass goes down.

An Age

Which schools itself to crucify
With steel, in her refinements,
The supplicant flesh, the cored bone.

We camp on the West's low promontories,
Where histories and dying fields
Wrinkle and founder in these leaden seas.

My hand still opens to a flower, a pen,
And look, my body's childish scars
Have outlived empires by their foolish luck,

As once, when over Europe's witch-lit stadium
The stiff, ribbed banners
Beat in the wind heraldic red and black.

That adamant mythology has fallen:
Those runes and talismans diminish,
Toys for the fingering of foolish children.

From such heredity, a long bleeding:
The banquet now lies spread in every street.
Sticky-fingered, we eat our hearts out,

And, unregenerate, watch incuriously
Each mage or dynast with his statue look
Trick himself out as the one avatar.

Beset by rumours of a single death,
Insisting on itself, protean, various,
We are too numb to count it;

Spell it away with a perpetual motion.
Driving widdershins through tumbled landscapes
We elide our origins and destinations,

Or, sun-shy, re-enact Platonic fabling,
Observing, in a glow of trembling silver,
The simulacra of our fellow shades.

When our lips move, what is left to read
In the lost texture of our languages,
Moving toward some Neolithic sound?

And when Miranda breathes her welcomings,
We, the survivors, hood our eyes against her,
Against the unbearable and receding blue,

Counting the years until we share our sleep
With that long armoury of outlandish bones
Folded and calcified in our slow hills.

The Hinterland

1

The summer opens where the days draw in.
Under the heat-haze, polished branches flock
To idle sound, and through a gauze-green skin
Cut sun lies lapidary on a book.
These are the instances a page retrieves:
A gravel walk, and a tall palisade,
The action of white light on the sharp leaves,
Tubbed oranges and lemons, placed and played.
The conversations of a house withdraw:
Birds walk among the foliage to uncover
Time's dark heart in the ash and sycamore
And all the summers counting lost things over.
     An urgent cipher through a wall of trees:
     Leaves pressing home their small advantages.

2

Leaves pressing home their small advantages
Beyond the sill, beyond the frayed sash-cords,
To this close darkness where the dead hold lease,
Their furniture impalpable as words.
From a green room they prompt the present play,
The ebb and flow of blood. Dust-crevices,
Where life is forced from an old sap. Each day
Our veins are charged with their impurities
This summer when the shagged elms tower and die.
Their played-out torches moulder in each hedge;
Maintain erect, under a changeless sky,
Their stumbled footholds and miscarriages.
     August, September, hang their weights upon
     The rim of summer, when great wars begin.

3

The rim of summer, when great wars begin
And Europe sprawls beneath her cavalries,
Licking the dust-bowl of a culture clean.
Ask for a rushlight, or a varlet phrase,
For woodcut figures cold as anchorites
In far cells of the mind? The dragon's teeth
Sown in a picture-book are Naseby fight.
What is the legacy these bones bequeath?
They were buried shallow, and the putrid meat
Soured through the grass, wept the green over
'So that the cattle were observed to eat
Those places very close for some years after.'
     We fat the dead for our epiphanies,
     But there's a no-man's-land where skull-talk goes.

4

But there's a no-man's-land where skull-talk goes:
She sits alone by the declining sea;
Winds turn continually upon their course
And all their circuits are a vanity.
To her slow heart-beat, frosted empires fail –
Bone-china bone, the watered eyes half-blind,
Dust hair. No living palmistries can spell
The bird-runes on the stretched silk of her hand
Which knows the loosening of silver cords,
Breaking of golden bowls. For her, the dead
Are a thrown captain on a sepia horse,
An old man with a nonsense at his head:
     Culled shades hob-nobbing where the airs are thin,
    A hinterland to breed new summers in.

5

A hinterland to breed new summers in,
And an old August working in the bones
Of children barefoot in a Northern town
Where windows speak in a long monotone,
All their black waters running deep. The ways
To washstand, jug and basin are dark shut:
Light climbs up to a silver bar, and stays.
Our children freeze; their urchin gestures cut
To crowded scarecrows on a cobbled field.
Their capped heads and their runnelled hands are full
With all our violence, and the stone is held
Which cannot fall; flung out, a dull arc pulls
    The locked sun down the road where elms turn brown –
    The unfleshed dead refusing to lie down.

6

    The unfleshed dead refusing to lie down:
    The favoured ones, the ephemeridae
    Who knew the enchantments of the lost domain
    And made a switchback of the ancient hay,
    Who played about the Rector's sleeves of lawn,
    Who won the Craven or the Nightingale,
    For whom the bright Edwardian summer shone,
    For whom Death was the Keeper of the Wall:
    'The sons of men, snared in an evil time',
    Whose luck ran out, whose claim was disallowed –
    The poplars all are felled: not spared, not one –
    Who lies in France under a cries-cross shroud?
        A great space, and young voices echoing.
        What inch of sunlight gilds their vanishings?

What inch of sunlight gilds their vanishings,
The harvests of our crooked scythes and spades?
'Huge, statuesque, silent, but questioning' –
Nobody, on his casqued and white parade,
Who left a name, a card, some ribboned bronze,
A song uncaptured by anthologies,
Whose flesh was eaten 'till the very bones
Opened the secret garments of their cartilages,
Discovering their nakedness and sorrow'.
One with all spun and all the spinning leaves,
The sift of man held close in field and barrow.
The eyes confuse: that rank and file of graves,
    Those dragon's teeth, those nests the birds have flown,
    Those penitential litanies of stone.

    Those penitential litanies of stone –
A prophylactic wreath lies bleaching there,
Washed by the sun, the interceding rain –
A granite finger to recruit each year
The dead, for whom two minutes can be spared
To make their speeches on the common ground,
To hear the feet withdraw, the hard flags bared,
The terrible trumpets for lost Rolands, wound
About the thinning heads of those who stand
Gathered and set apart, themselves the dead,
The citizens of the corrupted land,
The handful of old dust, the new seed-head,
    The may, the blackthorn, the November trees;
    A silence runs beneath these silences.

9

A silence runs beneath these silences
Where the shut churches founder in the green,
And all their darkness and their brightness is
One seamless robe to lap the creature in.
Bone-chamber, tumulus, the field of skulls:
The folded hands, and the high blackened helm,
Where honour and dishonour share the rolls
And night plays rook about the stiffening elms.
Here each arrival, each new harvesting,
Deepens the ripples in a strengthening pool:
The troubled fountain and corrupted spring
Find waters which must scarify to heal.
      Let the tree lie where the tree is felled,
      And there our conversations must be held.

10

And there our conversations must be held,
Behind the lettered spines, the faded boards,
Where a plain text of living is distilled
And old exemplars must correct new words,
Who saw the rose, sprung from its cloven hood,
Begin to put on darkness and decline,
Who knew the outworn faces and the weeds,
The vanity, the striving after wind;
Who spoke for those who set their hearts in print,
The pulped trees and the drab who hawked the rags,
The baffled cattle waiting to be skinned,
The blow-fly's rounder on the vellum page.
      Each book the substance and the shadow. Lives
      Where blood and stone proclaim their unities.

11

Where blood and stone proclaim their unities
Under the topsoil vagaries of green
Works the slow justle of the small debris:
The ruins of the Glacial Drift begin,
Driving the golden horns, the feathered shales
Over each crevice of the lost domain,
Making the way straight where the Blue Gault falls
To Greensand and her seams of Ironstone.
The skies are wind: spoil by a ruffled pool.
A perched farm blossoms on its ancestries.
Time's face exposed: the quickening muscles pull
Five fingertips across the centuries,
     Poised where the bedrock widens a dull gold
     And all the shadows cross on one high field.

12

And all the shadows cross on one high field:
A latter violence working in the grain,
The cockpit tangling on the shrouded hill,
The hangars closed, and the bent grass at noon
Twelve o'clock high. Bandit and Angel stand
And cool their wing-tips in a molten sun
Of Kentish fire, their long trails wound and fanned
Against a sky which cannot take the stain,
The lost crews working home against the wind,
Against new traffics and discoveries.
The elms are singled, failing one by one:
Earth entertains new archaeologies,
     Rehearsing each indignity of pain
     Behind the parched leaves glistening in the lane.

13

Behind the parched leaves glistening in the lane
Shade furs the cupboard rooms: heat piles a house
Of shapeless blocks where metal colours run.
Under a melting sickness, the obtuse
And ogreish language of a troubled sky
Flaps out its cloth of white and violet:
A speech where all the images elide
To pain of darkness and the pain of light
Till all the curtains rise, the whipped bough throws
A spray of ghosts across the hollow square:
A furious thickening in meshed foliages,
Blown droplets tingling as the flesh lies bare.
     The gathered waters drive for earth again,
     Diminished thunders breaking in new rain.

14

Diminished thunders breaking in new rain
And the rooms woken from a kind of dream,
The text and textures of their ground-work plain.
Calling each creature by its proper name
The conversations of a house unfold
One unremitting labour, which sustains
The open page, child's play and marigold,
The course the light sets in the hidden veins.
About the enclave of their pool, fish move
Across the shaken faces and the trees;
And through the air's refreshment all the leaves
Are congregating new-found silences.
     The chapter closes where the words begin:
     The summer opens where the days draw in.

15

The summer opens where the days draw in,
Leaves pressing home their small advantages:
The rim of summer, when great wars begin.
But there's a no-man's-land where skull-talk goes,
A hinterland, to breed new summers in.
The unfleshed dead, refusing to lie down –
What inch of sunlight gilds their vanishings,
Those penitential litanies of stone?
A silence runs beneath these silences,
And there our conversations must be held,
Where blood and stone proclaim their unities
And all the shadows cross on one high field.
  Behind the parched leaves glistening in the lane,
  Diminished thunders, breaking in new rain.

The Green Gate

The green gate leads to a prismatic world,
Strong mesh of flowers, interlace of paths
Extended from the living. Time and care
Create a stage complete and various,
Where properties of outhouse, cherry tree,
Can take each grandchild's breath away with love.

The trim lawn draws them, and the rituals guard:
Cold ham after journeys, jigsaws, clocks,
Those ordered rooms, signed by familiar smells.
The local gods, brown, wrinkled, silver-haired,
For whom the sprinklers and the children play,
Are one with maid, or wagtails on the grass.

Down each accustomed, gaslit corridor
They course like blood. Intent on dream and game,
They crowd the margins of an adult world
Whose text they cannot read. At Christmas time
The towering, rootless tree accepts their joy,
Lifting against the dark dim globes and birds.

All creatures move, dependent, to a death:
His first. Who makes that pilgrimage
From bed to bathroom? What yellow man,
Shambling and gaunt, extends his desperate smile?
Now flowers and lotions in a tiptoe shade
Bring sweet and sour infections to the air.

Playing in tainted sunlight, a child rolls
The faded croquet balls down private paths;
Charms time to a standstill. When spells fail,
Wears proudly to the town a serious mask,
Announces death with gravity, and, numb,
Wonders what lies behind the lowered blinds.

Soon she, felled by that hammer-blow inside the head,
Who lingers wordless, is a stranger too;
Lies on her double bed, smiles, weeps by turns,
While garden lights and sounds invade her room.
Dumbly the children sense how all things wait,
Poised on the obstinate beating of a heart.

Yet, as they grow, schooled by Spring funerals,
Or graves and gardens not revisited,
They learn the substance of the contract made:
That figured landscape, flowering in the mind,
Distant and perfect in unchanging weather,
Waits on their own deaths for true dissolution.

Garden Scenes

1 Paths

A garden tied
In pale green ribbons, lightly worn,

Where long-leg shears
Clip a fringe from dibbled edges.

Birdbath, sundial,
Station out these branch lines:

A thatched shelter
Closes a web of plaited wicker.

The margins crack:
Swollen asphalt bleeds out tar.

Yellowing box:
Wax leaves curl a dusty fragrance.

These grey reaches
Waver – fingers of old water

Where ants flicker.
A blue trolley grinds its castors,

Threading a maze
The august sun has stencilled in.

On blind alleys
A child pauses, always at the centre.

2 *Web*

Death is a dry-heart creature
Dangled at the light's corners.
Fly heads glister
Where the gummed silk swags,
Blurring the shed's dull eye.
A breath takes these backsliders,
Drifting their clockwork undersides.
Peacocks and tortoiseshells
Crisp; their charred wafers,
Unscaled eyes, dim marblings,
Fray at the latticed edges.
Spiders wisp and curl,
Trailing knuckles of bent grass
From hammocks of dust and frost.
As the door angles in a rod of amber,
Warm air flourishes the faded nerves,
Shaking dead fruit on a cloudy tree.

Trencrom

The salt brushed pelt of trees could hide them:
Ogres and witches who play pitch and toss
Or loose an apronful of clumsy pebbles
To stun the landscape into graves and kitchens.
Their lives are long and legendary as bones,
Their sleep deeper and harder than our sleep.

Quieter the gods of estuary and sand,
Holding their smoky fingers to our lips
And easing middle distance into distance;
Bruising the grass to a slow stain of brown,
Shimmering our goose-skin with mist fingers.

The dead men leave their sunken gates unposted.
An age of iron rusts into a silence
Made luminous, as evening light discloses
A cold intimacy we had not looked for.

As if even the stones could drop their veils,
Discovering some life under their scarred rind,
Or words form from a circumference of wind.

Rocks breeding chill in deep interstices.
The ferns darkening, and the lizards gone.

We are moving under, and beyond the hill.

The Spring Wind

The Spring wind blows the window grey and white,
Stripping the hangings, pouring out the rooms.
There are the dados, and the beaded moulding,
The gather-ye-roses on the children's wall.
Doors shake on their jambs: the spine of the house
Thrills as the sprung wood quivers, and goes still.
Something here high and cold, knowing old paper

And skirts of paint, flaking, and cream with age,
Grey floorboards, seamed and dry with mousy dust.
This loveless breath scours where a white face creases
And small hands knuckle over a yellow cot.
What calls is lonelier than wind, though wind is older,
Knows more, and knows it yet more emptily.
Ah, how the air fingers the pastel walls,
The shrinking webs; how the old house is blown.
The tussocks bare their silver undersides;
Under the warm brocades, the wings are pale.

The Old Pantry

Sun angles for a perch of glass,
Cups alight on their scroll hooks.

Life transfers to bone china
Her sparkling buds and lustres.

Oilcloth glistens to cut scraps of light,
A dimmed or glittering stillness,

But from the dark, the recessed silence,
White food floats dim surfaces.

Anchored at the pitcher's rim, a ladle
Swings a gleam over sweet milk,

Sugar crumbles a cold silver-sand,
New-baked bread swells under damp cloths.

An underworld, bleached and dumb,
Reaching into this fresh wash of air.

A Game of Patience

From 'La Patience' by Philippe Jaccottet

In the playing cards, dishevelled under lamplight
As broken butterflies, settling into dust,
Across the table-cloth, the smoke, I am aware
Of something best unseen drawing itself abreast
As the passing bell which sets the glasses tingling
Tells of the sleeplessness to come, the swelling fear
Of suffering fresh fear in the days' contraction,
In sharing flesh, the desertion of the sentries.
The old man wards them off, the long nostalgias.
There is a tremor at the heart to still. His glance
Turns to where chill rain drives against the garden door.

As the Rain Falls

They go about some job, as the rain falls,
Or to allotments at the town's coarse fringes,
Pausing for corner-talk in words rubbed dry
By the abrading seasons. Back home,
Dull boots unlaced, they cark at meddling children.
It is only that their faces, with the years,
Drift out of focus. The curtains close,
And each white stoneyard, set beyond the pale,
Riddles it out with yews and daffodils.
No amber preservations: now, the dwindling
Inflections of a voice pulled back from nowhere,
A stoop, the sun spread on a silver penknife,
A few honed surfaces – the barrow's handles
Polished and split, worked bare and to the bone.

Everywhere Light

Everywhere light, yet presages of evening
Dim briefly the burred gold, the crisp incisions
Naming the congregations of the dead
Who heard this clock's dull pendulum of sound
Drag the hours out through rubbed arcades of stone.
The heart-beat courses filtered sun and shade
Over the swell of shield, volute and scroll
Where Latin pins the dead against the wall
And a baroque hour-glass keeps equipoise.

Everywhere light, yet boulders dull to shade
This coarse grain milled from stone and shell, cancel
The glints of pink and blue on which a rock-pool
Suspends and half-composes her reflections.
The seaweeds level out their oilskin brown;
Secrete in lungs of pink, or charred magenta,
Baubles of silvered air: a bright ascension
To trouble the meniscus.
                                    Your hands are still,
Ageing more slowly at these intersections.

Old Lady

In the cluttered Regency room, her eyes cloud;
Stray over sampler, book and bowl of fruit,
Or the tumbled houses blurring beyond the pane.
Though the great bay still drags across the horizon,
Those Seine boats working it when she was young
Were smashed for firewood fifty years ago.

Here, she converses with the dead. The quiet air
Stirs to late news of our progenitors.
Names, anecdotes flow on. Such tribal lore,
The dry extension of their dust, stops here.
Their second death will come with our forgetfulness.
Outside, gulls lift over wet roofs.

She is tired now. Shielded from snuffing winds,
She has picked her way slowly down steep streets;
Must go to bed when Godrevy blinks her light.
Rain fusses the window. Offer her no judgement,
Who waits beneath the shadow of a greater one,
Sharing, with children, the right to our forgiveness.

Fore-edge Painting

Poetry of the Anti-Jacobin:
A sturdy quarto, whose morocco ribs
Texture the claret dye, the wide strapwork
Of burnished ribbons, looped informally.
Endpapers calm their whirlpools into stasis;
The cobalts, whites and azures of dried oil
Chart shoals and spindrift for an unsailed sea.

And as the Tory pages crisp and fan,
Shaking a landscape from their cockled gold,
A spectral blush of emerald and ochre
Sharpens to grass: a Humphrey Repton world
Which full-fledged oaks recede to punctuate.
An antique springtime rubs to sober autumn,
Tipped on a cut perimeter of leaves.

A stub of figures on the carriage-drive
Pauses past text and margin, their estate
Proof against any but the revolution
Of these equivocal false dawns and sunsets.
The scene dissolves into that wicked glow
Which bathes our childhood, our elected fictions:
All weathers in arrest, all edges gilt.

Scholar

He picked his way through life, to where
A strong-room and a narrow stair
Met in a pyramid of air.

Trinket and picture's dry parade
Patterned the funerary shade.
Cool were the silences they made.

His heart, rejected avatar,
He kept in a canopic jar.
Time cauterised, yet left no scar.

Blear, grim, he reinterpreted
Texts from the long Books of the Dead –
Their hieroglyphs amazed his head.

Before his cautious ink grew cold,
The tomb was robbed, the grave-goods sold.
The mummy-husk? Mere muck on mould.

Purifications

They have taken the flowers, and edged them out
To the churchyard wall; stripped the old graves
Of their scattered tokens. Sentiments decay,
At one with the shuffled grass, whose sand and ochre
Rustles with one voice, dries to skin
Over the blackening mat where the damp clings
And a moil of insects works all into loam.
The air purifies our affections.

Sun on the side streets. House contents cleared,
And the dust panes fanned with a new light.
Fingers pick at the told secrets, test
The trays of rings and brooches, the smooth crystals
Of the marketable dead.
                              But the cold briar,
A final ash knocked from its battered socket,
The sepia daughter, crushed into her frame?

Casts from the mould of a discarded life
Follow their shadows into earth or fire.

Somewhere, a wax face closes out the day;
A new cortège is leaving for the dark.

Effacements

The steady cedars levelling the shade
Bend in the waters of each diamond pane.
Furred cusp and sill: other effacements made
Where the armorial glass in bronze and grain
    Stiffens a lily on the clouded sun.
    The lozenge hatchments of the porch floor run

Far out to grass. The grave Palladians
Have gone to seed, long genealogies
Dissolve beneath their wet and gentry stones;
The leaves lie shaken from the family trees.
    As kneeling putti, children from the Hall
    Are playing marbles on the mildewed wall.

The letters and the memoirs knew His will;
All Spring contracted to the one hushed room.
White swelling grew, he passed the cup, lay still;
To the bed's foot she saw the dark spades come.
    They made such vanishings their deodands;
    The earth records what the earth understands.

Queen's May beneath his firstborn's coffin lid:
A lock of hair reserved, a brief prayer said.
'Each lifeless hand extended by his side
Clasped thy fresh blossoms when his bloom was fled.'
    Pain wrote in copperplate one epigraph,
    Then sealed the album's crimson cenotaph.

Behind locked doors, an audience of hymnals.
Tablet and effigy rehearse their lines
To cold light falling in a cold chancel.
Grammarians at their Roman slates decline
    Each proper noun. Bells close on a plain song.
    All speak here with an adult, eheu tongue.

But those frail mounds, brushed low by ancient rain,
Their markers undiscerned in the half-light …?
The last of day ghosts out a window; stains
The scarred porch wall, whose rough and honeyed weight
    Glows from the shade: stones so intangible
    A child might slip between them, bones and all.

The Doves

'Eheu, eheu,' doves follow to the close of March:
The white one blossoms, as on a Tree of Jesse,
Where the scaled mullions part the black-silk lights
On the tower lances. Sun eases the winter skin,
Firing her reds and yellows under membranes
Traced out by birdsong passing sweet and high
Through all the churchyard trees. Boughs come adrift
Over the splayed sword-work of spring flowers,
The superscriptions – Ballance, Mynott, Mellodey.
Rough marble lets fly her cold scintillae.
What were you for, who lie here in accord
With the erosions of this further season?
Light shivers from drubbed grass; then the stillness,
And the doves, as doves do, mourn, mourn.

Summer Palaces

The Cart

It is, after all, only a collection of leaves.
Hours bring them together; ends are not disclosed.
There is the work of hands, felt by their absence.
       They have taught the grasses

But the lesson is lost on them. The birds, though,
Know there is something that they have to do.
It is the way heads nod; they skip the air
       Which is not warm, not cold.

Is this, then, no-place? The wind might say so
As it feels its way through trees, draws down
A gauze of dust at the turning of a path.
       The sky makes itself plain

Upon the ground, and time shapes into seasons.
Their curls are shifted over here and there.
A chrysalis is cooled to the look of life;
       Wings fix, then dry away.

Earth over earth: here is the reliquary
Closed on a wheel chipped from the children's cart.
The talismans are scattered in the courses
       By which light answered them

When secrets were kept and the maze threaded,
The garden spoke with its one feeling voice
Through flowers which denied their own corrosions
       And had no need for names.

The Chain

Above us, numbing all our dreams with tales
Of bad islands, infestations of gulls,
The metal broadsides of our great ark tower.
There hangs the chain: sealed rounds of iron
Whose chafe and rust, they say, ensure our freedom.
Paid out with its reel of swollen fathoms
Something of us gropes there, where deeper, deeper,
The hook works pain into a muddy craw.

Allow us good days, when, in certain lights,
Waves ease links to invisibility,
Gleam slips from gleam, all the lithe flexure
Polishes to a haze of blue and pearl.
So the stump dwarves, gold-beating out Sif's hair,
Worked that obdurate element to a nature
Divine and animal: this was craft-work,
A clasp tendered by their slavish hands.

Our Pilot, arms akimbo, saturnine,
Rigged out in steeple hat and greasy frock-coat,
Stares back at us from his ancestral eyes.

The Dapples

Ripples break, widen, die – the solid pool
Cradling a raft of weed whose moorings ease
To the perceptions of a glancing wind.
Algae fume greenly, coiling their suspensions
Under the tension of a cold meniscus.
The chestnut dips into the apple-tree;
Grown crisp and luminous in the sun's affection,
Fingers of leaf-work clasp and ease apart.
While water-gleams, reflected, caught and held,
Wheel free their dapples into summer air.

A dazzle-paint, confusing space and time:
Waves, rocked about their clouded chequerboard,
Slip sunlight from the backs of Seven Seas
Which blows with silver music from a bandstand,
Twirls in a reach of sunshades, loosely wavers
From the spun roundels of a playroom stove
And shakes from frocks and flowers back to sky
Whose circulations gather and deploy
These glints which still and flicker in the leaves:
Young wings of light, working to fly, fall free.

Garden Lantern

Dry garden dust, wreckage of wing and case,
    Clings to the gutter-line, the ribs and veins;
Each ancient light splits from a slate of glass
    And Moorish arches rim the cockled panes:
A dull pavilion, mossed with verdigris,
    Storing dark nonsense in its cavities.

But lanterns call the light into a round
    On rainy evenings when the clock strikes wrong;
Glossing the laurel, patching out the ground,
    They speak of clearings in a forest tongue.
A searchlight swings its throbbing disc; once more
    A cloud of wings brightens the dancing-floor.

Now all the paper lanterns float it high:
    St Elmo's fire sits roosting on the mast,
A Jovial ball of light comes hissing by,
    And kitchen-girls quake to its thunder-blast.
A Jack O'Lantern aches at your desire,
    Hovering enticements over Grimpen Mire.

The pale Victorian lovers linger on,
    Though street-lights fray and crumble at the edge;
Rough jungle tracks of tar and metal run
    Past doubtful anacondas in the hedge.
Lianas of depression and despair
    Thicken their hold by Avenue and Square.

This metal socket for the groan of wind
    Makes room for absence, draws into its space
The darkness which will never comprehend
    Whatever moved upon the water's face
Or spins the globe in stoles of smoky light
    To cold antennae homing in through night.

Lighting Rehearsal

The old Wish-house wakes into our sleep,
Creaking its giant shadows round our heads.
It is Cold Lairs, the place of dead brocade,
Illyria, lady: always some Virgin Island
Whose caverns music must enter, and define.

The four winds drowse tonight, and will not strum
Aeolian harps. Our fields, our cloths of gold,
Are tacked down gingerly. The night draws on
Into its smallest hours. We prop our eyes
Against these brittle planes of acid light.

The Doldrums, and a spread of cold canvas. Space
Chalks out its miles to Cassiopeia's Chair,
Astir with dust-motes, old theologies,
Stage armies of the good and bad whose hosts
Admit the starlight on a curving course

To wash our pitched roof in its blended silvers.
Out there, the soundless acres grow obscure;
Here, we must clarify with our rough magic
Tropics of Cancer and of Capricorn:
The Islands of the Mighty, or the Blessed.

Spirits of Place, we beat these bounds again
At intersections of mysterious shade.
The diaphragms contract, expand, and throw
Their quivering roundels to the water-floor,
Bobbles of glow which skew the shape of things

Until the darkness gathered in the wings
Lowers all colours. Omnes exeunt.
Fresnels and floods cool their bright hutches down;
Someone brings up a pre-set for the dawn.
Our country waits to find its origins.

Stage Wardrobe

O pearly kings and queens,
Furnish your dusty thrones
From this rag retinue.

Chasten our nostrils
With corruptions of moth,
The fumes of grave-linen.

Here we exhale the dead
Whose talk is out of season.
They cloud the rafters

Or work a slow passage
To the fluff and nothing
Of their neighbour pockets.

What poor forked animals
Will cipher out these lendings,
Supply these unfleshed creases?

Cut him down, the hanged man.
With one brief kiss of life
Send the green sap rising;

Though your pale hands, reaching,
Sharpen to bone, to zero,
And your dress, motionless,

Fixes as bright things must,
Into a charcoal shade,
A puzzle of close air.

Three Sisters

for Phoebus Car

1 The Dry Tree

Baron, as your fingers untie music,
Four seasons ebb and flow, the migrant cranes
Wind their slow skeins from climate into climate

And the dry tree shakes in its dance-measure:
Green arms, brown arms, linked in amity
Though bark strips from the cracked and polished bole.

A hover of dust: the patterned air discloses
Leaves shivered with light, gardens whose pages
Open or shut as dawn or dusk require.

But then the dissonance, the stopped movement.
The room withdraws to its four corners
And no God speaks a word of grace or power.

For now the windows thicken to a snow
Obscure and vast, with powers to impress
The old and unborn armies foundering there,

And a green Maenad dances out her frenzy
About the sapless branchwork of her fellow;
The soldiers break step on the silting road.

A dead bird, loosed from the retaining sky,
Stiffens: a twig of clouded foliage,
Eyes fathomless beneath their cooling hoods.

2 Wild Grass

In corners where a bird repeats one note
And clouds make blank faces over garden walls,
Hoisting into the blue and beyond the blue,

Time is a study in continuations.
But for you, Masha, should meaning cloud and fail,
Life, you say, becomes wild grass, wild grass.

In such corners, that is the wind's concern.
The bird repeats one note chack chack;
The wall dangles with sour and vivid cherries

Whose notes are discontinuous, abrupt.
The child at the keyboard picks, unpicks a tune,
Coding the air with lost ends and beginnings.

Here is the wild grass: a speechless city
Where threads of life are plied into a sampler.
Errands are run by the quick-dying creatures,

Each movement bright and urgent as the call-sign
Of child or bird tapping their counterpoint
Against the clock, the poppy-head's oblivion.

Listen to the soft thresh of their ground-bass,
Time and the wild grass working, this way, that way,
Their tingling feather-heads, their cutting blades.

3 The Curving Shore

If only we knew. The garden fills with partings,
Rustling in summer silks and coloured streamers.
The green shell brims with music, and with pain.

A dance of insects, and the sun's gold beaten
Too thin for use: from all their cooling shrines
The little gods of place absent themselves

And broken paths return upon their traces.
A hopeless fork tricks out the garden seat;
The leaves are talking in dead languages.

Cloud upon cloud, the open skies re-forming:
Their echelons move off to the horizon,
Dipping westwards over the rim of the world.

Hand falls from hand; our eyes are looking down
Long avenues of falling trees. Apart,
The maple weighs its shadow out and down

On birds caught in a cage of air and grass
At work about their chartered liberties,
On pram-tracks lining out the sullen ground,

And music silvering the middle-distance
Whose bright airs tarnish as the bandsmen play.
The soldiers pass along the curving shore.

The Tragedy Of

1

He lays a sudden anger on the table
To fester with the ink and scratchy feathers,
His treaties, proof against all our entreaties.
We dress by mirrors which contain the gardens,
But the civilities of grass and water
Are fractured by a peacock's uncouth cry,
And a slow mildew breaks the quicksilver
From that perfection which our faces claim.

The coinage rings false, the guards are doubled,
And the Fool's head sits oddly on his shoulders.
An official artist has been appointed
Who doodles wolves, devises cold insignia.

This royal daughter, unfit for the game,
Settles her face into its hurt silk look;
Gathers flowers, listens to the harsh birds.

2

Yes, things here have been tripped to motion.
The tethered trees pull the winds close about them,
And their impartial heads fly East and West
About our furious riding. Metal hulks
Groan into mud. We shall impress the scarecrows,
Leaving the seeded ground to rook and rain.
Colour drains bare, our thinning bannerets
Are rubbed sore by many fractious weathers.

Somewhere, walls are hung with noble silences,
Justice is benched beneath the apple boughs,
A green field sets clown and shepherd dancing
And herbs sleep in dreamy underworlds.

A rusty beggar sounds his call to alms
But a fresh post delays us with stale tactics.
Our lidless eyes grow bright with resolution.

3

We have scraped out support and front-line trenches
In the proud flesh; wit and wisdom thicken.
Our heads nod nothings to the duckboard floor;
The lion's teeth glaze in a last rictus.
Some mouths are swollen with a foolish gold,
Some sticky with the crumbs of creature comfort.
A Tertian Ague: we shall sweat it out –
There are no gifts which remain ungiven.

Enter the giant sloth, a shroud of fur.
Death of brain-stem, cortex. Shall we move
Beyond the play of all our swords and cancers
Into a dust, into a valiant dust?

Lie, under the graveyard's airy gabble,
Careless of new command, the wheel of men,
The nimble flags which sprig about our graves.

The Comedy Of

1

A fickle spring, perhaps, or when the snowflakes
Fall and fall, but cannot chill young bones:
Under Gemini, when gentry sons and daughters
Exchange their habits, and with candid eyes
Wake to the marble of an alien city.
There the piazza, and the petty hucksters
Who ply their fingers, offer varnished fruits.
A stranger takes us to a house of shadows,
But the wood beckons at the city's confines.
The lady is green-sickly; her dark velvets
Fill with stale air – better leaves new-minted
When the dull ache of love swells breast and loins.

> The song carries,
> Holds its burden lightly;
> The furred scabbards
> Close on their unstained blades.

2

Our fears compel us to this place of changes,
These rash pursuits under old stars and branches.
The Duke is arbitrary: his tongue is taut
With sentences of exile, execution.
He tugs at the false beard of his unwisdom;
The currents of our blood flow otherwise.
A cap and bells plays mockers with the birdsong
And shafts of wit fly down the woodland rides
Where every tree is blazed with verse and chapter
From Andreas Cappelanus' Rules of Love:
His compass needle steadying our hearts
When signposts twist like wooden weathercocks.

> The song clouds,
> Drifts into the minor;
> A quickening stream
> Breaks open our reflections.

3

The stars have set, the longest night is over.
Hound-music on the hill; in palace windows
Threads of silver primp the morning light.
Tokens are fetched, the brass-bound boxes opened;
Captains and hermits tell their tales and beads
And voices break, caught between grief and laughter.
A father weeps, dressed in his careful finery,
As we exchange contrition and forgiveness.
Wrapped in the plainest of all silks and tissues,
One broods upon the night, his lean face shifting
Between lost youth and age. Some wounds go deeper
Than our new amity can probe or cleanse.

> The song gathers.
> Dancing in linked fingers;
> For a held breath
> The shade and light are one.

Twelfth Night

Our candles, lit, re-lit, have gone down now:
There were the dry twigs tipped with buds of fire,
But red and white have twisted into air,
The little shadow stills its to and fro.

We draw familiar faces from the wall
But all is part of a dismantling dark
Which works upon the heart that must not break,
Upon the carried thing that must not fall.

Needles are shivered from the golden bough.
Our leaves and paper nothings are decayed
And all amazements of the Phoenix breed
Are cupboarded in dust, dull row on row,

While branchwork set upon a whitened ground
Climbs out into a vortex of wild flame.
The substance of this deep Midwinter dream:
A scale of ash upon a frozen wind.

Our candles, lit, re-lit, have gone down now:
Only the tears, the veils, the hanging tree
Whose burning gauze thins out across the sky,
Whose brightness dies to image. And the snow.

Drop Scene

Theatrical: burnt cork and stave,
A basket hilt, wild cave.

Along the midnight esplanade
The sea's rhodomontade

Of blam, pause, blam. Underfoot,
Concrete sings at the root.

But each enormous head of foam
Breaks in a child's dream;

Condenses to a Flying Bomb,
And still they pop and come.

That Christmas Eve, when out was blacked,
Sirens sang Heilige Nacht.

Candle in hand, I tumbled air
The full flight of the stair

My mother, in her childhood, nose-
Dived – the high-pitched fracture shows –

To frozen faces, a stunned head,
Adding my drop to the raid.

Theatre of War, signed small and clear:
EXIT (pursued by a bear).

A Warning Against Sharing the Children's Dreams

Nothing's at ease here. Great soft armchairs roll,
Tumble and toss, dancing a cosmic dance
With numbers, matchsticks, clouds: white clouds
Teased out of clouds. Lumps swell in the throat,
Tongues weigh like years and toes are as far as stars.
The road goes smooth, then jumbly: the sun is calling.
Sick and crying, a girl kneels in the hay.
The landscape smells like a pack of playing cards.

Avoid, if you can, the strangers: the one with a bag
Who slips through the night looking for specimen bones,
The gnarled and veiny plasticine man, who hops,
Then covers and clings, the three unsmiling clowns
Who drift towards you on black motorbikes.
In a cool garden, a statue turns its head,
The play of muscles creasing a marble neck;
You are drawn deep into its empty eyes.

The dark dogs snuff your trail: the heavy air
Must be pushed away with straining, helpless hands.
An eye drops out in the chase. No time to find it.
Safe, but the other one falls to the floor of a cave,
Eludes your twittering fingers. Fire from the crests
Of the beeches, driving, driving. The valley is burning;
Shops and houses yield to a torrent of cars,
Fragile buildings thrust further and further back.

Lucky to cheat the outstretched arms, arrive
With two moons, a pterodactyl, an indigo sky,
Where the blue cold water and the shallow pink
Meet in their lazy curls, and a voice reads out
From its own Bible the quiet rules of water.
Here you can walk with a kind friend, sexless, nameless,
Whom tomorrow you will remember with vague longing,
Or alone on a bare green hill feel the absence of pain.

A Cambridgeshire Childhood

1 War Zone

The car goes wide about the bend
    Then fade, dissolve: the years rub down
The brightwork and the newest gloss
    To camouflage of green and brown.
        Under the magic apple tree
        Lie tracer and incendiary.

The tracks and half-tracks dip and sway,
    Break out their silver skirr and grind:
An endless convoy sliding past
    From fields of nowhere. Hoodman blind
        With ravishing stride moves like a ghost
        Towards an ever-burning coast.

White bulldogs cap the sentry-gate,
    And sad Italians, bound but free,
Patched out with lozenges and moons
    Dig for some pyrrhic victory.
        The camp's lines fade to a ground-plan,
        Lie Roman under shifts of rain.

The quarry lipped into the hill
    Silts up with scrub and masty beech;
Gathers on mats of dark and wet
    The spent rounds flicking from the breech.
        A pocky, tousled petrol-can
        Still justifies man's ways to man,

While osier and sallow grow
    Where diggers flay the gravel beds:
A blush of buff and emerald closed
    On belemnites with bullet-heads.
        Cold tinfoil bleaches on the hedge
        To set our pugging teeth on edge.

The windscreen vapours out with sky
   Through which, Ah God, the branches stir:
The light-washed reaches ebb away
   With Flying Fortress, Lancaster.
         A Lightning bolts the rainbow bridge,
         Sun caught on its twin fuselage –

Then the mill-stream. I overtake
   My doppelgänger cycling through
The ragged fringes of a war:
   The knowledge lost, if once we knew
         What song it was the sirens sung
         Among these cloudy trophies hung.

2 Pressed Flowers

— Nothing more empty than bright space.
   The wind runs down to a ploughed field,
   Sings a little in cold wires.

Time enough for two boys
   To pry about this chequer-board,
   Hedging and ditching April into August.

First flowers work their sampler:
   Pigments of sky and water
   Chalked on the freshening earth.

Then sun at apogee
   Glosses the full petals:
   The bede-roll lengthens.

The florets picked and pressed,
   Ichabod: the glory is departed.
   Here are their oiled silks,

Interleaf of veils and veins,
   The crinkled wafers fixed
   Against our transience.

Stained to moss and ochre,
   Fumitory, smoke of the earth:
   Picked on my grandfather's death-day.

3 Catholic Church, Cambridge

The spire climbs out of every vertical,
Its planes of stone dizzying to an apex
Where gold might be a blush of weathercock,
A nimbus, or that stern all-seeing eye
Whose level rays pick out conspirators
In the old prayer books: a vanishing point
Where the clouds' cataract, the smarting blue
Work to one end.
                The gantry clock leans out
A giant moon-face from this Jacob's ladder,
A court of numerals, where black long-hand
Goose-steps a dead march, and the dawdling sun
Visits the houses of its zodiac.
Under the aegis of that riddling gold
The horses turn their dipping carousel;
The convicts wheel the compass of their yard.

4 Cam

And Camus, Reverend Sire, comes footing slow
And I come footing slow to Mr Finch,
His burly priest. Though innocence is proven,
The only grace to make my merit grow
Is to drown weekly, inch by turbid inch.

God has appointed him a fisher of men –
Or boys. His rod and staff, they comfort me;
He dangles a clammy harness of grey canvas
To slap a chill on my goose-pimpling skin.
The sunlight lowers, degree by dull degree.

In draughty sheds, where ancient sweat lies stale,
And towels rasp a blush on skinny backs,
We, sectaries of some depressed devotion,
Strip for the dark immersion which prevails
Against the offending Adam. Dampish tracks

Cross concrete to rough steps of slime and gloom;
Refractions break about the smoky green.
I gasp and bob like some poor hatching thing
Through turdy puff-balls and a brown-sick scum,
My mouth agape into the fly-blown skin.

Oh, Father Cam, squandering your favours on
The sparkling reaches where the long punts slide
In summery indolence from Banham's Yard,
Accept from me a larval orison,
Rolling like Phlebas on your sluggish tide.

5 *Searchlights*

Shafts of light move in the dusty woodland,
Cleaning old skulls, re-surfacing the water.
The grass responds to them; the world lays down
Bolts of shot silk beneath their feather-weight,
Cutting glass roofs against geometries
Of sunlight building between cloud and cloud.

Night turns in her bad dreams. We are alert
To hedges thickening, the trees doubtful.
Men work about the fields with quiet voices,
Forcing a ribbed eye to this polar probe.
The moths are sealed; they quicken to a tumult.
Their wing-tips bruise on walls of ice and jet.

Over these columns quarried from ghost-stone,
The temple-roof hangs weightless, packed with stars
And other wings, brightening before they die.

6 Neighbour

She stands at the fence and calls me till I come,
Mouthing a message for the wind to lip-read;
Only my name stands in the air between us.
A slattern house, reeking with dirt and music,
A compound of long grass, drawn round with wire,
A summer sky, aching with Cambridge blue –
These are the substance of her misery
Which forces through our bonded bricks and mortar.
Her son comes home on leave; the sobbing furies
Thicken at night. Our lives become a part
Of that insistent voice, those wavering grasses.
Her garden burns, the red rim eating out
A heart of black which blows to feathery ash.
Low overhead the puddering doodlebugs
Comb the cold air, each weight of random pain
Clenched tight – these trivial ganglions on the nerves
Of a slow-dying war. My mother's love
Betrays her to the ambulance, and asylum.
All the doors close, but in the silences
Her message stays. There is no way to read it.

7 Summer Palaces

How shall we build our summer palaces?
Will the girls bring us sherbet, and our gardens
Brown to the filigree of Chinese lanterns?

The Emperor speaks in a long robe of thunder,
Bruising us cloudily; his combs of rain
Dance out a dance of more than seven veils.

Islands of bird-music; storm-voices dwindle.
Across the blue, cirrus and alto-cirrus
Draw out an awning for our shade pavilion.

Swallows will sew our flying tents together.
We live as nomads, pitching idle camp
Under the white sheets blowing down the line,

Or swing on ropes to somersaults of grass.
The hasps creak upon our airy gallows,
Roofed by light, floored by a crush of earth.

The strong leaves curtain us; we know each scent,
The deep breaths taken behind swaying curtains.
We have become the citizens of green.

Our walls grow firm in fruit and knots of seed.
A dandelion clock rounds out the hour,
Blowing our time away in feathered segments.

The night lies warm upon a wall of shadows.
We lie as naked in our drifting beds
As the close moon, staining us with silver.

H.J.B.

You might have seen him turn days over,
Looking, surely, for what he was looking at
And something else that could be there besides.

Appropriately, he kept a Walker's Diary
And climbed his Indian summers out in Fahrenheit.
Winter conferred degrees on him in ermine.

Clouds of snow powder blown along the fields,
An Ecceitas of greenfly at his roses –
Shocks enough for this confessional.

In 1942 the Christmas tree
Had 20 candles. The chicken weighed 6 lbs.
The temperature rose to 38°.

The role became him: an exacting scribe
In courts where Ceres and Proserpina,
Tardy or pushful at their rituals,

Would help him pencil in another year
With a total absence of pronouns.
He balanced their accounts of fruit and flowers:

Made timely logs of each unpunctual journey.
Chalfont, Banbury and Virginia Water
Took sober burnish from his book of hours.

His family: J and C initially.
To be followed by A. There were meetings
With close colleagues such as F or D.

At the last Christmas he told us all:
'I might not be with you another year.'
Delirious, dying: 'I seem to be covered with roses.'

The Waiting Room

We lie where she lay, feel the bed conform
To a shape not ours, a flesh grown thin as air,
And open her eyes again to the ebb of day;
Hear the gulls for her, find her conversation
In the crook of a stain, the shift of an awkward board.

Here she is close to hand, the stuff of her life
Pasted into the cracks of a room where pictures
Lower their oils to the dusk, dark upon dark,
And coffins of letters crowding the wardrobe floor
Look to her coming, after this long delay.

Now, the family voices gather her in
To bear her part in all their quarrel and fabling.
Her life a diary only the dead can read,
She takes her place as a proper name among names,
And we are locked out, in this, her waiting room,

Alone with shades, and with these, her comforters:
Lotions and bibles under a mantle of dust.
Night-thoughts of bone – a polish of wavering light
Reaching to where, still at the bedside table,
Lie Wesley's Journals, The Pleasures of Old Age.

The Box

The box he held seemed lighter than itself:
A space for air, a fence of brittle slats.
Its rooms were cubicles of dusty satin
Couched on by nothings, and the painted lid
A shade for shades. Under the varnished leaves
Two lovers, poised upon an equal lawn,
Tilted absurdly one high parasol;
The crackled glaze rubbed up their house to shine
As if all summer lay about their grounds,
Shaking ephemeral birds and flowers loose
To give them close delight.

               Then, a sharp sense
Of some dead language muttered under trees
Whose veils and canopies could not set free
The halting sun: vistas of matchboard rooms
Opened, and drew him in to squares of echo.
Against their darkness wavering sheets of glass
Made gardens tremble in a slow dissolve
Or faces form and re-form in ice waters.
He turned, and felt the small thing in his hand
So much dead wood: a token of erosion,
Things falling silent, faces turned away.

South Cadbury

A kestrel backed by fitful sun
Banks down a stiffish tide of sky,
And fluent shadows drain or fill
The pleated circles of the hill,
The sapless jetsam, high and dry.

Sour brambles cling, whose nubbled reds
Light rides awash with dung and mud –
A dark look to the squandered hedge,
The daylight blunter at the edge –
October shallows into flood

And flap of air: a beer-can keens
And an inconsequential ball
Makes orange dance-about and pass
Or canters over streaming grass.
The year leans outward into fall,

And through the film a touch of chill
From harebells late and luminous:
The crackled stems are dusted down
Into that prevalence of brown
From which old news might reach to us

Of press and havoc in the wood,
Of gated contours making way
And our conjectured pain laid bare:
The talk is rustled into air
Or scrambled into stone and clay,

And indecipherable, the scrawl
Of bent or briar's epithet
For hobnails or for chivalry.
The kestrel quarries out the sky
And life contracts: its terms are met.

The Inscription

It is the absent thing; there is no key to it,
        Rather no key the day provides
When catchwords and the text make no connection,
The table lacks a leaf, and the portrait
        Ghosts out the title-page.

You could not walk to where the distance grounds it
        In gatherings of blue and grey,
Or surprise it by your subterfuge
Where planes of moisture shelve among the valleys.
        Best be the stay-at-home.

Long shadows walking in the guise of light
        Keep it a secret from the hill,
And those who may at this late hour be working
To piece the table and the cloud together
        Still find the preface missing.

It binds, bound only by its own inscription,
        Chapter and verse. On the North fells
Two soldiers of the Second Nervian
Set up their altar. Genio huius loci:
        To the Spirit of this place.

Megaliths and Water

1 Menhir

Here, in the spaces between sea and sea,
Beneath refining decibels of larksong,

Come slow abrasion, and the clout of air
Whose unfleshed energy confirms the stillness.

The spores of sage and orange lichen settle:
Will you, too, make a virtue of all weathers?

The old gardener with his apron sack
Held his tongue; the leaves conferred about him.

I, Men Scryfa, the written stone, remain.
Do you read me? Read me. Over and out.

2 Stone Row

A long alignment stumbles into cloud:
The black and bitter groyne where we too walk
And feel ourselves drawn to an element
Whose voice is siren, ineluctable.
The markers firm their roots, passing us on and by.

Our footprints lightly bruise the skin of the world,
As cold and transient as the rippled wind
Nibbling at goose-flesh. The bents, the mill of shell,
Make signs for parting. At our nostrils rises
The damp sea-smell of our mortality.

3 Circle

A constellation of rough numerals
Is grounded in the bracken's cog and mesh:
A dial face, blind to our veneration.

Time breeds its long divisions at our feet.
The stone wastes to its own self-effacement;
Night will bring her furious clouds and spirals.

Stubs of impacted fire, these terminals
Trawl their slow shadows round a demi-lune,
Responsive to the sweep of unseen hands,

And hours go shouldered on, the countless grass
Is worked through all its hidden generations,
Stitching again the questions to the answer.

4 Henge

Somewhere the flattering garden slips away,
Green filaments are dimmed, and the occluded sun
Falters and checks: the lively pith goes dry.

Then blades heel over as the wind lays down
A silver course among the winter wheat;
The tree-heads close their giant separations

And Angels, flown above a painted manger,
Dance out the rounders of their zodiac.
The air is dressed with a particular light.

Beyond the legends glowing overhead
Love speaks one spacious word from his domain
To ease an answering music out of stone.

5 *Lake*

The curls of leaves hold water, a mercury
Which trembles greenly and is not spilled.
The garden keeps it in forgotten jars.

Hills cradle light, lowering its multitudes
To lake and tarn. Gathered, gathering,
Held to the brim, and held beyond the brim

The miles of sun loosen their shining figures
About the shallows, come to lively rest
On shelves of darkness, and of shifting cold.

The hung cusp quivers, and a clasp of silver
Closes the fissure of twinned elements.
Our breath is taken between lung and gill.

6 *River*

A tress of weed is brushed along the lie
Of water following its own pursuits
Where the spring frogs clump out the flats and shallows,
Their sand shapes mating in a drift and scrawl,

At the Mill's throat, a gravelled bull-head
Dawdles a spatulate shade. The grasses freshen.
We take presentiments of white and gold;
Life clarifies from shoals of ebony.

The river turns upon its pollard willows,
Each course cut cleanly; trickeries of light
Swing on their gimbals, these prevarications
Carried surely to the end which is no end.

7 *Estuary*

Meadows of water, where the nodding waders
Are brought to focus in a clouded glass,
And rain-shawls curtain off a dun horizon.

The casting worms tease out their tiny cairns
And voices carry over their own burdens:
Each indirection veers to indirection.

These are the silences to comb for shell:
We drag a shroud of bone from shifting sand,
A crumpled fuselage from Totes Meer,

Or find a witch staked out in her bleak pasture,
The rowers easy in their craft, the priest –
Salt words of God swell in the tilted throat.

8 Sea

Life, nourished from a primal green and grey,
Has logged these entries in your rolls and volumes:

Engines of plate and spar which work their passage
Over a cold brew thick with flesh and bone.

Creatures of plume and spray, their dark hulks buoyed
To those who are still busy about their dying.

One shadow mariner, who cannot anchor
Or grow to suffer the distress of landfall.

In spew and slick your ancient children gather:
Their draught of hemlock numbs you slow and through.

The Gatehouse

Late. And though the house fills out with music,
This left hand takes me down a branching line
To the slow outskirts of a market town.
We are walking to the Gatehouse. Mr Curtis
Will call me Peäter in broad Lincolnshire;
Redcurrants glow, molten about the shade,
The cows are switched along a ragged lane.
Tonight, my son tousles away at Chopin

And a grandfather whom he never knew
Plays Brahms and Schumann at the same keyboard –
Schiedmayer and Soehne, Stuttgart –
The older, stronger hands ghosting a ground-bass
Out of a life whose texture still eludes me,
Yet both hold up their candles to the night.
The Gatehouse settles back into the trees,
Rich in its faded hens, its garden privy
Sweet with excrement and early summer.
New bread and sticky cake for tea. The needle
Dances across: Line Clear to Train on Line;
The lane is music too, it has no ending
But vanishes in shifting copse and woodsmoke.
The levels cross: a light and singing wind,
Arpeggios, a pause upon the air.
The gate is white and cold. I swing it to,
Then climb between the steady bars to watch
The station blurring out at the world's end.
The wagons beat their poésie du départ;
The lamps are wiped and lit. Then we, too, go.

Signals

How could we tell the blaze, the patterans?
The chalk-marks on the self-effacing wall
Led us down Serpentine Street, and that itself
Was a true place, though less to us than some.
The barred arcades along the Brewery,
Tangy with fermentation and the dark?
A swirl of hop-scotch? But this was a thing
You could not do by numbers, so the dance
Would hurry you along some privet path,
Tying the grasses down to indirection,
Crossing your heart, laying your newest course
By pithless twigs, or when such markers failed,
Shredding a patch of paper to false snow.
It's true, return was always where it led to –
Though the trails petered out in Indian country,
And all the homing was as cats come home
Ghosting on feline automatic pilot.

As for the start of this mild wanderlust,
You could tune loosely in to that long thrill
When sound is shaken to a keen vibration
Before the engine grows along the curve,
Thrown on and caught by gantry after gantry
Down lines astounding in their verve and shine:
Empty and cold as metal in the sun.

Halt

Now, as clouds rag out over low hills,
The light sours between dead ground and water
Unfalling, about to fall. The windows work
Their shines, their dusty spaces, and we
Are gathered to this halt, where, long-uprooted,
The metal courses hold the flowers together
And a gas bauble in its Gothic cabin
Centres the sunlight. Now, that brightness moves
To open doors while shadows come to close them
Upon a sway into the tunnel's throat,
Each leather tongue tight on the stud, old smoke
Flocking its acrid wastes:
                        a rack and slide
Where the impossible couplings work upon us.
Here, all the seats were taken long ago
And soldiers fill the night with canvas ditties,
Their pile of arms impressed upon the blind.
Somewhere, the dazing halls of terminus
Where the clock lords it with a Roman hand.
We sit it out until one point of light
Probes an untreated green into the curve.
A signal's clack stiffens to monitor –
One cellophane eye held up against a cloud
Which still has not let all its waters down.

Three Couples on the Last Train

Her drunk, petulant voice lifts the stale air,
Quivering with self-indulgence.
'All day I've tried to glow for you.'
Introspections, recriminations.
His head hangs heavy, sad.
In this intelligent, clownish face
The large eyes do not respond
To the travelling play of shades, reflections.

They look on with understanding,
Taking the ironies, in delicate amusement
Exchanging light glances
Which come to rest like birds.
These tokens show they are not threatened.
Their bodies make gentle love,
Nudging, parting,
To the carriage's uneven sway.

Head-scarved, sober,
Her worked face empty, she sleeps
A settled sleep no rhythm but her own
Can now disturb. By her side
He sits monumental, trailing a hand
Heavy with blue tattoo.
Unmoved, he looks beyond or through them
To a lit, hammering darkness.

The Site

Here stone was tackled, and the sum of labour
Handled about by long and clumsy weathers.
The mystery gathered underneath its caul,

Brimmed the dark conduits, the untiring song
Raised by processionals of blood and wine,
The unpicked rose, furled in a high window.

A life uncaught, whatever sketch-books came
To brush away dissolving rainbows, play
On figured surfaces to sound the deeps.

Enactments cloud the air. A catch of breath
And flurries of great scree bring the work down.
An absence welds its presence to the grass

As ineluctably as in Hiroshima:
Man, scored upon a retina of stone,
Struck by black radiance, light incalculable.

Horace Moule at Fordington

Distinction flowers on the darkened lawn;
    Sash windows open, the soft tassels shine
Where velvet rooms wait till the blinds are drawn
    On scents and silences. The heads incline
By their own gravitas; the tones exact
    Allegiance to a Church of England norm
Which has no need of this brief ritual act,
    This pause, outlasting all their hands perform.

Nobody smiles. They feel the sunlight there,
    Leaning across our shoulders; time unfurls
And we look back at these who look elsewhere.
    Their clericals absorb the light; two girls
Bleach out the summer from their swelling dress.
    A strength to set about the work of God,
This quiver-full of sons; quickened to bless
    Their strong maternal staff, paternal rod.

A neat, pale face, bare to the clearest bone,
    His eyes mere patches of uplifted shade,
The gifted one, the friend. And here alone
    All sight-lines meet, before the swerve and fade.
Our shadows will not press the grass apart,
    Or stir the cord on which their love is strung:
His finger still invites us to the heart,
    His throat uncut, the bastard son unhung.

Die Ahnherren

Close-lipped, severe, well-fed, Herr Doktor stares
Bleakly across a hundred or so years,
Self-centred in gilt-edged security:
A Lutheran Pastor in his gown and bands,
Partnered by mob-capped wife, pallid and angular.

The Old Ones – two awkward pieces which must fit
A complex tribal jigsaw. Some second cousin
Or genealogic frowst might, perhaps, place them.
We have no skill in family connections.
Disgraced, their custom is to face the wall.

Naming is primal. Features without vocables
Are monstrous as long men without their shadows,
And though names muster to encumber rolls,
Old churchyards, deeds, out-of-date almanacks,
No syllables we try give back identity.

Their loss is irremediable. A teasing flotsam,
Improvidently lacking who, when, where,
Riddles no serious person cares to solve,
They may, with luck, become their time's exemplars:
Minor and tongue-tied ghosts, dwellers in limbo.

To dealers, even such continuance dubious.
Gloomy, unsaleable. By this prognosis
Their stolid self-appraisal stands condemned;
Unlucky ones who chose a black profession,
A dignity which shrouds them to decay.

Moving

That is the course we shall not travel by;
The road sheers off where hedges put in doubt
A finger-post for other lights to claim.
They have moved house; we could by moving try
To work the cats' eyes home and find them out,
But all would call itself some other name

And in a slide the place goes into shade
As if a crust of nettles or old stone
Were cropping out a lost Tom Tiddler's ground;
And that sharp turn we could or should have made
Gathers a cavern look: all the unknown
And windy nothings live inside this round

Of orange lamps which underpin the cloud.
Our stake is at some crossroads far ahead,
Though clumsy tear-drops on the windscreen dim
Each destination, known or disallowed,
Each circuit flashed between the quick and dead
Or pulsing darkly like a severed limb.

Natura

1 Water

A few glint beads, prisms of shaken life.
Against the window, fusions, intersections,
And a world whose edges have dissolved again

Under a fresh persuasion: the spring rain
Whose light cordage brings down the heavens,
Whose greys are only fitful shades of blue.

Water, whose runs are runs of broken music:
A trill played quick and far, a slow fingering
When the house lies asleep, its dream unbroken.

Or down there, on some early morning lawn,
Each web is lit and purified by dew –
No net so frail it will not gather her.

And in still flower-heads, the wax gradations,
The reach of pistil, stamen, these cool transients
Delay their globes against a film of colours.

Where cusps are strung on branch or guttering,
Distillations of thunder and of chasm,
The lineage is traced in clear succession

To those far crystals where a child, gazing,
Descried nothing but a sense of crystal
And trembled, though in the glass no shape would stir.

2 Cottage Flowers

Courtesies of childhood,
Their clouded whites and blues
Are restless with breath
Drawn in another country.

Light in its infancy
Knew them as visitors:
Their hold tenuous,
Their growth wayward.

Frail singletons, whose scent
Links evening, evening;
Whose names are threaded
On webs of rain and shine.

The packet breaks
Its rainbows open,
Sprinkles hard dust
On fingered ground.

And the shades follow,
Beckon from crevices:
Nodding familiars
Skilled in the one season.

Under a stone sun
They flourish, fade.
We endure the reproof
Of their knee-high conversations.

3 Sky

Seamless: a fiction of blue
Whose deception is absolute.
Only this pale inflection
Reveals the tension we are under.

Lucid as the Virgin's robe
Our garment of untextured air:
An innocence betrayed by time
Only to further innocence.

Tabula rasa. No chronicle
Of dawns or witless thunders,
Pencillings-in of larksong,
Dull scrawl of turbines.

Bombstick, meteor,
Clouds at their shape-changes –
Such clear denial
Deepens to affirmation.

Nine spheres elide:
Law consonant with justice
In the perfected stillness
Of a flying wheel.

A blue to which eyes lift
Fixed scars in constellation:
A drift of tracks, recording
Where angels fell from grace.

4 *Lanes*

Night, and the car poised.
Under a lunar gauze
Ash-tints, charcoal,
Cloths of scrim and velvet.

The labyrinth wakes:
A slough of dark skins,
A stretch of shadows.
She plumbs her own deeps.

Nothing, up sleeves
Cuffed by mouldering lace.
Ragged gloves haul in
A spool of light.

Brief revelations:
The air moth-flaked,
A spectral rabbit
Stuck in a white throat,

And one red planet
Steadying a compass card
Of pewter fields, deployed
In polished sequence.

The engine croons:
Rough dip and rise.
Sealed, centreless,
Time hangs by a thread.

5 *Natura*

How should her creatures best express her,
Her own brush-strokes being the more painterly?

Meads enamelled under the sun's cloisonné –
Leaf-gold laid on the still trellising –

Or sketched and frayed at every wind's decision,
Tethered grass a flail of grey and silver?

A push of wheat softens the sprawling field,
The bones' complexion, gentled into green,

Ghosting a crop whose plaits and bunches thicken
To summer, working slowly with the grain.

Savours of juice: blent acres of harvest
Come home and dry under a tawny moon.

Then the felt absence of the stubbed hedgerow:
Tans and ochres harrowed to the horizon.

Under the tides of air she breathes, exhales,
Move all nomenclatures of birth and death

Who share this ark, who ride our zodiac,
Swung on a course which seeks and makes no landfall.

Her veils disclose only what they insist on.
She works the swelling truth of these deceptions

To one great canvas, drawing our compassion:
Each atom locks upon its perfect fury.

6 *Woods*

Not the expanse of pine,
The Sibelius music
Whose dragging winds
Move darknesses about.

More, these stands and hangers:
Snippets of lean fur
Where the packed fields
Fall away to roads,

To be passed, repassed
In light and half-light:
The night's fullness
And the day's contraction.

Clenched on rises,
Their bent backs brushed
By feckless weathers –
Slow colours come and go.

Sun mazed in branches,
Bird-skull, beech-mast,
And the doves, who talk
A language of otherness.

Best, for the most, unvisited,
Their siren privacies
Calling to sentiments
Green, lost, deciduous.

7 *Grass*

Floored by tall grass,
Where greenish light
Balances about
Its fades and coruscations,

Your eyes brush
The feathered reaches:
Bodies hook and eye,
A wing-case cracks to film.

Air passes you over,
Draws to the field-edge
Slow blurs of down,
A float of sound.

Now, a long strike of heat.
The veils thicken;
Under the drowsed fringes
Earth stirs in her good dream.

And you, suspended
In that grave clasp,
Are light as the high cirrus
Yet carried further, and away.

Bound, with all travellers,
For the sack of summer palaces.
Gold thumbs to ochre.
Birds become their shadows.

8 Stubble Fires

Contours break the skin.
Acres of dust air
Drain from scraped fields:
White sheets bleaching to the hedge.

The rims harden
To bruised copper, violet,
Summer dead things,
A still shake of leaves.

East replies to West
In hems of ragged flame;
The darkening oils
Drift, merge, dissolve.

Ragnarok for the small gods.
Twilight wavers; cloaks
A shrivel of insects,
Morsels, burnt offerings.

And summer falls back, slips
Through policies of scorched earth.
Nostrils wince and prick
At charred rounders and striations.

An old ground-plan
Settles and clarifies
Land hurt and cleansed,
Picked to the black bone.

9 Frost

Arcades: a stand of silences, columnar.
Grass in her coarse furabout of silver,
Orange berries, blurred in their small shrouds –

Here are the hollows of night where the mist swarmed,
That dull annealing to a lodge of trees
Teased into shocks of wild and risen hair.

And, as we climb, pressed to a grey breast-work,
Air, poring over these chalk undulations,
Disturbing no pleat in the land's graveclothes,

Slips over lynchets cut against the light:
Rings counting out the centuries of cold.
Flesh creeps under the hoar skins of down.

Curds of ice block out each rut and furrow
The clouded rind fosters a blackened eye
Resolving nothing in its basilisk pupil,

While overhead, a scarified sun displays
A disc inscribed with no identity,
Outfacing a segment of declining moon.

Yet when the hill, tiring, inclines her head,
We find, returning, there on the scrawled hedgerow,
A few glint beads: prisms of shaken life.

The Beach

And Langland told how heaven could not keep love;
It overflowed that room, took flesh, became
Light as a linden-leaf, sharp as a needle.

Today, the stone pavilion throws a window
Into the morning, that great strength of silver
Shawled from the climbing sun, and on four children
Alive to rippled beach and rippled water
Swaying their metalled lights in amity.

Hands build an airy house of meetings, partings,
Over a confluence of the elements
Here, where there is neither sex nor name,
Only the skirmishes of dark and bright,
Clear surfaces replenished and exchanged.

Black dancing in a hall of spacious mirrors,
Far voices, and the hush of sea on sand
Light as a linden-leaf, sharp as a needle.

High Summer

High summer spills and swells.
Her airs alternately are smoothed and stirred
By collared doves and the complaints of men.
Machines prick, point and scar. Each creature's vagrant mood
Dizzies and handy-dandies. Staunching her green blood,
Self-healing, she binds up her wounds again,
Denies continuance to groan or word,
Slackens her decibels.

Perhaps our lesson is
To learn by heart her light: the dominant,
The reach on which shade flutters when hours tow
Dark over. Is the day, the night's pre-eminence
Assigned by tropical or polar temperaments?
The chequers on the windowsill allow
An Alice eye to tease or circumvent
Their old antinomies.

About the furniture
These travelling breaths and coruscations flow
Through muted intervals of flight and rest.
Cup, wine and table's cool mosaic now invite
Us to consider well, according to our light,
Whether an action or its lack suits best
A still-life, balanced, feigning not to know
A hand, alert, unsure,

Can trick and touch this room
To a new mood; rouse pen and ink to fret,
Create a minor and a shifting scene.
What heartbeat stirs where that Corinthian Skyphos stands,
Redeemed and purposeless, stolen from votive hands,
Next to a Roman flask, whose pale sea-green,
Flaking to pearl and crusted violet,
No longer can perfume

The air? Light seeps away,
And fading colours emphasize that weight
Chafing the watcher at the barricade.
Between the first symptom and the diagnosis,
Between the faint hope and the hard heart's prognosis,
Come those considerations of the shade,
Night-thoughts which must be managed, soon or late,
With such grace as we may.

Again the shades relent:
Allow slim quarter-lights and silver gleams
Their possible, unreasonable joy.
A friend combined an iron and a river bed
And lay all summery there, his somnolent head
Tickled and cooled, the merry waters' toy,
Lapped in his rhythmic, amniotic dreams,
Mithraic and content.

Mere metaphors at play,
This shift of enmity or harmony
About the paintwork? Trees are laced with airs
Of various refinement. We are dumbly walled
By tall blue skies on which no warning signs are scrawled
Until an August cloudscape stiffly bears
Its load across; reminds us vacancy
Is execution's stay.

High summer interlude,
A calm to fear, a calm to celebrate,
When no wind stirs, nor any tongues intend
Plain questions, crooked answers. Our soliloquies
Relieve and distance all those harsh complexities
Of suffering and laughter at each end.
Now, ground is dead or holy, and we wait
Both chastened and renewed.

Song

The wind that winds the weathercock
    Pours down his golden throat;
He braves it out by shine or shock
    And plays his song by rote.
        All weathers twine away from him
        Their sweet or sour, ablaze or dim.

On parson, pedlar, man or maid
    He keeps a weather-eye,
His tail's a tumbling-bright cascade
    Where rain and rainbow fly.
        For he's the Golden Vanity
        Who spins about his thrice-times three.

The skies may beat him black and blue,
    He rides them out mast-high,
And whether weathers fly to him
    Or he makes weathers fly,
        Is held in balance by his art,
        Who knows his head-in-air by heart.

The changes ring from hour to hour,
    The bell-notes ply, reply;
Planted upon a shifting tower
    And in a shifting sky
        His weathers, too, will serve our turn,
        His sunlight cool, his showers burn.

Winter Quarters

The Christmas Tree: 1944

1

Complements of the season,
   Fire, Fleet and Candlelight,
A curtain-work of velvet,
   The web and pin of night.

Out in the grey garden,
   The paths go nowhere at all,
A fruitless net of branches
   Holds to the frosted wall.

It is cold wood and silence,
   Unshapes of flint and loam,
Ground weathered into absence,
   And the bright sap called home.

The New Year brings a stranger,
   His shadow stains the land;
He waits upon your threshold,
   A live coal in his hand.

Against his throbbing advent,
   Flare-path and Bombers' Moon,
The sweet must of the fir-tree,
   The branches thick with rune.

Your roots are cut and broken,
   Your star is finger-high;
The mast-tree plumbs the centre,
   Its tinsel splits the sky.

2

There the brocades, woven against the darkness,
Quiet bevels of glass and figured walnut
Making their change of substance into reflection,

Calling the child, who, propped against his pillow,
Presses his eyes till they swell against the knuckle
And stares from his bed into the swarming pitch,

Alert for the jewels pinned on processional air,
Trinkets of light, a more than royal progress,
The unlocked treasuries of a ghost-kingdom.

The child slips down to the room where nobody comes,
Lured by a siren tongue to a virgin country
Where every contour is a familiar strangeness.

There are the robes hung over black-ice windows,
The tree which has decked itself, and sings to itself,
Blossoming there, O rich Arabian tree,

The Phoenix tree, rising each year from the ashes,
Freighted with ice and flame in a twist of glass,
Whose delicate birds are the birds of so, and no other,

Whose flowers and fruit are sufficient, sufficient still
For the child who stands, caught in the wavering crystals
Which foretell all: his image diminished, untarnished.

3

The life caught in its branches
    Crumbles in drying air,
A shiver of dark needles
    And a year stripped bare,

As cold as a clean bed-sheet,
    The stubbed wings in the sky,
The ache of an old floorboard
    Or the snow's white lie.

'Give me back my legions,'
    Cry Emperor and Child,
'That box of pretty soldiers
    Whose bones lie far and wild.'

Long miles of sighing forest
    Reach out, out and away;
Break ice on a birdbath,
    Scatter the crusts, and pray.

Dusk, and the twisting candles
    Blend shade and flying shade,
The quick and the dead link fingers,
    Their circle made, unmade.

The box is packed, my children,
    Gone where the dust-motes go;
Under a crease of tissue
    The softened colours flow.

Nights Turning In

Nights turning in, fold upon awkward fold,
Leaves of a burnt book whose dull pages crumble
Their brittle edges and discolorations.
The stitching weakens; flesh and spirit split.
Black epiphanies: a spring of night-sweats,
A text of dreams, a dance of matchstick bones
And soundless windows opening on no-place.
The hour-glass nips my sand against its fall.

Somewhere, across a street, a woman dies.
The knowledge drugs all childhood into sickness
And curtains flap out sharply at the bedside.
Nothing, nothing. A boy's head turns about
And elm-tops thresh across the greying light.
Cold bowls of spew: the shake, the severance
When something old and wrinkled can be still.
Love hovers there upon the slipping years.

Commotions of the dark, the soldier's time.
A faceless private twists against the wall,
Coughing small blood. A stretcher, swing of doors.
The neutered smells parade these corridors
And night softens a bruise upon each corner.
My sentry paces with his greatcoat stiff;
I take a prisoner to the sour latrine.
His grin shines there like a clutch of handcuffs.

Old bombers throbbing in, the gunfire tumbling.
Between this wake and sleep my sister sings
'A Bobsa sat in a little box bed,
And this is what the Bobsa said':
The winds blow hard through all your bricks and mortar,
They carry harm, though harm makes long delay,
Settling its spores against a full fruition.
The horseshoe at your door spills out its luck.

Conscriptions

National Service 1952–4

1 Cleanliness

Is the one song of our innocence.
We have become that which it is next to:
Every mess-tin has a silver lining
And greatcoats mint pure bobbles of fools' gold.
Is not the sun a high armorial fire
Which angels burnish into excellence?
Down the long barrack-room our bedding-cakes
Repeat their candy icing and grey fur.
Beauty lies one skin deeper. Look, the broom
Is pared and pared again to spectral white;
The bucket is, no doubt, intangible,
Whose cusp is moulded from the freezing air.
We have ascended Plato's giant ladder,
Worked our eyes free from sensual mote or beam.
Each cants a virgin rifle to the light,
Whose shining gyre repels the wanton dust;

The ghost of a flea would not escape our scrutiny.
We dream of purity: a myth of coal
Whitewashed to some immaculate Everest,
The world's grass trimmed into a uniform
By scissors neat and crisp as a wren's claw ...

'Take his name, Sergeant, and dismiss.'

2 *Scapegoat*

Who are you there, huddled on your bed,
The sum and cipher of the awkward squad,
Your unbulled boots as round as innocence?
Nothing about you that will take a shine:
A soggy face, whose creases will not harden
To stiffening rubs of soap or these hot irons.
Unserviceable one, we circle round you,
Trimming our tackle to the Spartan code
And licking the parade-ground into shape.
Your fingers are all thumbs, your two left feet
Are mazy as your tangle of dull webbing.
Our silence covers up for you, our hands
Work your fatigues to parodies of order.
The small Lance-Corporal stares you cold and white;
His fingers itch to knock the silly smile
Off that dim face. You are our crying need,
The dregs and lees of our incompetence,
A dark offence, a blur on the sharp air.
These squares will not assimilate you now,
Whose discharge, something less than honourable,
Leaves our hutment stripped of all reminders
That something in the world could be in love
With pliant, suffering things that come and go.

3 The Square
(Blackdown Camp)

Can you draw from cold spring air
That whispering host which hovers lightly
Over the strutting heads of our brief Stentors,
Who rasp and wail with bulled and brazen throats,
Bothering our confusions into order?
Here the old regiments were brought to heel,
Dressed, and dismissed into the common clay.
Rosenberg knew it: nineteen-sixteen.
'Slow, rigid is this masquerade',
And the May Queen out of all her finery.
Something passes for sunlight on the Square,
And fading away in combes of Hampshire sand
Guard-room verandahs twist their Indian tricks.
Tongues fade, cross-fade; the air is empty,
Drilled hollow by the legions of the damned
That in the crossway and the flood had burial.
We are the soldiery of the nursery-floor,
The rasp of khaki coarse at neck and thigh,
Our heads held high by plasticine and matchsticks;
Who grow in grace, perfecting symmetries,
Learning to stand at ease upon the carpet,
Ready for Floor Games, and the Little Wars.

4 Sunday

A choleric sun, nailed to its meridian,
Bothers the lazy hours from slipping westward,
Idle on their afternoon parade.

These are the lone and level sands of time.
Asphalt, the old sweat, glisters a mirage;
Angled shadows drawl and dawdle.

Slow, slow, the reined-in coursers of the day:
A nest of lorries, fender snug to fender,
Bounces the aching light from glass to metal.

We yawn our backs upon the iron bedsteads,
Cupping our hands to cradle shaven heads.
Eyes hold nothing of the sky in them.

Someone writes the world a long, slow letter
Which will be sealed with a loving kiss.
A twisted tune breaks like a bad-luck mirror.

Unhappy pin-ups freeze in their chaste lockers;
Barrack the green shade with their secret curves.
Bad minutes drift their ciphers into years.

5 *Range*

'Your weapons are given you to kill the enemy.'
Corner him in your eye; his name is legion,
Or Boredom, or the Sergeant-Cook.
He jumps like a grasshopper from the breech,
Tinkles among the pebbles of the range
And dies there in a little spill of brass.
As sights are notched up, he appears again
Under the zoomorphic guise of Bull or Magpie,
Travelling by Inner and by Outer Circles.
We splay our aching legs, shoulder the kick,
And ask again for a report of him;
Riddled, he returns a dusty answer.
Don Quixote leans there at our shoulder:
Gestures and angles underneath his whiskers,
A furious windmill of small arms and cane.
There, where the flapping tic-tac of the Butts
Confuses hand and eye; there, there his tricks
Appear and disappear in shreds of cardboard.
This is your enemy: the aching sun,
That baulk of sand, the estuary's blue sky.
He is the slipping knot of bedclothes
Whose linen face collapses at your feet,
The man of straw, pierced by your pigmy lance,
Who dies his death: a thousand thousand cuts,
To bob and come, to bob and come again.

6 *Night Exercise*

From Inferno's lesser circles,
    Imps of darkness, sooterkins,
Crack their cloven hooves to sparkle,
    Barking at each other's shins.

Chilly fingers knuckle over
    Till the skin's as blue as woad:
Pin-up moon's a lonely lover,
    All the signals are in code.

Stars loose off their ammunition:
    Rounds of blank. Our comic turn
Leaps from its jump-off position,
    Frights the butter from the quern.

In a burst of Chinese crackers
    Fools make circles to Ducdame;
Walking dead go to the knackers,
    Hamlet's father doffs his armour.

Disrespectful groundlings grumble,
    From their traps the devils rise;
Thunderflash and thundergrumble
    Rub the sleepymen from eyes.

We are midnight's mischief-makers,
    Dreamers dithering their dreams:
Sectaries of quakers, shakers,
    Mice agley in best-laid schemes,

Lambs gone ravenous for slaughter –
    I kill you and you kill me;
Tell the Colonel's dirty daughter
    'Twas a famous victory.

7 *Assault Course*

Tarzan is swinging, all his ululations
On undulant display, but Jane is waiting
Somewhere in Italy: I trust and love you.
We flounder after him up scrawls of netting,
Tricksy reticulated interstices
Which catch a shoal of twitching fins and fingers.
Our pendulums of flesh on rope lianas
Soar like Lieutenant Robin and his Batman;
Piranhas, non-commissioned, coast the waters,
Apt for our boning and our filleting.

These are sad tracts of sand to founder in:
Limpopos set about with fever-trees,
Free-standing cliffs of absent-minded wall
And a Cloaca Maxima to drain us.
We sink with Carver Doone to the abyss,
Tipple with Moriarty to the Falls,
One with all those who lost their feet, and fell,
Whirling their cloaks about the Eiffel Tower
Or joking as they passed the nineteenth storey.
These are the ups and downs of exaltation,
Small dodgems of the flesh. We dive through tyres:
Hoops of old fire to set the tigers blazing,
And under catacombs of rolling canvas
Shake hands with Alan Quatermain, Tom Sawyer.
Through, over, under, off – a stocking stitch:
There's no doubt left that we must pull our socks up.

8 Guard-Room

The New Guard forms, is present and correct,
Stamping its dolly boots, slapping its rifles.
We dress according to the ancient lights.

I am their Corporal; at my conscription
They take their stint of turn and turn about,
Conjuring for me their forgotten faces.

Lights out in barrack-blocks: Alma, Dettingen.
The sky has moved into its winter quarters
Over this coarse plain, bruising to the heel.

The sentry's breath disperses a still plume.
We have dismissed the sun to his great arc;
The pendulum moves deep and slow beneath us.

Should some goodfellow come to bless this house,
He must be challenged, were it the Prince himself.
Even our shadows have offended us.

My lubber-fiends deploy and stretch their arms
To the one bar of our electric fire
Whose raw scrape intensifies the cold.

The Guard-room mirror plays its monkey tricks
And small hours crawl towards the edge of light,
A sticky silt brimming our mouths and eyes.

We are the tutelars, our field-dew consecrate,
A smear of cigarette-ash on the floor.
Even this dull ground needs a libation:

This staging-post for Somme and Passchendaele.
The Square whitens towards our armistice;
In France, their markers steady the parade.

9 *Sentries*

The inspection of shadows is our trade;
It is a business like any other.
Their stony faces are their misfortune:
Scratches of chalk on streaky blackboards.
When they speak, they do not raise their voices
And their complaints are blear and frivolous.
We know the fret and chafe of swinging iron,
The high wind slipping through a stretch of wire,
And little devils twirling in the dust
Abouts and roundabouts of wrinkled leaves.
Underneath the lamplight, the barrack-gate
Admits an air of cold authority,
Winking at our buttons, flickering ice
On swollen toecaps, lustrous ebonies.
We stamp their seal into a crush of gravel.
Let it all pass: ay, that's the eftest way.
We would rather sleep than talk;
We know what belongs to a watch.
Our relief is at hand; he will undertake it.
Wrapped in our winter pelt of pleated greatcoats
We fall into the consequence of dreams,
Careless who goes there, borrowing the night,
And will not stay to be identified.

10 Prisoner

You have fallen through it all: a cipher
Among the ranks you are reduced to,
The untamed residue of our glittering bull.
I watch your cropped skull bob between two Redcaps,
Those fresh-faced bullocks of our *Staatspolizei*
Stiff in their creases and their icy blanco.
We shall survive, but you are the survivor,
With nothing left to lose, or do, but time.
Your conduct prejudicial; crimed, impenitent,
Inured to having all the books thrown at you,
You do a Buster from the sliding train
Or slip your skin between the gated walls.
Your number's up in all the Standing Orders;
Our colours cannot call you. Your presence here
Is merely another absence without leave.

I link our wrists, trapping the bracelets on.
How shall we celebrate our Silver Wedding?
You flick a grin, strip with a knowing eye
My poor sleeves bare of sundry birdshit chevrons.
Oh, thing of darkness I acknowledge mine
By the conscription of a signature,
Your lightest word is ponderous to me,
But I will take you for the night's duration
While Moon ticks off the hours on her demob chart.
We shall walk out together, much in love,
For such a petty pace as you would creep to,
And hunt the shadows with a pack of lies,
Fusing the blue ghosts of our cigarettes
Till sleep takes you, and a sallow lamplight
Bones your neat head to cunning innocence.

The tents brown out a Scottish hillside:
A canvas of cold water drenching down
From all the tops into the lagging valley.
We drape our beds and rust like iron things.
I would not know that soldier's face again:
Merely a wedge, a pallor from which talk
Breaks out and runs in darker rivulets,
Working its horrid nonsense into corners.
Night after night he picks a sentence over
Until we riddle out the half-told secret.
His fingers are the draw-strings to a knife
Which keens and wakes with him beside the pillow.
He swears that it will get them, do them in;
The knife knows better as it sleeks a blade
Which never will let blood, or cut the knot
That tied his brother's neck to breaking-point
At the fixed, formal hour. That guilt must be,
Can only be, a blinding innocence.
His twitching face settles against the dark;
Rain courses down, icing the cold cheeks,
Fretting its runners deep into the clay.
What kindness in the world loads him with this:
An amulet to cut and come again,
Peeling the running air to slips of light
And tender for the dead, surrendered flesh?

12 Envoi

There lies your way, Major,
    A year of the old parade
Before the ribboned tunic
    Must gather dust and fade

As the hung smoke of battles
    Fought in the long-ago,
Memories of sap and salient,
    Tobruk or Anzio.

Now, our final parting,
    Neat, dry as your hair.
(The newest batch is wheeling
    Over the sun-struck Square.)

'Yes, sir. Demob tomorrow.
    No, sir. University.'
'Missed all that. Never made it –'
    (Staff College, Camberley.)

Somebody else in the morning
    To serve, to stand, to wait,
To type Battalion Orders,
    To keep the long files straight.

'Too long in the tooth, Corporal.
    Shake hands. Good luck to you.
'Thank you, sir. Are you sure that...?'
    'No ... Nothing else to do.'

Farewell to all our greatness,
    To musket, fife and drum,
Before the new lean armies,
    The new lean missiles come.

Samuel Palmer: The Bellman

1

So many loves and passions in the dust;
The city black and swollen, a bad dream
Shaping the night to its own lumps and savours.

Its river-voices will not come to rest
Nor its tumultous brew of humours clarify,
Though keys to courts and tenements rust bare.

Tongues run blind far out into these reaches;
Days are laid waste by this trafficking.
The moon rising tells another story

To Samuel and his nurse, there at the window.
Its metals blend in the ascendant;
The garden fills with smokes of dusty silver.

An elm crosses its shadows on the wall;
The motion of its growth is held, opposed.
A plying web gathers its strength about them.

The two of these share Milton's words with us
'Vain man, the vision of a moment made,
Dream of a dream, and shadow of a shade.'

2

'Seclusion without desolateness,' he wrote,
'And darkness without horror.' In this place
To which his working hand and eye have led us
       We are made freemen.

Ancient, you renew the hills and valleys;
They will confide the secrets of their dancing.
Your inks have run into a spire of smoke,
       The houses' foliage.

Old England is a pile of matted shadows,
A plaid of deep grass; where the meadows draw
The little threads far out into confusion
       Our footsteps follow.

Your hatchings cross and thicken: falling ground,
Breastwork of thatch and clay, a brush of leaves
Where all the sharp, sweet voices of the day
       Hunch in their feathers.

The rising moon describes her magic circle;
Mushrooms pry blind among the pricking dew.
The Bellman's chime gutters our lights away
       From country matters.

We rest in darkness, darkness which has come
Out of the grave to tell us that the dead
Are undivided, and their absent breaths
       Are fruitful for us.

La Primavera

In this, her kingdom, fictions of light gather,
Suffusing the pale flesh in a grave trance
Which is her thought, and whose desires are other;
The light airs hover over a ring dance.
The grace-notes hold there, and the hung fruits glow:
The riders all are fallen at San Romano.

The garden shaped my steps to her consent;
I read the text of her inviting hand,
Knew time to be dissolved, the censors absent.
No city shook its bell-notes on the land,
No New Jerusalem: mere trembled gauze
Whose veils disclosed and hid the garden's laws.

Then, when I turned, light lived from edge to edge
And each defining line became the source.
The glancing room conferred a privilege
To enter silence, follow out its course,
Turn to a window and exchange a stare
With frost laid cold on paths: untrodden, bare.

I knew this light, those breaths our dead resign,
That gift of tongues which holds authority,
Those dancers on some gold horizon-line,
That chosen ground. Her kingdom set me free
To share an hour unmeasured by the clock,
A space drawn freely between key and lock.

How, though, to judge and weigh the shift of planes
Or tell the climbing foreground from the sky?
Under the music come the dragging chains
And we are littered under Mercury.
Arrows must hedge the Saint; the pearl flesh dulls,
And Mary weeps there in the Field of Skulls.

La Derelitta bows her head, life thrown
To one eternal gesture of despair:
The flawless courses on unyielding stone
Pave the twinned elements of earth and air.
Savonarola burns; the scorched tears run,
Time throws a black smoke up against the sun.

Yet the globes hang there, and the star-flowers spill,
Speak mortal names on an immortal ground
Which is the ground of being, printless still;
The grove still sighs with music beyond sound.
Hortus Inclusus, and there is no stir
From haloed leaf and turf announcing her.

Transformation Scenes

1 Evening in the Park

The groundwork fading, shadow crossed on shade,
   A no-man's-land of cold uncertainty:
The crooked sunlight breaking up the glade
   And something ciphering from tree to tree.
      Low tides of night-dressed wings,
      Flickers and pesterings,
Enhance the opiate of ruins ruinous,
   The burst of star-shell fallen to the floor,
   The spectral ravens croaking 'Nevermore'
      In tones most ominous.

Back at the Hall, red drugget leads the maze:
   A ghostly peepshow of embroidered rooms.
Though sometime bones of little good-dog Trays
   Whiten the wet mould of their chamber-tombs,
      Each stuccoed altitude
      Gold-frames a buxom nude –
But all the garden gods have smudged into the rain.
   Such absent-minded tritons in the lake!
   We wait, and feel again the long light shake,
      But will not come again

To tease the trinkets from the jewel-box,
      The baubles from a Georgian Christmas-tree:
The must and rust of humming-birds and clocks,
      The filigree, the tat, the pedigree.
            Time now to stump the hill
            Where stone is dressed to kill
With bobbled obelisk and dumpy octagon,
      Where some sly toad lifts an unjewelled head,
      Revisiting the mansions of the dead,
            Each son et lumière gone

Which might, perhaps, throw a bewitching light
      On these dishevelled fictions of an age
Diminishing, kaleidoscopic, bright,
      A minuet on a revolving stage.
            It is the moon's affair.
            Her blue blood washes where
The frost of cardboard castles thaws into the grass,
      Small pyramids tell tales of smaller kings.
      Oh, button mushrooms in your fairy rings,
            Tout passe, tout casse, tout lasse.

2 Scott's Grotto, Ware

'From noon's fierce glare, perhaps, he pleased retires
Indulging musings which the place inspires.'
So, Scott of Amwell, fearful of the pox,
      Shifted his garden ground;
Quarried his Quaker frissons from the rocks
Till winking, blinking, Dr Johnson found
A Fairy Hall, no inspissated gloom.

But slag and pebble-bands decay and fall,
The glimmerings and lustres fly the wall
Whose rubble freezes to a dull cascade.
      The flint-work strikes no spark
And its begetter dwindles to a shade
Composing, decomposing in the dark,
Scribbling an Eclogue in a candled room,

Turning from Turnpikes or Parochial Poor
To the close circuits of this tilting floor,
Caves editing a Gentleman's Magazine
    Of cold and fading shells
Eased from their chambers of pacific green
To ride the beaches and the long sea-swells,
Then pressed into this ragged, alien womb

Which closes its dark backward and abyss,
Its miniature, yet Stygian emphasis
Upon your childhood voice, its terrors crossed
    Upon their own reply.
'Oh, if you're lost, then tell me *where* you're lost,
I'll kiss away the little deaths you die
And bring a light to raise you from the tomb.'

3 *Ornamental Hermits*

Veiled melancholy, mid-day accidie,
    Improvings of the landskip sheathed in rain:
We dwell, not live, shifting from knee to knee
    In robes as uncanonical as plain,
Nodding, like Homer, over knucklebones,
    (Cold vertebrae a starwork on the floor)
Serviced by birdsong: vespers, compline, nones –
    The cycles of unalterable law.
Our eremitic dirt, our nails prepare
    A mortifaction close to Godliness;
Under the tangled prayer-mats of our hair
    Each sours into his mimic wilderness.

The desert fathers, locked into each cell,
    Knew all the pleasures that retirements bring:
The succubus, the tumbling insect-hell,
    Assault of breast and thorax, thigh and wing.
Our bark-house windows, open to the sky,
    Show vellum faces, blind-stamped and antique:
A glaze of rigor mortis at the eye,
    A tear-drop crocodiled upon the cheek.
The unread Testament aslant each knee
    Will not dispel the simple moth and rust
Corrupting us, degree by slow degree,
    Into the scattered frictions of the dust.

We beck, we hoist our creaking arms, we nod,
   Blessing processionals of cane and fan,
Attuned to Paley and his tick-tock God
   Or swung in gimbals pre-Copernican.
And who dare call our observation vain?
   The celebration, not the celebrant
Will keep the ancient order clear and plain;
   We too are arks of His great covenant:
God's weathercocks, upon his axles pinned,
   The beads of an industrious rosary,
Tibetan prayer-wheels turning in the wind,
   Imprisoned things which float the bright dove free.

4 *Portmeirion*

A slatted nest of pastel boxes hides
   The unfrocked Emperor of Considered Trifles,
Who, from some frolic cubicle decides
   New dispositions for old sacks and rifles.
     Gardeners, with water-can and paint,
     Furbish each rose and plaster saint
       With fresh bravura.

Or have these cracked and speckled eggshells hatched
   The frippery Princes of High Cockalorum,
Preening themselves about the gimcrack, patched
   With paper marbling and a fine decorum.
     We courtiers swell a scene or two,
     Feather their nest, improve a view
       Stippled as Seurat.

So what's to do but pace and pace about,
   Wearing our motley, and our Welchman's hose?
There's something déshabillé in our rout;
   The Buddha's stomach flows and overflows.
     Alice won't play. Why has she come,
     All frumpishness and suck-a-thumb?
       The place can't lure her,

Though the gold-leaf is laid upon the green
  And night will see the uncomplaining air
Gauze our its pretty transformation-scene,
  Swish rockets leaping from the tiny Square –
    That way the Old King left the town,
    His ashen blessing powdered down –
      Such sprezzatura.

5 *The Makers*

The dinky castles slip into the sea,
Though primped in paper flags and button shells;
A deckle-edge of ocean lips and swells,
Mining and slighting all our quality.
        We see
Their looped and window'd raggedness decline
        Into a sift of sand,
Hardened and barred as wind and Eastern wave design.

The scarlet toadstools pack themselves away,
The Christmas Cakes are crumbling to the plate;
The royal icings of their blood and state
Are one with all the snows of yesterday.
        The tray
Still keeps the touch of sweetest marzipan,
        Though little tongues of flame
Nibble the tissues into which their colours ran.

Gardens and gaieties are blown to seed,
The nymphs are crying down their party frocks;
The peacock straggles back into his box,
The secateurs are rusting in the weed.
        Agreed,
The gnomons are in shade; each gnome's expression
        Feeling the rot set in,
Is weathered slowly to a deepening depression,

But Homo Joculator starts again.
Though dyed in sinks of great iniquity
His mackintosh is black for luck, and he
Is whistling as he potters in the rain,
        The pain
Absorbed by cupola and curlicue,
        Those inching distances,
Castles in Spain which lend enchantments to the view.

Or

To step out into the drying garden,
Or rest greenly under the swarming branches –
The question rests in its own equipoise
And blue weighs out its great indifference.
Droit de Seigneur: the springing sunlight,
Here, or upon the antique Malvern Hills,
Will choose Copernicus, and Ptolemy.

To turn the first page of the great unread,
Or idle down a long-familiar margin –
The fingers know direction as they move,
And we will take their curious attention
Closely to heart; observe the Brimstone's flight
Who must explore mansions of air and light,
For his crisp yellow is definitive.

To follow shadow's course along the hill,
Or lift the eyes to dazzles of plain sky –
We wake to ceremonial chorus, find
Each blade of grass resolving Hamlet's question:
An old cat, fuddled in the border dew,
These flowers, half-opened and appropriate.
On a May morning, the word is golden.

Possessions

1
(M.R. James)

Shy connoisseur of ogee, icon, rune,
    Professor Prufrock ruminates decay:
Old Crowns and Kingdoms, food for thought and worms,
    All preservations held beneath the moon,
All sleeping dogs which can be kept at bay
    By gloss and glossary of well-thumbed terms.
His monograph extends by one dull page –
The last enchantment of his middle-age.

A fugitive from groves of Academe,
    The salt groynes running black from sea and sky
Betray his buried life down miles of sand.
    Low-tide: the beach is ebbing into dream,
Cold bents and marram-grass hang out to dry
    On swollen dunes. Deep in the hinterland
The calf-bound pages fox in white-sashed Halls
And stonecrop tightens on the churchyard walls.

Oh, blackthorn, unassuming country wear,
    Oh, modest rooms booked in some neat hotel:
Such pleasantries of the quotidian
    Are crossed by a miasma in the air.
Though bridge, or golf, might make him sleep as well
    And better than thy stroke, why swell'st thou then?
Bell, book and candle fail: the shadows mesh;
He counts the dissolutions of his flesh,

Appalled by faces creased from linen-fold.
    His textual errors thicken into sin,
Sour skin and fur uncoil about the night,
    Grotesques are hatching from the burnished gold
And countless demons, dancing on a pin,
    Repeat *a real fright, a real fright*...
Brandy, the first train home. The past dies hard
In stench and flare of bed-sheets down the yard.

2
(Walter de la Mare)

Grave summer child, lift your unnerving eyes:
Black bird-beads, drinking at the fluid light.
Whatever sifts among the unread leaves,
You pick your way, no Jenny Wren so neat,
Through Brobdingnag, here where the old aunts traipse.
Billows of shade, each face so loose and vague:
The stuff and nonsense clinging at their lips
As dusty, musty, as an antique wig.

A Conversazione. Old affairs
Flutter in broken heartbeats to decay,
Their ribbons fading into family ties.
Only huge, grown-up clouds for passers-by,
Cooling slow images in Georgian panes
Which close on rosewood, darken up the glaze
Of Dresden, and that chandelier which leans
Weak lustres over unplayed ivories.

The daylight shutters down, the white moths climb,
The house aches into whisper and desire.
You lie in bed, prim as the candle-flame
Pressing against the wing-beats in the air,
While nodding flower-heads and scents grow pale,
Mist curls where willows clarify, or dim.
As murmurs thicken in the Servants' Hall,
The callers gather; you are not at home.

3
(Rudyard Kipling)

The skull's base burning, and a swelling pain.
    A migraine of the soul: the Gods withdraw
Who made their Headings plain, and plain again,
    Whose word was Duty, and who spelled it Law.
        All slips beyond his reach – in the dark wood
        Where a wild nonsense claws substantial good.

The Lord was not there when the House was built,
    Though strength lay in the Mason's grip, the Sign,
And some who knew lie out in France, the silt
    And regimental headstones hold the line.
        Air thick with sighs; dead children stretch their hands
        To the Wise Woman, she who understands.

Is this the end, is this the promised end?
    Strange voices travel by Marconi's wire;
The crooked cells proliferate and blend,
    The cut runs counter to the hand's desire.
        A high wind wraps in winding-sheets of rain
        His House of Desolation, closed on pain.

They work about him at the razor's edge,
   Coax the indifferent stars to purblind sense:
Green simples, grounded by an English hedge,
   A surgeon, wiser than his instruments.
      He is returned, in ignorance, from the Gates.
      Under the draining tides the Day's Work waits.

Fachwen: The Falls

1

Green upon green: the crag discloses
Oak leaves over coronals of fern;
In quick vernacular the Fall rises,
The field's tilt makes clear and plain

Its puzzle of gorse, rough cups of harebell,
Ling and heather bonded to the height,
Soft crosses of yellow tormentil
Fringing a crop of split slate.

These flowers of the high pasture,
Grazing colour from a chancy sky,
Swell stem to blossom, become other.
Time adds, and cancels out, another day.

Butterflies in a coarse garden
Twirl clarities of white and red;
Poise and fold, the life hidden
Under the brief stain of a shade.

And arms, crooked on a grass terrace,
Ease to fronds of the sun's fire,
Warm as longing, a kept promise,
Or cool, mortal and beyond desire,

While the loose bolts of polished water,
Letting their silks and satins down,
Preserve in tricks of light and amber
The seeming of a world of stone.

2

Innocence: a stud of more-than-pebbles
Under their late-summer pelts of moss –
The unlicked cubs, Pliny's bear-shapes
Fostered by boulders, cumbersome wet-nurses
Lurching about a chatterbox of water
And hung with tingling webs, each crack and hollow
A choke of mould, a nest of quick decay.

Passage: a pack-horse bridge, the dolmens crossed
On stretchers of cold iron, their flat maps
An iconography of nowhere, traverses
Where wood-ants tease and flicker out their angles
Over the spread and eddy of the Fall.

Decay: the broken body of the hill,
Sulking a bruise of green and violet shale
Over the gritstone and conglomerate,
Twisting a cottage beaten to its hearth,
A floor wafered with an absent roof.

Bedrock: the Quarry Hospital, which bares
A mortuary slab of dressed and guttered stone.

3

The animation and suspense of water,
Where swelling stones, which rolled and gathered moss,
Point their white flocks the error of their ways,
Steady the channels' cut and counter-cross;
Where spinning threads pay out about the maze
Of time before, of time to follow after.

Here, Gothic slime, coagulate and brown,
Hung stiff above the brabble and the foam,
And blocky boughs peeled off to the half-nude.
Matthias Grünewald at Isenheim:
The landscape struck into its attitude,
The melancholia of the North set down.

Above, blent green against a chalky blue
Whose fiction reaches to a distant star,
And branches levelling those fans across
Which carry space without a spill or jar.
The plunging light is held against the press
Yet slips a trifle of its substance through

To quiver on a needle-point of grass,
Sharpen a saw of bracken, patch a stone
Whose ghosts of lichen bleach into the air.
The films of shaky white are on the turn
Where foliage lays a shaft of hillside bare,
Narrows an eye through which the waters pass.

The mid-point view: an equipoise of shade
Clouding the oaks which crutch down to the lake,
The yaffle with a cry stuck in its throat,
The heart of water, at its fall and break –
A glass which fractures to its own clear note,
A bright thing lost among a darkening wood.

4

Spread shade rusting to mould, turns of a no-track
Pulled hard, and against the drive of the waters:
That sullen tone of a voice confused, Brythonic,
Void of sense – a fool's reply to a question
Long fleshed in the grounding of church and chapel.

Then a cut to the bone; now, the brief whip-flick
Of bramble or nettle, skin's hairline fractures
Which heal, as this heals not, though green disguises
The hill's hurt: that probing, dressing of gangers
Bargained into the grave as the rains rubbled
Waste and spoil to the lake and its grey deceptions:
Fish-tunnelled hills, quarries of blur and quaver ...

Ling brightens. Somewhere off to the right-hand
Sun plays to an empty pit and gallery:
Gouges brimmed with half-light. Topping the incline,
A smashed hut, and a spool of snaking cable
Angling down its bait: a dead thing rising.
Riding light on the ridge, thickets of hazel
Speak of spent lungs reaching into the freshets;
Small things hover or dart, swim in a shoal of bracken ...

The Fall scores the hillside a little deeper.
Waters of Life, of Babylon: cold, unfailing.

5

If you could read this Chinese charactery,
Ideograms of twig crossed in the plash,
Grasses which rune 'Wish you were here',
Or 'This is a dry house shared with midges',

Then we could make the landscape our device,
And spell messages, such as 'Yes, I am waiting
Under the mountains by the falling water',
Or 'I expect your letter with impatience'.

As the Provincial Governor has left town,
I, his clerk, must write his letters for him,
Juggling, with such Mandarin as is at my command,
Flowers and absence, seasons and expectation,

Noting the brilliance, versatility,
With which the waterfall adjusts its dress;
How screens diminish to a single thread
But seem to find no trouble in maintaining

A style beyond all doubt or criticism.
The grass, now that I look more closely,
Is what is lost in the translation,
But says, so far as I can follow it:

'We have here a true voice at last.
Minor, no doubt, but perfectly in key.
I think we can say water has found itself
And will now go on to break new ground.'

Such, perhaps, is the letter I shall send.
No doubt the Governor would have more to say
Than this, entrusted to a cockle boat
Of stanzas rigged a trifle carelessly.

After Ovid, Tristia

Deeper the drifts now, rain and sun won't ease
This crabbed and crusty land a north wind scours,
Each snowfall hard upon another's heels
And summer elbowed from the frozen year –
These Arctic gales brew up a special fury,
Whipping the tall towers down, whirling our roofs off.
We shivering men, in pelts and galligaskins,
Put no more than a bold face to the world:
Each hair's an icicle, a shaken tinkle,
And blanching frost makes all beards venerable.
Our wine becomes its jar, stone-cold and sober
It stands its round; we break our drinks off piecemeal.
More news? How rivers lie in manacles,
And how we quarry water from the lake?
Our feet trudge in the wake of summer boats;
Our horses' hooves ring hard against each wave-crest.
Over new trackways bridging secret currents
The Russian oxen tug their simple carts.

Kingfisher

December took us where the idling water
Rose in a ghost of smoke, its banks hard-thatched
With blanching reeds, the sun in a far quarter.

Short days had struck a bitter chain together
In links of blue and white so closely matched
They made an equipoise we called the weather.

There, the first snowfall grew to carapace,
The pulse beneath it beating slow and blind,
And every kind of absence marked the face

On which we walked as if we were not lost,
As if there was a something there to find
Beneath a sleep of branches grey with frost.

We smiled, and spoke small words which had no hold
Upon the darkness we had carried there,
Our bents and winter dead-things, wisps of cold.

And then, from wastes of stub and nothing came
The Kingfisher, whose instancy laid bare
His proof that ice and sapphire conjure flame.

Night Walk

We found night in her tower, lifting each veil
And stain of cloud; our space grew full and bare,
The midnight blue tempered to ash and haze.

There was a crush of light on seas of grass,
Two faces bitten by a Chinese moon
And Venus making play with her small mirror.

Cold was crouching, huddled into shadow
Where trees displayed their pearly barbs against us,
Staked at the taut rim of an aching lawn.

We learnt the skills of frost, moved in our absence,
Ghosting our thoughts upon that polished bone.
The clocks were struck into profound silence.

And as we walked, bruised on the rigid ground,
The blood was bitter ichor in our veins,
Though singing in its courses with the spheres.

Saturnalia

The steward robs the orchard,
Strips birdsong from the year;
Io Saturnalia,
And a great paunch of beer.

Merry Andrew, tall man,
Your face cold as the snow,
Maria, sweet vixen,
How does your garden grow?

What should you burn in winter?
The dry stuff of the heart.
Hung with a wicked tinsel
The boughs cut and part.

Clouding the horn lantern
Time goes by on the wind;
The flame shakes, is shaken,
The snow is left behind.

A cloth of cold canvas,
Breath molten on the air,
Marriage of shade and shadow,
And the Fool crouched there.

Ship of Fools

The spindrift took us, and a chancy blue
    Twisted our compass from the homeward tack.
No spirit moved upon the waste; each knew
    The chafe of motley salt upon his back.

There was no thought, in the dead reach of night,
    Our timbers pitched against a sure decline,
To find the water sliced with careless light,
    Our lean hold parcelled out with bread and wine.

Field Glasses

Clouded beyond repair,
Each lens, whose purple bloom
Once zeroed in on air
And filled the prismed room

With O's and eyes of light,
A shaken moon or flare
Which slid across the night
And left its absence there,

Or eased a rainbow bridge
Across the migrant dawn
To bird and foliage;
The magic circles drawn

Round planes, their vapours trailing,
A cricketer's white ghost,
The Admiral's plain sailing,
The first one past the post.

No wonder, brought to light,
The weight deceives the hand,
With life brought down in flight
And lost in no-man's-land.

The landscape filled and sealed:
The long horizon's round,
The visionary field,
A thicket of dead ground.

And each cold retina
Holds, as the victim's eye
The leaning murderer,
A scratched and swelling sky.

Notes from a War Diary

(H.J.B. 1918–19)

1 Madelon

This is the song the poilus sing,
    Madelon! Madelon! Madelon!
'Et chacun lui raconte une histoire,
    Une histoire à sa façon.'

A captured goat in the Canteen Car,
    Driven by 'Darky' Robinson,
Magpies, poppies and marguerites,
    Crosses are wreathed among the corn.

'Glorious weather all the time',
    (Shelling of Ablois St Martin),
To a walnut tree, by the Villa des Fleurs,
    Faux-Fresnay, Vaux, Courcemain.

He's never seen two prettier girls,
    With manners to match, pink dresses on,
Little Monique, Jacqueline,
    Mme Pinard – or is it Pinant?

And a stolen flight with Paul Scordel,
    (Back in time for parade at 9),
'Regardez à gauche pendant la spirale',
    (A mustard-yellow A.R. Type 1).

'La servante est jeune et gentille,
    Légère comme un papillon,
Comme son vin son œuil pétille,
    Nous l'appelons La Madelon.'

But seven die at the Aerodrome,
    (Spads, appareil de chasse, monoplane),
'Forget your sweethearts, forget your wives',
    A Bréguet dives on a Voisin.

'Adieu Champagne, Villa des Fleurs',
    To the Airmen and the waving corn,
The convoy leaves the little Square,
    Beaumont, St Omer and Hesdin.

'Hope for a revoir bientôt',
    Thirty-eight years, to the day, in June,
Back 'en passant' to the Villa des Fleurs,
    To Faux-Fresnay and Courcemain.

Canterbury bells in the garden still,
    The house closed up, the shutters on,
And Monique dead at twelve years old,
    And the walnut tree cut down and gone.

What was the song the poilus sang?
    Madelon! Madelon! Madelon!
'Et chacun lui raconte une histoire,
    Une histoire à sa façon.'

2 Echoes

    Like him, a survivor,
        His notebook lays bare
    The exact words cut
        On the Picardy air,

    And Vanished Commanders
        Are echoes, catcalls:
    'Well, any answer to
        Captain P's "Balls".'

    A parade-ground whispers,
        Under August sun,
    Of deeds, decorations:
        'There's more to be won.'

    From a field in the field:
        'Very gratifying to me.
    I'm proud of you, and I want you
        To be proud of me.'

That intolerable, urgent
　　Intent of the dead,
Now light as a high-summer
　　Thistledown head,

As his own unheard voice,
　　Lips shaping 'C'est bon',
With the wind in his ears
　　In that A.R. Type 1.

3 *Armistice*

Epernay. Took lorry along Dormans road
Under shellfire, dodging shells for a joke.
For no purpose took 7 cars for a ride.

Supper with 'Flamande', Jeanne, et le petit chat.
Saw 2 dead Germans, one with skull blown off,
Lying in house, partially gnawed by rats.

Scene over lights with Sergeant-Major Ford.
Headquarters moved now to Valenciennes.
Remain, pro tem, reading 'Sylvestre Bonnard'.

No guns audible at night. Ceasefire?
With car on Arras road. Hindenburg Line.
'Rindfleisch Westphalien', dead gunners, wire.

Walk with Smethurst down by the canal.
Graves, Château gardens, pansies and 'last rose'.
M's birthday. Weather keeps rainy, dull.

Birthday parcel and letter arrive from home.
Felt seedy and weak. Many cases of flu.
Put panes and canvas windows in the tram.

Rain continues. Heard death of Corporal Gosse,
Heard 'Jock' Kemp, 18, died of 'Spanish' flu.
Heard German envoys arrived for armistice.

Gunflashes still visible at night.
Terrier 'Judy' foully done to death
By Cook. Canine attempt on 'Nan', the goat.

Noticed flags out at Escadoeures.
Told news of ARMISTICE at Scotch Canteen.
Kings in flight. Unloaded Canteen stores.

Cambrai Park. Statue to Blériot.
'L'homme est un puits où le ride toujours recommence.'
Contemplations, Victor Hugo.

Trouble with Lieutenant Alec. Under arrest
For setting bar up in the Troops' Canteen
And selling whisky meant for Sergeants' Mess.

Revert to Private at my own request.

4 Convoy

Fifty yards between the Sections,
　　Epernay, Courcemain, Cambrai:
Soundless convoys grinding on to
　　Hesdin, Abbeville, Beauvais.

Sleep in fallowland in grass,
　　Sleep out under apple tree;
Vauxhall, Talbot, Thorneycroft,
　　St Pol, Meaux and Couilly.

Six by six the Sections close
　　To their five-yard interval,
August sun, and rubber molten,
　　All remaining cars on call.

'Freddy' Williams, Holdaway,
　　(Offensive on the Amiens Front),
'Jock' Kemp, 'Darky' Robinson,
　　'Paddy' Lloyd and Corporal Hunt,

Keeping date and keeping distance,
　　Flesh and metal paper-thin,
Fère, Laloge, Forêt de Crécy,
　　Tyre-tracks lightly pencilled in.

Still the harmless shells dip over,
    Where long-gathered harvests wave;
Sergeant-Major Ford is picking
    Flowers for his Corporal's grave.

5 Fin

Madelon is left behind,
Her dispersal papers signed.

Spasmodic progress, mile by mile,
'Feeling pretty seedy still.'

Mons, Cambrai, Valenciennes,
By moonlight through Poix, Amiens.

Train-raid. Sleeping officers
Relieved of whisky and cigars.

'Khaki baked, new underclothes,'
Bread and bully, jam and cheese.

'Walk to Obelisk. Fine View.'
See 'Yes Uncle': a Revue.

March from the Delousing Camp
With books, flint implements and lamp –

'A trial for me.' Full marching order,
Kit-bag slung upon the shoulder,

Columns of four, and keeping step
To the harbour at Dieppe.

Channel-crossing. Dull, mild night.
South Foreland and North Foreland light.

Wait for tender. Disembark.
Fenchurch Street from Tilbury Dock.

Thetford under snow: the buzz
Of twenty different offices,

Buns and chocolate and tea,
'The Padre's curiosity.'

Cambridge station. Home at 10,
Lift on Royal Mail Van.

Soldier, scholar, he arrives
To what is proper: 'great surprise',

And ends the tale he never told:
'Wake naturally. Stiff bronchial cold.'

The Cottages

This is a day for things that are not there,
    Or there as lightly as a water-skein
Which dwindles back into the summer air.
    Appearances are flitting once again,
And cottages which cobbled out a street
    Stumble to hammers rocking through and through,
Forcing the sky to patch what's incomplete
    With scraps of rain and cloud, and raggy blue.

The orders all are down, and what we own
    Slips from our fingers; time takes us in hand
And finds our reaching fingers slip to bone.
    It's bone and broken bone can understand
This smell of woodsmoke coarsening the air,
    The secret voices ghosted to desire,
The little semblances of life laid bare,
    The hives and combs flooded with light and fire.

Strange that the dead should carry so much weight,
    Their last corruptions come of moth and rust,
The street grown strange, and strangely intimate,
    Their footsteps rising on a stair of dust –
And on the common ground which props the scene
    A chimney pot takes root in moils of clay,
Curling a rim of soot, easing a green
    Out of the darker houses, the decay.

Incident Room

'Police. You haven't heard, then?'
A pause takes breath. 'There's been a body found.'

The two stand burly, gentle at the gate.
Here, bones clean over in a shifting ground
Where deep, medicinal roots are intertwined;
Thrushes leave picks of shell on the back sill.
Though days confuse and motive works awry
Leaves measure out some strength; the roses
Cluster forgivably, cerise against wet light.
The language of flowers is not all hidden from us.

    'Down there, beyond your garden.
A woman. Some children found her.'

Our places. The Jungle, silky once with poppies,
Now run from seed into a greenstick scrub.
The Saddlery – gone: a nest of curling tack
Blind-stamped back into the limy mould.
Higher, the Sweet Little Garden: old haunt
For white-webbed blackberries barbed about the dew.
Solid with life, all seasons in accord –
Till the Contractors flayed it to the clay.

    'No. Yesterday afternoon.
She could have been there since the weekend, though.'

We have our shrine: Genio Loci, a lay figure
Crouched and wrinkled in his niche of shells,
Weathering it out by his own calendar.
Our paths lead to his particulars;
His wave-soft pebbles offer us assurance.
Tutelary, but asleep; blind as the sunk pool.
The flower-heads cup for sun till evening
Draws down unsafely at our patchy fence.

    'Slim, dark hair cut short.
Did you hear anything, anything at all?'

A net of sound is trawled about these rooms:
Carriage of clocks, the stray and fret of tongues,
A pearly mutter from the kitchen screen.
The collared doves complain about our weathers,
Footsteps, checked, trip the hill-path down
Or climb against the grain by dusky lamps.
Pain reached no threshold. In small discourtesies
Our brick and woodwork wear themselves away.

      'There may be photographs.
They won't look very pleasant, I'm afraid.'

The house labours under our care, our love.
The speechless books and unframed music fail
As in the garden strangers pause and stare
At the vague underworld of grass and stone.
The glass drifts out of focus; bounds are beaten
Where the wild wood and the wild world make one,
And all is absence, absence without leave.
Uniforms glister in a gathering rain.

      'Thank you, sir. That's all.
And if you should remember something —'

This is no Incident Room, here, where spread clouds
Drive their load over obliterate ground:
Only a place drawn down into a past
Which will contain us all in dark solution.
Raindrops bounce and hover on the paving
In quick, unhealing rings; a sepia tree
Dries out behind our windy shawls of green.
A cold scent quickens in the formless air.

The Chestnut Tree

No Sandman, no soft-shoe shuffle
   About the garden,
    Just light easing, the small quiver
Of small creatures.

The shrine suffers a god's absence,
    Webbed and creviced:
A shell held to a green ear
    Where traffic hushes.

Dusk shakes out her pale children,
    Bits of life
Sidle across the cooling air,
    Smaller than angels.

The pond surfaces, the fish
    Nudge and wrinkle.
Another sunset works us down
    And down further.

We cannot name those four
    At the lawn's corners;
Night draws a hedge of fire
    Across our eyes.

The tall horse-chestnut sings
    About its dying:
Ring-marked, a house of knowledge
    Primed for the fall.

Next Door

The house empty next door,
    Snow a dullish blur
Caught between freeze and thaw –
    And emptier

That space pushed out from us
    Where the pulse faltered.
Absence, dust, terminus,
    And all altered.

Plates wiped into silence,
    Time beyond minding,
White on the garden fence,
    Clocks unwinding.

The daylight going, gone,
  Settled into night;
How strange our rooms have grown
  Bubbles of light

Where conversations run
  From the walls we share,
The life, the voice, withdrawn
  Stripping us bare

With talk of pale china,
  Cold bits of iron,
Sticks of dark furniture,
  Scraps written on.

Caught between thaw and freeze,
  Snow breaks branches down
As it did, as it will,
  Eighty years flown.

The Candles

A candle at your window, Reagan told us,
Light it for Poland. Forty years ago
A Polish airman taught me his 'I love you',
Breaking strange language out for me like bread;
His red and silver lynx badged my small palm.
Salt on a childish tongue: under the stair
Our fat soap candles lay; they lit the climb
To bed, and winding-sheets as cold as wax.
Their black wicks lifted to an oily stain,
Then sirens howled the moon, the chopper came;
The barrage lifted, and we still had heads.

Now, the Advent Calendar counts down
Shutters of light on swiftly cooling earth,
And what is known becomes a blur of wind,
A stretch of grass, dressed with the death of leaves.
The candles for our tree are boxed and still,
They nuzzle blind, delaying their soft fuses,
And though white blossom and the red of blood
Are twisted hard against our expectation
We shall not light them for a blue Virgin,
Or for a country where the luck runs out.
We press against the echo of a word

And think of English trees, an All Saints' Night,
The mists taking the conifers apart,
The mortuary chapel shut, but the gates open
For congress of the living and the dead.
There are the candles, glimpsed and guttering,
Behind the iron curtains and the wall:
Slight fires upon a shelf of Polish graves
Whose marble crisps to angels, crucifixions,
Names cut from the roots of another tongue.
The letters dance in black, and under them
Crimsons and whites of silken immortelles.

The celebrants, the host of lesser lights,
An autumn Pentecost, a gift of tongues,
Flutter themselves away in cells of glass
Against the cities: Wilna, Warsaw, Cracow.
Their slim flames, fuelled by the airs we share,
Still say 'I love you' in the grass and chill.
Here the sad suitcase and the paper bag
Are finally unpacked; our shadows lean
Across this pale of loosening flesh and bone
Which knew, that for a space, candles would flower,
Whatever comes with night to put them out.

Out Late

Looking and Finding

for Geoffrey Grigson

In this close island, hung
With cloudy ghosts and rain,
You quicken us again

To signs and seals: a ring
Of pocky stones, bare sky;
Old litanies, the lie

Of wind and land, the long
Lit naves, and, at our feet,
Green graves, cool meadow-sweet.

This is where we belong,
Who have inherited
The parish of the dead –

That dark substantial thing
Which hugs itself alone
In rubbled brick, flint, bone,

And speaks with riddling tongue
Of what we were, and are:
Memorial, avatar.

The Gardens

You cut the garden where a garden grew,
And surely as the calendar made days
Appear and disappear, his borders, beds,
Became a waste of ashes, wind and weed:
The little sherds and prints of china knew
That he and others threaded out this maze,
And long-lost flowers puzzled out their heads
Before the silks and satins blew to seed.

Your garden cut into those gardens, where
Old spade-work went to ground: a saddish blur
Of brick and half-brick, fingerings of green
Which made their lack of substance all too plain.
You shook the memory out in tides of air
With such Spring-cleaning, such a leafy stir
Of blues and whites, such branches tossed between
The sky's conspiracies of sun and rain.

But country ghosts will talk of country matters
And show their skills in sign and countersign:
Their broken pipe-stems chalking up the clay
Through which rust nuggets of cold iron climb.
In any song a thrush or blackbird chatters
Of what is his, or hers, or yours, or mine,
You'll find the resurrection and the May
Of those who had their world, as in their time.

Cat's Cradle

for Tim

A cradle made of string
    For hands to ply and plait,
Teasing a see-saw thread
    For one old journeying cat.

We swung him down the night,
    Mewed in his wicker ark;
His dancing eyes lit up
    The soundless dews and dark.

Summers of goose-grass led
    Down paths we had not made
To nests of tabby gloom,
    Soft play of sun and shade.

Long absence held our breath;
    The house grew wide and bare
Until he called us home.
    I cut out of cold air

His face with its sharp look,
    His fur grown stray and dim –
For these long miles of sleep,
    Let the earth cradle him.

Ragtime

He moves about his traps of light,
This errant and unerring thing,
To catch the dust with double paws
Or damsel flies upon the wing,
    And certain of his small terrain
    Will cut and run and twist again

To take, as due, bread from the hand,
Or flash his coat of cinnamon
Across cut grass and sun-stroked stone,
His come and go, his came and gone
    Exacting from the summer air
    A sense of being here, and there;

Or sleeps, as if that sleep was all
That sleep could be: a loose repose
Where all the garden's coloured quilts
Conspire about him to disclose
    Their buzz and bloom, confusion clear
    To one inconstant pricking ear.

In all these rituals and rounds
Each sinew, nerve and sense agrees
That his mysterious web of life
Should traffic in simplicities,
    And offer belly, throat and paw
    As hostages to human law,

As if such trust were possible,
As if his amber, secret eyes
Held nothing in their narrow glass
Of revelation, or disguise:
    Clay woven into voice and purr,
    Caressing hand and molten fur.

The Pool

The flying light fixes to leaf and stem,
The moon is grazing every tender skin,
The hours grow small, and the night gathers them.

A scattered surface locks upon the pool,
And webs which steal across that dreaming eye
Bridge darkened life, cradle this golden fool.

Cold mariner, your fins tremble to stone,
Caught in a brief amber preservation.
Bright shiner, cloud into the morning sun.

Genio Loci

Brick and mortar for the ghost
Slipped between our first and last,
That beneficence which came
When man called his hearth a home;
From a roaming wilderness
Cut the mystery of place.

Overhead the star-beasts pass
This loose gazebo, winter-house,
Patched with glass and cockle-shell,
Cobbled up with flint and tile,
Where the garden guardian
Hosts his feather, fur and fin,

And, as coloured lights go down,
Glazing rime upon the green,
As the winds blow colder through
Spaces leaded bough by bough,
Keeps at this dark terminus
The empty nest, the chrysalis.

Too Far Away

Too far away, the green, the white on green,
  And all that lift and fall of dark and bright,
The bottle-rim rubbed out from earth to sheen
  Coaxing the summer to a knot of light

Where gatherings of ray on careless ray
  Swung in their cradle, while the garden knew
That this was where the sunlight had to stay,
  Teaching the shadows how the garden grew.

And still it holds: the elders leafing down
  Their musty clouds across the reach of day,
The broken glass which tricks a dwindling sun
  Till all the garden slips – too far away.

A Borderland

This, then, is where the garden fronts the wood,
Where broken palings can be plucked like weeds
And thrown in brittle jigsaws on a fire
Which eats the heart out of good neighbourhood:
The nettles overgrow: the rusted wire
Follows the garden where the garden leads

Which is to nothing much: discourtesies
Of rags and mats which sop into decay,
A kind of murder where the clues lie down
In nests of earwigs and antipathies,
Dismemberings of green which stain the brown.
This is the place where children come to play,

To crouch their dens upon a borderland
From which the kitchen-door can just be seen,
A gravelled path, some garish flower-heads.
Here childhood and the trees make their last stand
About the half-bricks and the foundered sheds,
Play out their let's-pretends and might-have-beens.

Thick-set beyond Tom Tiddler's Ground, the wood
Is run by dogs — there it might start to snow,
Old Shaky-fingers pass his poisoned sweet:
The place where mother said you never should.
Its otherness might sweep them off their feet;
The wood itself has nowhere else to go.

The Houses

The houses are cut out in ones and twos
Of something blacker than the night is black,
Advertisements for simple happiness:
Their window-squares are perfect, and we choose
Those counter-panes of yellow to express
Kept promises, gemütlichkeit — but back

In this dank brake where leaves and branches blur
And nothing helps that pure horizon-line
To steady us into simplicity,
Where beady eyes and meat dressed up as fur
Peer out into the grip of vacancy,
Our pallor and the wind are what define

That salesman's pitch of gables, missing street,
Those beacon-lights which pin the distance down
Dissected by their little glazing-bars:
A conversation-piece, exact, complete,
Beneath a random scattering of stars,
With no dull glow to make us dream a town

Could back that cardboard propped against the dark,
Where citizens of Flatland pay their rent
And stare across, untroubled by our doubt
At this unchancy tangle's question-mark,
Where what is out tonight is always out
And love is still the uncontrolled event.

Late

Everything is left now to its own intent.
The hero stars are rubbed of nerve and sinew:
Only their blue bones glare through special spaces.

The leaves are shifting black stuff out, about.
Paws and eyes hook life into rough meat,
Little things collapse into brief stains.

Light leaches from the grass; marram and bent
Pester and hiss about the swollen dunes –
The North Sea dragging, dragging at the land.

The moon slabs out the ground with shaky marble,
Coasting her skull across the sleepy wakers,
The objects of desire on tradesmen's altars.

Night watchers prop their eyes on light and silence.
Behind the patient screens, the tang and barb,
A question slowly rusts into its answer.

For ever, for ever: it is being worked out
In the blind nosings, the secret lives
Of creatures who do not know that they have secrets,

In the tall avenues, the bolted cloisters
Where tongues find out new mouths, beds ache and sigh,
Flesh is purring between salt, damp sheets.

The Glow-worms

It's an old tale: she set a candle there,
Hope against hope, to keep the watch with her
Till all the sadness of the night made clear

That prisoner in the glass, fetching lost love
Out of stopped clocks, and the disguising sand,
Sure that one dwindling flame had strength to prove

Something was deeper than the dusk prevailing
Over her cottage garden, and the wind,
One with each lonely fire, each long beguiling

Of what surrounds us, came with us to birth:
A world of shade which plies about the heart
Its threadbare webs of nothing and waste breath.

A love uncurtained, sure, holding its own
Against the voice which whispers 'Late, too late,
Accept the clouded sun, accept the pain.'

And these green stars, fallen in such high grass?
Over what absence, from what distances
Wings life towards us, lover and incubus?

Dead Wood

Not a breath of wind to set the grasses talking,
        But rain, unsteady, thin,
Which promised something more than a mere soaking
        To more than skin,
And the wood crumbling through its own fingers.

No pictures, conversations: a saurian sky,
        Beech-mast underfoot,
The keys of the sycamores rusted into their places
        And the doors shut
Where the wild things were, which were there no longer.

Leaves dead in their thousands, the sapless tangle
        Shivered about, and blown
Into a witch's parlour of insubstantials,
        The pallors of bone
Ghosted upon a mulch of pith and marrow.

All this dishevelling, the slow unpacking
        Of spore and seed,
The clotted ash and char of a pointless fire –
        No one to read
The text of rings, and the close-hauled centuries.

And nothing to try for, not much to regret
        But the wood being down
To the dark stubs, the rags and the tattered metal
        Something had sown
And left about for the ground's consideration.

Walking the Earth

You are all we have to steady us, confirm us
In the knowledge of our lost footsteps.
On such nights, and in such unpleasances
Toes are the poor man's fingers, stubbed on shapes
Securely based on shifting premises.

We put down markers where the trees confer,
Their finger-posts crooked by an indecision
Which veers us off into a new nowhere
Compounded of your shadow and your substance.
Gaia, mother, out of your contractions

Come the hard children we must bear with:
The cold thorn-bush dragging at our skin,
The pit's declension, where the blind and half-blind
Fall head-over-heels, but not in love,
The Sisyphean hill we push our flesh up.

Reduced to our extremities, we know
The swollen ache your body-contact fosters;
You throw us back upon ourselves, and we,
Who have no best feet to put foremost, watch
For parted clouds to paint you, warts and all.

Your stuff becomes our nonsense, and while you
Stretch out a life of pure circumference,
Littered with births and the returning dead,
Pity us, a blend of your poor simples,
The slipping sand in your dark hour-glass.

Tonight

Only kings and fools would be out tonight,
Such threadbare crows as trip on wires, go crutched:
Tricks of black plastic, and the moon's quick gloss,
Bruising her light against these terrene craters.
A shattered sky brews nothing in its cauldron,
Only this head of cold steam, springing branches,
Beating the bounds of every parish vagrant.
Loose wrinkles ruck about the marrow-bone:
Clubbed thickets, plainish fields of plainer water,
Slight gardens – prayer mats in the wilderness.
Life there: lashed to its frail mast,
Rocked, rocked in all the cradles of the deep.
Stumbling uphill on the level ground,
Sharing an old coat which swells and flattens,
Wind and man twist in their double harness.
Oh, things unwelcome, thorned, unvisited,
There is no remorse that we can offer you,
Our best words broken into syllables,
The black box closed upon its coded secrets.

A Midsummer Night's Dream

for Margaret

1 Prologue

One tree will make a wood, if you are small enough,
Watching with parted eye and double vision
Where Herne the Hunter, antlers caked with moss,
Rattles his withered chain, and quick as lightning
Knocks a green canopy to stump and crater.
You too can lodge there, rain and shadow falling,
Where the ants cross their tracks, puzzle your eyes
With the quick flicker of a coming migraine,
And, over pale saprophytes, the bracket fungi
Pull water out into brown cloths and cushions.
I crouched there once, upon that draughty landing,

Intent upon two ghosts who once were lovers
Rubbing fierce salts into their open wounds.
The darkness of the tree, the darkness of it,
Fostering such musty stuff in its own sickroom,
Twisting its accusations into mould ...
    'Keep promise, love.'
                      Here am I still,
Patient upon some tryst, some assignation
With those I cannot meet, but must pry out
At midnight, posted by a blasted oak –
The pencil licked and purple with love's wound,
The message scrawled in childish capitals –
Time bleached those lovers into grey, then silver,
Easing their passions into frond and tendril.
Now only witches nest here, cut from shiny paper,
Cloaks ample, capering legs as dry as broomsticks,
Their mumbled chins tight to their Roman noses,
Their cats in silhouette, fur jagged and standing.
Night passes round her boxes of black magic,
Crinkling a prelude to her puppet-theatre;
By the slight pricking of my thumbs I know
That things are coming to a head of branches
Whose windy rut rubs all the velvets down.

2 Wind

The trees push their loose heads about,
Dark hair angry with bee-voices,
The sob and growl of the unwelcome dead.
Fingers to fingers, feeling the world slide,
We call again, 'Have you a message for us?'

Lost Uncles, prim Victorians
Frou-frouing in the dryish grass,
How easily our flesh parts for you,
Admits your sea-shell conversation
In the heart's echo-chambers.

These oracles are bare of priestcraft.
Only the deep-drawn sigh, the gusty breath
That there is no disputing.
We die into and across your voices,
The light fading, and ambivalent.

3 The Elementals

Bouts of quarter-staff, and the wind rising:
The soughing and the sighing start again
Under a clouded sky, an acid rain
Eating the heart out of the sluggish lake;
Over a ground whose flesh is gone, clean gone,
The trees must fail, their checkerboard is down;
The fairy-feller plies his masterstroke
And Delville Wood, High Wood, the Ardennes keep
The floored earth sour with an expended metal.
Carols and carollers have gone their rounds,
Church-doors are locked on prayer and profanation:
Wild-fire in stubble, swollen granary,
November windows garnished with false snow,
A ribboned maypole blunted into missile –
Is this arrested by a quilt of bluebells,
A stand of beeches blurred by your soft focus?
        'Do you amend it then, it lies in you.'
'And here we are, and wode within this wood,
Whose dark, unseasonable hearts congeal
To summer frost, sweat fire at winter suns,
Lovers whose tinsel chafes the tender skin,
Who know their nakedness, and are ashamed;
Our dance is broken, past our remedy.
Who will restore the changeling child again,
The coronets and cloths which keep a court
Of Lords and Ladies dressed in green and purple,
Fatten the pale hearts of the Shepherd's Purse?'
Unskilled in crisis-management, I wait
Under the Oak, whose Government is Jupiter,
The Vertues of whose fruit and bark will stay
The spilling of blood, and the bloody flux.
This I can tell, with sixpence in my shoe
And a sweet milk-tooth stolen from my pillow
When I was a boy (before these Civill Warres).

4 Shadows

Our shadows have disarmed us:
We rehearse their satyr-play,
Tumblers in the chalkish light
Which leaves a little of itself behind
Turning the corners of the leaves.

Such sweet and bitter fools
Caught in this rippled mirror,
Angels who dance on nimble pins
Where dry twigs fail to crackle,
And suffer the occlusions of the moon.

We are in love with our familiars
Who kiss with absent passion,
Undress our kindly flesh
And point, with close-webbed fingers
To grave and graver silence.

5 The Court

An old man's gums mumble for justice, justice,
Where trees decay to cloth and painted column,
Unhealed, unhealing: merest twists of gilt,
Alloys of tin and copper. There will be justice
Perched on a furred bench under apple-trees
At the conjunction of more fortunate planets.
Here there is bread and water: common, stale,
Wrapped in cliché, sickening to green.
Justice of walls. I too have known it,
Sent to my bed at noon, scaping the whipping
Until Our Father came, with a case of briefs,
His smoky chariot bolted to its groove,
Walking briskly under the sooted planes.
God must administer his own creation,
Confirm his delegates to their sober suits,
Fix their crisp eyes on fluid situations.
    'I never may believe these antique tales.'
Here, woods are stained, polished to artifice,
Bright in their inlay; in their deaths they curl
Cold, unresponsive to the play of flesh

Which works its passions out against the grain,
Intent on cupboard-love and closet-secret,
Confabulations of the cabinet.
The floorboards tick as Love's old Counsellors
Trip down wrong passages, tap bedroom-doors
Behind which skirts are lifted, stockings bare
Their dexterous enchantments, their bend-sinister.
At stud the bitches couple and uncouple:
Castlemaine, Ariadne, Lily, Aegle ...
Out in the fields, beyond the swerving headlights,
The bears are bushes and the bushes bears
Where the white girls are sobbing in the wind.
Under the aegis of oak, ash and thorn
Even these halls must suffer consecration.

6 *The Green World*

The green world, figuring it out,
    Renewed, Arcadian,
How could these couples ever doubt
In snowfall, hail or waterspout
    That Spring would come again?

For Aucassin, for Nicolette,
    For Darby and for Joan:
The sunlight sharpening the wet,
The Gamut, Octave, Alphabet,
    The softening of stone.

Obedient to natural law
    The folded lovers lie,
Their senses quickened to explore
A Masque of Brightness played before
    Conspiring hand and eye:

The cuckoo's double-fluted trick,
    The lanterns in the grass,
The colours of May's rhetoric,
And, fire from Winter's musty wick,
    A chestnut Candlemas

For Flora, ribboning the scene,
   Enskied in white and blue,
Who reconciles each might-have-been
With was, to come, and in-between
   To make it new, and true.

7 *The Lovers*

'Whose voice is this, shouting the wet woods down,
At home in a goatish sabbath of black smells?
The flailing branches in their russet suits
Know that our tongues are tripped, and all they meant
Runs idle messages into sodden ground,
For all the lines of briar and vine are crossed
On which our words were strung, by which our fingers
Trailed their unlucky scrapes into this no-place.
The ground, puck-hairy, coarse with violence,
Whips out its barbs to suck hot beads of blood
From blue love-bites where snapped thorns rankle.
By the slung moon's pale ignis fatuus,
Mounted upon some bucking lubber-fiend,
We are led all night a byway, hunting down
Forgotten courtesies of the drawing-room,
Triangles of dark hair between pale thighs.'
   'Follow me then
                 to plainer ground.'
'The Puck is busy in these Oakes, rough Robin
With all his saplings sharp in Lincoln Green,
Their bows drawn at our ventures, clouded now
Into old scarecrows and a creaking darkness.
We will turn out our tattered coats upon him,
Loosed from that School of Night in which we studied
The shameless quarters of our hearts and loins.
Now, strewn with strawberry leaves, we hold our flesh
Against its resurrection: careless limbs
Stroked upon limbs, the breathing easy
And our own voices dreaming us to sleep,
Spelling us out more clearly than we knew.
Above our heads, kind stars will steady us.'
I watched their waking from and waking to
On a bank sweet with natural grasses, dews,
And a pied dawn to bless their mortal houses.

8 Constellations

Out of their fixed sphere now:
Free-fall of beast, girl, hero –
Lost in O Altitudo,
A space beyond all spaces
To take our breath away.

As a child figures it out,
Tracing the master-plan;
Joins up the dots again,
New bearings taken
On signs, houses, occultations.

Throned, garlanded in fire,
They lean their absences
Over our old gods, guisers
Whose speech becomes ellipsis.
Each to his chosen star.

9 The Mechanicals

The problem is, how to disfigure moonlight
And keep the accidentals of the moon,
The onceness and the hand-in-hand of it.
The green plot thickens, and her clouded globe
Bears witness to these rings and roundelays.
Ovid is banished where the Black Sea moans
Tristia, tristia – still the mulberries
Fatten their milky drops on Thisbe's blood:
Lovers must die, and garden walls must crumble.
I knew you, Peter Quince. One careless summer
I, tender juvenal, watched your hands at work,
Wood in sweet flakes curling in whitish dust.
The bat you made me sent your daisy-cutters
Out to the boundaries of childhood.
Old friends, the wood was a fine stand of timber;
The Carter's bells have jingled it away.
   'So please your Grace, the Prologue is addressed.'
Only the barest boards, the rawest deal –
But as you spread about your cloth of gold
The tuppence coloured and the penny plain

Make harvest landscape, all its fecund light
Fingered by Midas with his ass's ears.
I have no fears for you as you troop in.
I, too, wore glad-rags, held the wooden sword,
Dubbed carpet-knight by a grave audience.
Something can be made of any lines
By those who, tinkering in draughty sheds,
Patch up the broken to the whole again.
It would be good to leave a window open
When bushes, dogs and lanterns go to sleep
And the late brands are wasting into ash.
The great oak bressummer, the hearth's roof-tree,
Will hold enough of moonlight to get by,
Struck from the adze-marks of your shaping fingers.

10 *Moon*

It is radiance on its moving staircase
Parting the drapes of always night,
The tide slipping her floodgates,
A gravity which draws us out
To clear silver beyond our pale.

Expert with wound and bow
She runs her circles round us;
Littered under this mercury
We must accept her ground-rules.
Our glances travel at the speed of light.

We offer her no histories,
No white slow-motion surgeons
To graze dry pastures.
Rather, the simple love she mirrors:
For ever new, for ever at the full.

Observe the rites of May, betake yourselves
To wakes, summerings and rush-bearings,
Wash with hawthorn-dew on a bright morning
For beauty's preservation; hugger-mugger,
Enveloped with a mist of wandering,
Lose your virginities in wayside ditches.
Your lavish Queen, made bold in this Floralia,
Sits in her arbour by the painted pole,
Under whose standard Justice is agreed.
Dance for Jack-in-the-Green, your high roof-boss,
The oak-leaves foaming from his wooden mouth,
Before your bonefires, garlands, junketings
Are levelled by a thundering ordinance,
Your landscape raked by new theologies,
Your hedges rip-sawn and the wood stubbed out,
Dragons' teeth sown in the poulticed gums.
　　'Think you have but slumbered here
　　While these visions did appear.'
I walked in the astonishing light of trees,
A tenant only of their close estate,
Where the Great Oak, scored and furrowed,
Grappled his roots through subsoil into clay;
His branches, solid in the rising mist,
Have housed us all, and burned our oldest dead.
The Wodewose, with matted hair and beard,
Who knew the springs of love, walked there beside me,
As dark as any heart. Night fell again;
I took the key to her dark wardrobes,
Fingered the sloughed skins, the heap of cast-offs.
The spars fell loose; their sails were nets whose mesh
Caught nothing more than a little dust and air.
Now, out of my text and out of pretext
I pray for amity and restoration,
Who have dreamed waking-thoughts, woken to dreams.

The Plantations

The air, drifting in those cold plantations,
Made no impression on the yellow grass.
Ground seemed steady enough, packed with damps,
And a small culvert pulled its low brown water
Into green pastures – there was no restoration,
Only leaves turning: forty seasons had confirmed them
To fit the sky with the same duns and ochres.
But the wood crossed its fingers: no thread there
To follow footsteps I could half-remember –
Chambers of echo, twists of the impossible,
The rides trailed out, and the earth stopped
Where the trees followed an old branch-line
Towards the Gatehouse –
                                    The Crossing Keeper
Turned his head, dark as the Button Moulder,
Loosened my flesh and bone to standing water.
His indirections to house, ruin, rubble
Could not be followed then, or perhaps ever.
He groped the past with pennies on his eyes
That I had flattened under the engine's thunder,
Cutting a smoky course past dykes and levels.
The trees grew tall, swollen with ripe foliage –
Mr Curtis, he knew, was dead, long dead.
Cars threw me glances from enamelled skins
Nesting in leaf-mould for the stranger lovers
Who gazed through screens of glass at closer screens.

I had not looked for this: the tracing fingers
Losing their hold where new light met the shadows,
A blue diesel shaking line and outline
On its mild swerve from nowhere into nowhere.

Boy 1

He's watching something in the summer light,
Which is as drowsy as an old cat's fur:
Perhaps that thrush, whose breast is Friday's colour,
Or small airs rocking in the apple-tree.
The room smells of velvets, thickened life,
And nothing stops the birds from chirrup chirrup
Or grown-up voices from their break and murmur:
Rivers of lost language among pebbles.
The fabric of a day lies loose about him
Where colours run and fade: old roses, corners,
Lengths of stuff whose patterns can be threaded
By a mind fingering them in its own slow way.
This is what lasts for ever; not bands of angels
Or the great God-face, mountainous with spiked hair,
But a disc of milk in a brown jug, gathering dust,
And a sharp fly, twinkling its cold emerald,
Poised on his arm, grazing the window-pane.
In this long pause between the tick and tock
Of a simple clock whose hands refuse to move,
His hands, too, are corners and old roses,
Spreading their webs of blood against the sun.

Boy 2

He sees, but what he sees becomes unfriendliness;
It's queer the way the night breathes over him,
And though it's cows, they're less and more than that,
Muddled with trains hooting the dark like owls,
Thundering a rush of iron into cloud.
Best shut his eyes upon the ticking floorboards,
The streak of light, the press of flecks and bars
Which make things not, and wrong as his own hand
Weighed thick beside him on the bed: strong beast
With five fat fingers like old sausages.
Heavy, too heavy to lift ...
                    He opens them again to find his father,

Quiet as a tower, a lean, tall shade
Smiling beside his door. But all the stillness
Grows not, and wrong. The face breaks into riot,
A turnip-head of pocky pits and swellings
Pasted and scratched upon a swinging mirror.
The cows groan softly in wet fields; his room
Eases a swarm of usual, pointless things.
They creep beneath his eyelids, nest and settle,
Rucking the sheets where bad dreams dull and glow.

Leave the Door Open

Leave the door open, let the landing through
To stop the room from being itself tonight,
Part of the rain, the leaves, the outer darkness
At odds with the particulars of sight.

Leave the door open, for the air is close:
A kind of heat rubbed on a kind of fear.
Aimless things are about some urgent business,
The safe and far is dangerous and near.

Leave the door open; though the kitchen voices
Climb and fall back, all they can ever say
Is that they have no spell, there is no meaning,
Nothing is further off than break of day.

Leave the door open, let one golden bar
Sink a cool shaft from ceiling down to floor.
Light: steady and simple, an assurance
To make the door's assurance doubly sure.

A Box of Ghosts

Shall we break bread with them, make our communion
With these who smile at us from scraps of film –?
Motions of life, but this, this is not life:
Quick sprigs of garden, garish greens of summer
Where plastic balls are thrown, fat orange cats
Dawdle across the purr of the projector,
Grandfathers poke sticks into blurred hedges …

We run the years and colours out, to find them
Slipping their generations into albums,
Holding us to their breasts, our swaddling-clothes
Dull ivory on muted furs and sables.
How we illuminate these books of hours,
These long autumnal gatherings, pressed leaves,
These paper hands condemned to fondle us.

Cassette and tape expound their resurrection,
Come from the grave to say how roofs need mending,
How well we look, how tiring their long journey.
We know those coughs, that cast of amateurs
Who say the one thing that they still can say,
Who speak their lines, then go to bed at noon,
Choked on a dust that has become habitual.

Ours, ours. The patina of flesh and bone
Dwindles to pasteboard: burnished gold and sepia
Flourished with whiskers, a pale balustrade,
And some slight tripod crowned with leaves and brass.
They have become such studious lay figures
That all their talk is but of how light lay
Upon the crease of silks, or buttoned tunics,

Though once they heard, and cannot now recall,
Such press of echoes, such a to and fro
From the bright years whose darkness now enfolds them
The bat-squeaks from some huge, enormous horn
Flowering carnivorously in a drawing-room,
The mordant romance of a violin.
Their rest is silence. We respect and fear it.

And all dissolves into impossibles.
We are such natives of a promised land
As those, hemmed in by sullen seas and mountains,
Who, when the white prospectors came for gold,
Heard from their wind-up toy, their box of ghosts,
Strange, unappeasable, ancestral voices;
Danced with the singing dead, made their communion.

Visitor

'Please, ma'am,
It's the man with the darkness, come to put the candles out.'

Our table-talk ran out in shifts and corners;
I saw the patch on her grey worsted stockings,
Such homely things, down to their last mending,
And a face tired out by years of resignation
To its own image, wrinkling as she cleaned
The stain of living from our host of surfaces.

No draught of sound came down the corridor,
But where we sat we felt the lustres dim
From the best china in its box of mirrors,
The keyboard yellowing softly into grey:
That presence, bringing such an absence,
Now welcomed, not wholly unexpected.

It was, perhaps, more a kind of wonder
Where he had gathered it: prodigious, rare
Like Moly? Dredged or scavenged for?
Nourished and fostered by secluding fingers?
I thought myself of an old coal-sack
Dropped stiff and shining in the summer road.

Meanwhile she stood there with her usual patience
Laid out before us like a supper-tray,
Our faces unresolved between the last of day
And anything the clock kept as suggestion;
Our eyes lost in chambers, vaults of candles,
Each tiny flame bolt upright, still unstirred.

Paste and Satinwood

The silent ones you offered bed and board

Were simple stuff: delays of moth and rust,
Odd reach-me-downs, the counters of the trade.
'Lay not your treasure up …' It was a trust

And neither by the other was betrayed.
It's hard to see where hands end, things begin.
They made loose rings about you: undisplayed.

You knew their worth. Soon they were living in,
Doing the little things they had to do
And fitting closely as a second skin,

Collecting light and shade, ways in and through
To other rooms and faces, holding sway
In paste and satinwood. They'd chosen you

At some brief market-stall one shopping-day,
And brought you home to make the patchwork square.
Not old, not new, but yours; and you away

They dance a little on the heavy air
And show themselves for what they always were:
Mere calling-cards. The message plain and spare

Repeats 'Remember us, remember her,
Before we spread our wings and fly abroad,
Before your memories drift out, and blur,

Another kind of silence is restored.'

A House of Geraniums

It is calm work, remembering their names
In a house of geraniums and white stucco,
Looking at death and looking at the sea,
Salt on the wind filming its weather eye.

Each photograph is purest ectoplasm,
Part of the way lights crease the window-sill,
A teacup's ring is glimmered on the table,
Kind thoughts lie pencilled in a Fairy Book.

But all these wishes, all these visitations?
'I know she was with me on the day she died.'
Sheet-lightning: air stuck in sultry vapours
That she dispersed with a particular joy.

And other, simpler wraiths who keep their patience
As we arrange a mystery about them,
Who, if we find them voices, only say:
'We were; you are. Why should you ask for more?'

The dead are anything that sighs in millions:
The tossing flower-heads of Queen Anne's Lace,
Moths trawling the dark, those waifs of snow
Flocked against glass, formations of the night

Which grows towards us: ghosts talking of ghosts,
Compounded of old walls, old bones, old stories,
Watching an inch of sun slip to the West,
Playing the revenant to this house and garden

Sleepy with cats down a remembered lane
Where unaccustomed eyes look cleanly through us;
Pity our grey hair, unfamiliar pauses,
Our tongues which trip so lightly over our graves.

The Key

Neither leaving, nor wishing that they were staying,
    They stood at the gate,
Cinnabars on the ragwort, the wind crossing
    Swords in the bents, the light
    Moving about.

There was nothing else much that needed doing,
    The key under the stone,
The stone under the grass, the grass blowing
    Under time gone,
    The fences down.

And already the rooms were changing, the ochre curtains
    Fading to blue,
The carpet figuring out a forgotten pattern,
    Leaves learning to grow
    As they used to.

Cows grazing their shadows, a clock ticking,
    A pause to share
The hour with anything else that needed saying.
    A note lay under the door
    To be read last year.

They stood there still, as if time, the grass tossing,
    The white stone,
The key to the blistered door that was always missing
    Could ask the two of them in,
    Or wish them gone.

Green

The garden laced green stuff about the two of them,
    Soughing, shaking its points of wet light;
Under and over, leaf upon quick leaf,
    The seasons following, folding them out of sight.

And the web shook: quietly, sometimes fiercely,
    The branches high-strung over long grass;
The back-gate was choked by the Zéphirine Drouhin,
    It became easy to sit and watch days pass

Leaching colour from the deck-chair canvas.
    He was unmanned by what had vanished; she,
Under the spread and weight of the blue sky,
    Set out the bright things for a late tea.

One year goldcrests came; another summer
    Herons took two fish from the cloudy pond.
The gate, the green, the cool rooms had decided
    There was no future in looking much beyond

Bees in the hyssop, a wild honeysuckle
    Cupping its warm crowns against the wall,
The mild whispers of things growing, being, dying,
    Fingers of light slipping into the front hall

Where the house, chastened by wax and cut flowers,
    Split all the green to something without a name,
The sun and the moon stretched out their warm and pale
    On the spare bed to which no visitor came.

Erotion

1 Lachrymatory

Lachrymatory, tear-flask,
(A doubtful ascription
Say lexicographers)

We make you tributary
To cold Cocytus,
River of mourning

Where suffering strikes
A chord, responsive
In the dull circles

Of Dante's Middle-earth
To the Angelic birdsong
Of a Celestial sphere.

Lacrimae rerum:
All mothers know
It will only end in

Warm indignity,
Puckered faces,
Rictus, defecation –

Though your blank centuries
Chambered in sand
Bring to our light

A crust of green and violet;
Brighten those dark
Associations of small bones.

2 *Martial V 34*

Father and mother, now
I trust this child to you –
Erotion: all my thought,
My kisses, huge delight,
Who lived but six days less
Than six cold solstices.
Fronto, and you, Flacella,
Take your best care of her,
So small, and out so late,
Lost, scared of the night
And slavering Cerberus
Gaping his monstrous jaws.
Help her to play on,
My name brightening her tongue,
Frisking beneath the heads
Of those old greybeard shades –
And earth, your lightest turf
Will be enough
For one whose flying feet
Carried so little weight.

3 *Martial V 37*

For lost Erotion
Heap on comparison:
A voice to mute the swan.

Skin softer than fine wool,
Purer than whorled shell,
Snow, ivory, lily, pearl,

Hair a more golden fleece
Than any girl's cut tress,
The quick fur of a mouse,

And breath a sweeter balm
Than rose or honeycomb,
Amber, warm in the palm.

The peacock shone the less,
The squirrel fell from grace,
The phoenix – commonplace.

But Fate is bitter, sure;
All that is left of her
Lies ash on a fresh pyre

And Paetus mocks my grief:
'My wife dies, yet I live –
And you cry for a slave!'

What courage, my old friend,
Sticking it to the end,
Blood-money in your hand!

4 *Martial X 61*

Here lies a childhood lost,
Quickened into a ghost.

Six winters brought their snows:
Fate spun the bobbin loose.

Stranger, you who inherit
My small protectorate,

Bring, to confirm your reign
Gifts to her marker-stone.

Honour your Household Gods,
Respect the much-loved dead.

Be happy. No dark years,
No further stones. No tears

To stain your patch of sun.
Think of Erotion.

5 *Hourglass*

The rarity of common clay,
Lost, and whispering to the sky,

That cloudy converse of the dead
Who in the heyday of their blood,

Caught between wind and water, knew
By heart how bright things come and go;

Those ledger-stones and leaves which cover
The separations: loved and lover,

The child who for a breathing space
Became the genius of the place,

The poet who defined a song
By what came native to his tongue –

For all, the bravery of the sun
Could only make the hourglass run,

Its grains, refractions of the light,
Slipping westward into night.

Christmas Games

1 *Blind Man's Buff*

'What can you see,' say fingers and thumbs,
Coaxing the fluttering eyes to shade,
'When voices brighten out of the past
Which could sing both high and low?'

I see brown boards, a tasselled hem,
A threadbare maze of reds and blue;
Rafter and roof are scarfed in shine –
The powdery wishing-dust of stars.

'Oh, Hoodman blind, and blind again,
Whose lips are sealed, whose lids are tied,
Where are you now?' say the swaying clock,
The long, slow sigh of the mantled gas.

In the dancing squares, the pulse of blood,
The land of birds with spun-glass tails,
Where the dark is only a trick of the light
And faces hide on the backs of spoons.

'Twistle him, twistle him three times round.
What silken ghost in a crease of air
Will you catch, let slip from your wrinkled hand
Under the spice of the golden bough?'

2 *Pass the Parcel*

Fold back December night,
Curled moons and angled stars
That print the wrapping sheet.

Let drifts of longed-for snows
Thaw back to ditch and grass.
There, by the leafless trees,

Particular, complete,
A house, a garden wall,
Lamps lit, the table set …

Nothing you do not know;
Again, the Kindly Ones
Hold out their hands to you,

And, for your share in them,
They lay their small gifts bare.
Take, thank, and read your name

As thicker the snows come,
Then shawls of sleet and rain,
Blurring the candled room,

Bringing the deep night down
Upon your hands, which pass
Their part and parcel on.

3 *We be Three Men* …

'We be three men come to seek work.'
'What can you do?'
'Eat plum pudding as fast as you.'
'Show us your handiwork.'

What can we do, but whisper at the door
In the cool hall, beneath a moonish clock?
The heavy coats are hanging there like skins,
Umbrellas hide the simple shepherd's crook.

We are beyond the pale, the outside ones,
As robins are, damp sticks and the iced wind
Licking its lips across a hairy mat,
Purling at keyholes, cornering the blind.

Life waits for us in courts of paper crowns,
Warm as old rugs, made welcome and at home
Where nutshells crackle under slippered feet,
And crinkly rainbows tack across the room,

But we must beat the bounds of landing, stair,
Rehearse our clumsy skills to yellowed walls,
Mending slow punctures, cleaning window-panes,
Dipping bright buckets into darkened wells.

How still, how strange, this dusk and browniness –
The wind is animal, and pricked with fear,
Daring us now to show our handiwork,
Fling the door open – find the palace bare.

Observer Corps: 1940

Here, at a missing bunker God knows where,
You could drop in, leaving a push-bike propped
Against coarse meadow-sweet and stinging nettles
To find a summer where the bad light stopped;
Re-plot the arc of sandbagged walls, prepare
A working surface where the small dust settles.
   Behind the frontiers of the radar scan
   The proper study of mankind was man.

Your props – a sight, a memo-pad, a pail,
Gas-mask and helmet hanging in their shrouds,
There on the board, neat fuselages pinned
Of Heinkel, Dornier, Junkers – but the clouds
Plane to the west, shake into vapour-trail
As innocence and blue go loose with wind
   Scouring the spaces where a hedgerow stood
   Or bubbling fingers clawed a cockpit hood.

A distant coast slides nothing but wild air
Through magic casemates opening on the foam,
And little stirs upon those yellow sands
But pewter tides which work their passage home –
Which is, as this was, living-room somewhere,
A match-light trembled in its cupping hands.
   Only the cool-darks of great shadows pass
   Across that buckthorn, holly and salt grass,

While those who made this post their own affair
Until their watches ticked them out of bond,
Have left its unfrequented space ajar
And slipped out at the back of their beyond.
Deaf to the church-bells' old invasion scare
They take an outing in the Sunday car
   Or pry on border countries, which disclose
   New blackheads clustered on a folded rose.

By drowsy hangars, tractors take their turn,
Scrambling an orbit round the lost control
Whose wires are cut, whose telephones are dead.
Though your binoculars make wide patrol
It's getting late, and far too late to learn
Where bombers lair upon the cold sea-bed,
    Or where, beneath these restless, grassier waves
    The dead are harnessed to their deepening graves.

The Poets Call on the Goddess Echo

1 (Emily Dickinson)

Identity — an Is conferred —
No Syllables express —
It sharpens to — a Solitude —
The Stiff Look — of a Dress —

In Crevices — and Rooms to hide —
It brims its Panic full —
An Inch of Fame repeats it —
Its Crowds made — plausible —

I tried its Measure on my Tongue —
Where only He could see —
A Moiety of Self returned
In blank — Indemnity —

2 (Robert Graves)

Was it Arcadia, or Whipperginny?
I knew the sea, bristling with fin and trident
Under the aegis of a hooded moon.
I paced those cliffs, and with a sharpened eye
Knew Olive-tree and Ilex clasped in shadow.
There I, Narcissus, in my downcast pride,
My body pestered by this threadbare cloak,
Came in a new-found awkwardness to seek you.
The sea boiled rudely, and I raised a voice
Which broke against the rocks of topsy-turvy,
My tears more salt than any brine. Ah, then –
And this the miracle – though I could speak
Only that name by which the Gods afflict me,
The clouds drew off, the Goddess raised her hand,
Your name, my love, came flying on the wind.

3 (Wallace Stevens)

The nymphs are a shade of grey
And the light is of mouse and ash.
Their tongues express the shade,
And the shade is a state of grey.

It is a hissing, a hissing of leaves
Under the vocables of air,
A featheriness of winds
Where creaturely things dissolve

To conversations of pearl,
To susurrus, tinnitus.
The seams of the day make corridor
For frou-frou of chlamys and tunicle.

Ratachak. The woodchuck buries them.
Here we shall make palaver
Whose syllables cluck in the throat.
The birds too are shades

And the shades are a state of grey
Twisting the leaves under and over.
Light and air. Chickahoo. Echo.
Io. Oho. O.

4 (John Crowe Ransom)

With such alas and absence in the weather,
    The drifts of winter cautious in their going,
The nymph lay frozen, light as any feather,
    Chattering her teeth to names there was no knowing.

Deeply she slept, and far beyond my waking,
    Upon a couch of snow, with more snow falling;
I could not move the little heart to breaking,
    Or thaw her sweet throat by my harmless calling.

Ah, you bright girls, won with such hardihood,
    Long may your graces ward you from such durance;
Flutter your white hands free from that dark wood
    Where your high beauty can find no assurance.

5 (Robert Frost)

It's not that the way was hard,
    Though the rocks and the boulders there
Had guessed that another yard
    Was a step too great to bear.

It might have been right to go,
    It could have been wrong to come,
Though no one had let me know
    That the place was deaf, or dumb.

So how should I be to blame,
    Whatever the height or steep,
For giving away a name
    That was never mine to keep.

6 (e e cummings)

i sing diminutives of i
(which is the wee of smallest small)
that find their one amazing way
to be as hugest as the all

for every kind of saying is
as much (and more) as leaves are green
and what they know of take and give
tells taller tales than might-have-been

which you in millions do repeat
as true as two as true can be
to let the buds and springtime know
how you are most the i of me

7 (W. H. Auden)

Oh dial her number, but lover, remember
   The switchboard is burning, the wires are down,
The high-stepping dancer, the lucky sponsor,
   And all the good fairies are bounced out of town.

Tall chimneys topple by the ruined chapel,
   The typewriter jumps on its capital I,
The grass looks entrancing through the Squire's fencing
   But the factory hooter has no reply

For the night-club bouncer, the girl with cancer,
   The Duke of Dandruff in his double-bed;
The drums are all drubbing, the robins are sobbing,
   Your name is as heavy as feathers, and lead.

8 (Marianne Moore)

Alive to this terrene haecceity, Gilbert
   White, of Selborne, could not find
'a polysyllabic, articulate echo'
   until a friend chanced on a
   'very adroit polyglot'
capable of crosstalk in decasyllabic metres.
   Her purities engaged them, though her tongue ran to
quick dactyls, rather than 'slow, heavy, embarrassed spondees',

for to stand at an angle to one's name, at the
    exact 'centrum phonicum',
commending its propriety without being
    'as it were entangled, and
    embarrassed in the covert'
is, in itself, a 'rule for distinct articulation'.
    (Lucretius disdained a complex reverberance:
the single flute-note become the 'pipes' wildwood rhapsody'.)

9 (Sir John Betjeman)

The Tower Captain calls to order,
    Sallies pass from light to shade,
Covers follow on the changes;
    We have erred, and we have strayed.

Civic benches, civic willows,
    Services in Series Three –
Blazoned windows, black in sunlight,
    Pardon our amenity.

From the gilded Radcliffe Chapel,
    Up the precinct and parade,
Charity and chimes diminish,
    Tesco, Boots and Interaid,

Till, in the aubretia'd crescent,
    Final echoes fall and die,
And the Flymos and the Metros
    Whirr and idle in reply.

Blessed bells of Great St Mary's,
    Hunting through the April air,
When He speaks among your tumult,
    Grant my name may find Him there.

Fireworks

This is light which has the idea of writing,
    Breaking it out in rough calligraphies,
Cutting Quadrilles and Lancers, figure-skating:
    Blue flecks of ice burred off on the damp skies,
    Those draughty grounds of being, fearful spaces
Where silhouettes and shadows bounce together.
Under this crackle, fuss and utter pother
        We know our place is

To strike such postures, buzz with such bravura,
    To say so little and imply so much,
Twisting a double helix in the water,
    Working the blackness up to such a pitch,
    Tossing green balls for long-dead hands to catch,
Our frozen hands and hearts all but forgotten:
O Altitudo, etchings freshly bitten,
        Game, set and match.

But there the dark, the dark uncomprehending
    This legerdemain out of close cabinets:
These filaments and webs at their unwinding
    Of loose-cut brilliants, of dying trinkets,
    These crenellations, crumbly towers and lancets,
The rose-windows twirling against the night,
The writing on the wall: crisp, aureate,
        Which must advance its

Case against our backdrop of slow motion:
    Rays, arcs, auroras, pyre on beckoning pyre,
The galaxies at their long diminution,
    Red giants and white dwarves, the tigerish glare
    Of Sirius, Algol and Denebola.
There Nero angles in his endless lake
And mysteries breed about his pleated cloak.
        The near; the far.

But here a glossolalia, the expression
    Of all we never said, but thought of later,
An open-air performance, free admission,
    The set by Piper and the words by Oscar,
    An audience who in a first fine rapture
Can only moo and groan in their submission.
The perfect book: pictures and conversation.
        How can we capture

This nimble falling from and into grace,
    These nonce-words tumbled from the Tower of Babel,
The sprezzatura of this party-piece?
    Watching the fires burn, the cauldrons bubble,
    The shafts of wit, the Chinese gibble-gabble,
We too are bound upon our wheels of fire
And all our little stratagems laid bare.
        We scratch and scrabble

On this dull clay, our bend of space and time,
    Hunting the perfect marriage, the true fusion:
Ormazd and Ahriman, half-rhyme and rhyme,
    The Question and the Answer in collusion,
    Rabbit and hat one truth and one illusion,
Our burnt-out cases littered on the grass
Made one with all the flames which we must pass
        To our conclusion.

The View from the Hill

At the kite's tail we tethered in the sky
A landscape hung, and wind, oracular,
Thrummed in the cord, keeping a weather eye
On what was far but near, and near but far:

A sibyl's voice, whose dark enchantments ran
Loose in the chequered birdsong of the shire,
Singing of youth and age, of boy and man,
Breaking the clay to green, the ash to fire.

I felt new powers, old principalities
Renew the contours of the land, and then
The spit not dry upon my purblind eyes
I saw men as trees walking, men as men.

Barnacle Geese

Giraldus told us of their fostering shells,
Leeched on old timbers where the seas ran high:
The feathered oars, the beaks which clung and clung
Until the combers took them, or the sky.

Fish, reptile, bird – slow in their transformations,
And yet obedient as the spirit moves
Upon the waters, and those darker waters
Whose deeps and breakers salt our human loves.

The Air Show

for Ann, who was there too

Toy Chest

With a slow, makeshift groan
    The toy chest swings its lid,
Nodding dull rafters
    Over stuff hid.

I trace the knotted wood,
    The paint's untroubled skin,
Toy chest; blanket box —
    Their rough squat settles in

Folding like summer nights
    Over dead games,
The struck and puzzling hours,
    The bright, unwanted names.

There, jammed in the cracks,
    A smell of other rooms:
Young, sharp voices,
    Quick tear-storms.

Those years that pulled me by,
    Caught in their apron-strings,
Crouch in odd corners
    With hugger-mugger things

Black, lumpy as sacks
    Worked-up by Burke and Hare.
Blindfold, I guess the weight
    Of all that's gathered there

Refusing to come out
    In this pale April light:
Tongueless, hot, obdurate,
    Packed in too tight.

BACK

Back

I drew the car up in the land of was;
It did not seem to mind the different air,
But shone, its dials playing fast and loose,
The mileage clocking up another year.

I recognized my voice. The gates had gone,
And someone odd was snicking banks of green,
Softening the path down which my footsteps ran
With softer shadows. I was back again.

The house was smaller, shrunken on the bone;
He turned and walked through what I could not find.
I was his future for an hour, he mine;
We watched each other printing out the wind

Which slipped across to nowhere as we smiled,
Huge cloudy summers piling up behind.
I praised the shipwrecked garden he had filled
With stupid, alien stuff, and stood my ground

Where shining levels, ordered beds, a sun
Immovable and steady in its fire
Let all his pleasant gossip trundle on
Past savaged trees, the dense and loaded air.

'But tell me, was it haunted? There's a ghost ...'
I laughed: 'Unless it's me ...' and stared past him
To where some prying fiction of my past
Inked out the shadows in that upstairs room.

'Come in, and have some tea.' I would not go:
A summer child, out in the garden late,
Who knew that in means talk, not much to do,
Just sitting, watching grey things draw to night.

The Air Show

I think I can see myself – a small animal
Doing a hop-dance over a patch in my head
Which is called summer and grass; where light is cut
Into bits and ribbons. I name this space The Air Show,
And most of it now is perfectly dismantled:
The whirring, the whining, the scratches laid on the air
Spin from a gramophone's headpiece rocking its needle
Over and over into those neat ellipses.
The song has run itself out at the end of the line
Into the blackout, past the unreadable label,
That frog-voice gone which croaked so briskly
'In a Quaint Old Normandy Town', or groaned in vain
For 'Amy, Wonderful Amy'. The summer is thick,
Here, in Grandad's Office. I dowse the flies with Flit,
Gunning them down upon the dazzling window,
Watching them buzz their clockwork, kick up their legs,
Stiffen into burnt raisins, crumbs, dustiness,
As their stuck-up friends drown in yellow flypaper.

At The Air Show, beyond the bobbing heads,
The buzz of flies and voices, bits and ribbons,
A tri-plane bellies its fabric into the sunshine,
Wing shelved on wing, engine shelved on engine:
Stuck monstrously on the grass. High overhead,
The little silver gnats tow rolling banners
Lettered with huge but cryptic messages.
The sky is very open, very endless,
And lying on my back with my head cupped
I feel the world go twirling softly round
Like an old waltz: 'Destiny', 'Romola',
While my mother in white dances into the 'thirties.
These deeps are blue, the stuck specks in my eyes
Are looping loops in fields of vertigo,
And that prodigious, glittering machine
Rests delicately on a sheet of emerald,
Being itself, The Air Show, gathering light
As the years grow smaller, tucking themselves away
Under the steepling ledges of its wings.

The Path into Avernus

The Christmas Grotto lives inside the tent
Of darkness childhood pitched inside my head,
Where someone else, whose hair is neatly parted,
Is walking hand-in-hand, and with the dead.

The airs are green, the path into Avernus
Wavers through light which bulges into rock,
Against the heigh-ho's and the cardboard larches
The seven dwarfs are working round the clock,

Swinging their axes into wooden billets,
And goggling back with huge aquarium eyes
At Innocence, her white dress falling, falling
Softly as snow into her own surprise.

Along the golden mile, illuminations:
The golden road, and far-off Samarkand.
Under preserving ice in Xanadu
The child, the dead are walking hand-in-hand.

The Spanish Train

The little Spanish train curls in the hand,
Its coat of many colours; the June garden
Will blow to seed, find new snows and sierras.
Somewhere, beyond the phlox, the cherry wall,
Goya etches: *tristes presentimientos.*
And though his rooms are hung with all misfortune
The train draws down a truthful patch of sunlight,
A radiance not yet underpinned by shade
Or lost in the earth-closets of the garden:
Neither the last mile to Huesca taken,
Nor the fixed siren set upon the Stuka.

Now, on a sofa, the child holds a word:
Spain, where the rain goes, and a wooden train
Quite serious in its unclouded paintwork,
Its yellow bright as any Star of David.
While the small fingers look inside a carriage
Or hook and eye the polished dolly-waggons
The flowers prepare their faces for the night.
Shutters and bolts are drawn. There are long journeys
Which must be made. *No saben el camino.*
There is no remedy. There is no time.
The little Spanish train curls in the hand.

1 Crich Circle, Littleover, Derby

I'd like to pull you back into the sun
That beats the boundaries of your patch of lawn,
Your swags of elder, poplars, privet-hedge,
But you refuse: unable to dislodge
The load of night which presses on your roof,
That crooked, dismal, half-enchanted life
You share with an abandoned garden shelter,
Old corrugated iron and black water,
The colonizing rats who scamper still
Up the forsythia pinned back to the wall,
The tamped and piggy sandbags swollen thick
Against french windows always on the sneck.
You like to keep your smoky head well down,
Bunkered against your neighbours, but alone,
As if night had to fall, and fall again
While you, the trap, coax all the darkness in,
The Deco flowers blazoned on your glass
No prophylactic against dream and loss.
You are the ache, the hug and cloudiness
Of ghost-life pressed and whispering between
The day's undressing and a greyish dawn,
Cold knobs and corners stubbed against my head:
A labyrinth, and now my only guide
This pocket torch whose battery runs down
And dwindles to a fleck of yellow shine,
A tiny frizz of wire which focuses

On a child's book where all the small print dances
Out of my reach. You drift into the moon:
A twist of shrapnel, silver at the skin,
Coldish and rough and crumbly further in.
A humming-top, you spin the bombers on
To one deep-throated and unsteady drone.
Between the first Alerts, the last All-Clears,
I cannot place you: one of ours, or theirs?

Diet

They gave me bread and brains and buttered porridge
A dusty glass of water, stale and sweet,
To take away the sickness of the roses
That climbed the bedroom walls and could repeat
Nothing but roses, roses, till their nonsense
Crept sweating round me in a winding sheet.

They pushed their gravy trains into my tunnel
And stuffed me up with garden slugs and snails.
My salad days were crisp and limp as lettuce,
Then all the clockwork toppled off the rails,
The little foxes jumped from all the foxholes
And ran about the world with blazing tails.

They rubbed their hands in sorrow and in anger,
Then put the crumbs out on the window-ledge:
The crows preferred to gobble up the eyeballs;
And all the children's teeth were set on edge.
The devil spat on all the plumpest brambles
And sharpened up his nails on every hedge.

They laid the tables with their best behaviour,
And stuffed my manners in a napkin-ring.
I told their boasting turkey it was Christmas
And sang that I was happy as a king.
Then when it lay in bits of skin and rubble,
I cracked its wishbone, wished like anything.

They never thought, when wishes turned to horses,
And all the beggars rode away, a set
Of crows and foxes, eyes as big as saucers,
Would fight for any sweetmeats they could get.
I egg them on by eating to remember;
I buy them off by drinking to forget.

Double

She says he came back that night. She lay awake,
The usual skeletons propped up in their cupboards
With best-china faces. The guns began to bark;
The shrapnel pattered. When more stones fall than usual,
Consult the Sibylline Books. I do consult them,
But the pale snapshots in their padded albums
Are ancient lights, ambiguous oracles.
We know, though, he was out, and at his post:
One of those Augurs in their stencilled helmets
Reading the scrawled sky, the city's entrails.
Stoics and bombs whistle as lightning strikes;
The skeletons crooned, bouncing up at keyholes.
She, hoping, praying that we would make old bones,
And, as she swears, with all her wits about her,
Turned to find him there in the smallest hours,
Moving about the room he had shored up
With baulks of timber. Under those auspices
They chatted together for a little while,
Her fear draining away, the heartbeats gentle,
Before he closed the door upon himself,
Blacked out his shadow on that darker shadow
So tightly they grew indivisible.

Later, much later, she got out of bed
And laid a breakfast of crossed purposes,
While he, rubbing the fires from his eyes,
Wrote out a testament, alas, gone missing,
To clear himself of presence without leave
That night when Love and Duty had his name
So clearly down upon their distant rosters.
Martial says 'Dream of yourself, or stay awake.'
She says that he came back; he still denies it.
I was asleep. What I saw I will not tell you.

A House of Dolls

Someone who spilt salt, walked under ladders
Has wished bad luck on Mr and Mrs Brown.
Who cracked the mirror? Who sent a letter
And stammered the King's head on upside down?

Their smudgy faces have been cried upon –
We will not say by whom – and though they tell
Make-believes about cats in the lonely evenings
The mainspring is broken: nothing is, goes well.

Someone took pennies from a someone's handbag
And was shut in a high room till the devil went;
The car lay on its back with its wheels kicking,
Chocolate money grew scarce, and was soon spent.

It was scrimp and save from now on for the duration,
The breakfast scraps tacked to the dinner-plates,
The children wriggly and skinny as young rats,
The calendar a migraine of blind dates.

Whose tongue and lips on the battery's terminals
Felt the juice tingle as it ebbed away,
Pulling the light out of the clickety windows?
God found somewhere else where he wanted to play,

Bored with banging life shut or swinging it open,
The doll's house bared like a split face
On sobs and dust and bits and wet corners,
Something missing, and nothing in its place

But the Brown family, mended and making-do,
Propping their pipe-cleaner headaches against the wall,
All the invisible stuffing knocked clean out of them,
And nowhere to go to get away from it all.

The Old Frighteners

When the impossible grottoes hunch their backs
Under the crinkled stars, we dream to find
The sirens blowing down the bedroom chimney,
Far, far away, and paler than the wind

On darkness hanging from the window-panes.
A pail of water and a pail of sand
Will keep the devil in, and devils out.
What is it that goes round the house, and round,

Dragging its tarnished ribbon off the spool,
Creasing its wicked face upon the moon?
Unsteady things call to unsteady things;
All the slack fur is rubbed against the grain.

Whoo-hoo, whoo-hoo go the old frighteners,
Their clammy sheets twisting between our toes,
Banging the doors about in the grey ghost-house,
Pushing their long dull fingers into eyes

Sticky with sleep, half-opening to find
The sad lights fluttering their yellow-brown
Off the soft edges of the bannisters.
We float downstairs upon the ache and drain,

The unison, the dying aah of things
Traipsing their nonsense back into the grave.
Then the bristle of night standing on end:
The guns chuckling out in the witch's grove.

'Once there was another sun and another moon.'
They shine through the pages of a battered book
Where I and Heimdall keep the Rainbow Bridge,
Hearing the grass grow, watching a hundred miles
Over these branching streets, dark snow, lit trees
And stars silverily adrift over the houses.
In Christmas basements train Brock and Sindri
Forge me Skidbladnir, my pocket-battleship,
Scuttling itself about in soapy waters.
Like them, I know the underside of things,
The brown roof of a table, drapes, rock walls
Which echo to Thor's hammer, huge Miölnir
Storming its way down gloomy roads to nowhere.
I must be Ratatösk, the Squirrel of Mischief,
Slipped between the worlds of the dead and living,
Between the seconds of the front-room clock,
Between the grains of sand which pad the sandbags
Layered like drowsy pigs against the window.
I rehearse the names proper to my fable:
Hugin and Mugin, perched on Odin's shoulders,
Riding the night with Junkers, Dornier.
Hitler flings his right arm at the air
And Baldur drops, struck dead by mistletoe
Whose waxy clusters drip over the doorway:
Dull shrouds for seedy candles, oily lanterns
Lighting the forest acres and more snow.
I will lie on the Fields of the Dead, Hela my bride;
Half-corpse, half-woman – she will gather me
Out of the daylit world into the flight of things
Riding in from the East, over the North Sea.
Behind that other sun and other moon, wolves run.
Their jaws are open; they will eat the light,
Leave me for ever in the dark, the cold.

Jungle Book

Cold Lairs: the sheets are fighting like ghosts tonight
Under an eiderdown prinked out with stars,
Brilliant stars cut from a wambly night-light
Shiftlessly trembling into its pool of wax,
Sheathed in a ring of card. The Bandar-log
Swing fast from dream to dream, their jungle-stuff
Twitching the shadows out of secret corners.
I live under the white of the lost Queen's dome,
Her palaces of pleasure oiled by darkness.
At my feet, a stone water-bottle
Nudges its blunt head, ominous as Kaa's;
Under the bed the nestling cobras pry,
Swelling their black hoods, readying their fangs,
And lawless beasts are banging about outside
Where reservoirs and memories crimp the moon,
Dowsing the shaky night and all its fires,
Turning its bones to water. In the cities
There will be burning, bodies under blankets,
Wallpaper dangling like wet skin from a scald –
Here, minarets and lattice-work in stone
Under the night-sky of an eiderdown,
Heavy Baloo and lemon-eyed Bagheera,
Warm your kind fur out of the bedclothes' ruck:
It is Cold Lairs: I know the call-sign,
'We be of one blood, ye and I…'

Glory

Things lie on their sides, mainsprings uncurling,
Kicking their wheels up, buzzing with awful rumours
To dandelion-clocks and stumpy daisies.
The garden spreads its nets of camouflage
For *Britain's Wonderful Fighting Forces;* here,
The life of insects and the life of grasses
Is smudged aside by our advancing armies,
The caterpillar-tracks, shed tyres, jumped-out-of skins.
The *Men of Steel* leap from their photographs
Into this humming, fluttering summer cauldron,
Commandeering chipped green dinky-wagons,
Their heads propped high on pride and broken matchsticks.
Held in reserve *Our Unchallengeable Navy*
Lurks in Davy Jones' thick-lidded toybox,
Its thin grey line patrolling those dark emperies,
And somewhere night's black exo-skeletons
Wait to pounce with their cold magic claws
On all our silver *Warriors of the Skies*
Drawn up in squadron at the lawn's far corner.
I watch my veterans with their squared-off faces
Lidded with steel like ancient Chinamen,
Moving in quick slow-motion through a smokescreen
Of high, impossible words and windy leaves.
When our campaigns dwindle and die at sunset,
The Children's Encyclopedia calls *Make and Do,*
Opening my cats' eyes to its *Book of Wonder,*
Its *Magic String,* index of exclamations.
All these words pump up a special glory
As hard, unpinchable as my bicycle tyres.
I stick a fan of paper between the spokes
And soldiers, history, I, my garden-friends,
Race like wound-up motors into our futures.

JOURNEYING BOY

Journeying Boy

The train, of course, is absolutely still,
Or sliding oh so slowly home again,
Bouncing its brittle gunfire up and down.
Kitbags wobble: the dark sacks
Of tonight's resurrection-men,
Stencilled with simple names and broken numbers.
Down the corridors black concertinas
Play the floor sideways, out and back:
Facilis descensus Averno. Under my sandals
The shining parallels race on,
Haul our lost luggage into nowhere
Over cinders, torrents of oily stone;
Our stuffed compartments, weary cubicles,
Whistled dolorously downwind
Under the gantries of the blinded Midlands.

A hanging door sucks at a cold platform;
The steam blows a long kiss to the stars.
Brekekekex, koax, koax, croak the porters,
Peremptory, forlorn. Where are we? There?
But our smoky dream-boat punches up the night,
Which smells of battledress, and I crouch,
Wedged over an empty packet of Wills Woodbines.
A pack of cards flicks and whispers;
The light slithers on a helmet's curve.
As the train dances roughly on its points,
Sleepers keep pace with their reflections,
The dull lanterns of their heavy faces
Nodding, shaking between yes and no.
Calmly, as if incurious quite, they ride
This ebb and flow, the endless of away.

There for the Taking

They are still there – how could they fail to be?
The tree loaded with plums, its sage-green fingers
Knuckled on purples, mottles, bobbles of gum,
The pale snail-shells footing the garden wall.
The brass plate by the door at the end of the drive
Polishes itself away summer by summer;
Its shallow letters tell the most perfect strangers
How fiercely a name burnt for a few short seasons.
Now such things must be left to be themselves,
Things which have lapsed, which have fallen out of love,
Out of the nets we cast so lightly about them,
Greeting their simple natures with eyes and fingers.
Signed like the money-box closed on childish pennies
'For Holidays', 'For Rainy Days, Mine and Others',
They are still there, for others, there for the taking:
The frosted glass at the top of the stairs, the doorknob
Angling again for a child to map its contours,
For the hug and share of the new, tremendous secrets.

The Old Bell-board

The old board's not used much: a panel of glass
Up high on the wall, a square of windows
Where the tremblers shake about in their tiny lairs,
Wagging their tongues, red whirling dervishes.
Someone is holding a bell-push down and down,
Threading the house with a cobwebby scrape of sound.
From a numbered room above or below the stairs –
Bedroom One, or Two, or the Breakfast Room –
A lifeline twitches the coverlets askew,
A muscle ticks away at an eyelid's corner.
Who is to fetch and carry, to come and go,
Swishing the air at the twist of a hand or door?
Grandad trims the gas lamp under his breath,
A terrier, cloudy-eyed under rugs of hair,
Is down at his heels; Granny, bobbed with pearls,
Loops her Waterman over her deckled paper;
Evelyn works the kitchen full steam ahead,

Shaving the runner beans to a quick cascade.
The bells can tell you the special smells of things,
The way time picks at the crumbly bones and mortar.
Is it set fair, or storm? They have no lives,
These citizens of a sleepy house and garden:
This doll's house, weather-house, where grown-ups do
The things that a child imagines they have to do.
Their work is a special kind of play and feasting
As they busy away at their sunshine, letters and dust,
Building and filling the ark that I keep in my head.
It rings like the long note held by a rubbing finger
On the rim of a glass, the rim of a memory.
Those tremblers waver and slow, going nowhere,
Coming so lightly to rest, the current warm in the cell.

At the Stairhead

Your feet could not get colder than this,
Your head hung over the stairwell, the carpet-rods
Pure slips of gold gone into powdery dark.
The shining of things goes down, and always down;
The bed is marooned by acres of crackling board.
Tonight the house is bandaged like a mummy,
But sharp with edges of reflected light.
Waiting, here at the stairhead, crowded pictures
Char on the walls: cold ashes, distant voices.
You grope for them; they are proper to the night,
Voices from catacombs, bone Roman voices,
Voices chinking tipsily in their cups
Or ripping softly down the corridor,
Growling in dullness, rising, slipping, falling:
Kennelled things. Your ears sing with blood,
Alert as if the stars could make frost music
Or bats shake silver chains out of black thickets.
The voices too are making a bad song
Where light might live behind the closing of doors.
There is nothing here for you, just the white cold
Pressing itself on flesh, on the gold slips
Which travel down and down to the powdery dark,
To the nothings of velvet, the stupid voices
In a long house of thin glass and throaty curtains.

Magic Lantern

The magic lantern show is nearly over.
The bilious frog in his tasselled smoking-cap
Croaks and goggles fubsily in his box;
Ageing monkeys, faced in gold and scarlet,
Twirl themselves off with their barrel-organs.
Goodnight to monocles and waxed mustachios,
Priggers and prancers of the Victorian order.
Light now draws perfect family circles,
Grey as smoke-wreaths, dim as muddled homework:
My mother, profound and sleepy as a doll,
Grandad, young and bowlered, slipping himself a grin,
Granny laughing, a dog – wild shreds of hair,
Long nose, black eyes come from the dust
To see nothing that once saw something.
Now for the tailpiece: Grandad's fingers
Twitch past a small black train, mad as a spider,
Tiptoe across a bridge across a ravine
Across green tumbling across to a blue river.
The train pulls gruffly out of Lincoln Central;
My eyes choke on coal dust, search the wind
And clanking signals for some huge delight
Cloudy as last year's pain, bright as a dewdrop.
There is a handle, polished as a nut,
The key to the last slide lifted from the box.
Turn it, the arcs and lozenges dissolve,
Spinning the good dreams and the humpbacked night
To overlapping folds of pink and violet,
The Rose window high in Lincoln's transept.
Granny, the frog, the little tiptoe train
Open and shut, the dog's blind, lustrous eyes
Bright as the eyes of spiderwebs and flowers,
As the next lucky thing hoped or counted for.
The magic lantern is hot silver tin
And if you touch it, it will burn your fingers.

In the Boxroom

The papers are going their special kind of yellow
Up in the boxroom, which is made of dust,
Half-light, and dust, where all the deadlines follow
Their tide-marks back into the cool, undistant past.
The closeness of things is what the boxroom knows,

Keeping its out-of-season Christmas baubles
In cardboard a little too high without a chair,
Locked up with an odd summer or two, and fribbles
Fingers have not yet put to waste or fire:
Hatboxes closed on a twist of empty tissue

Which could be what spiders hang in the high angles
Where the corner line and the ceiling lines converge.
The air dull, but holy. My skin tingles
And the small space is large enough, as large
As its reserve, its kept and unkept secrets

Waiting for nothing, as I stand there watching,
Because they have had their world, as in their time:
The blue yacht with its sails set, the points switching
The ghost of a clockwork train, that thickening ream
Of newsprint faded and dry. I riffle it through

And the *Royal Oak* and the *Graf Spee* go down,
The Old Codgers write dead letters to the dead,
And I pull the headlines back, line upon line,
'The Navy's here!' A hatch battens its lid
Down on the hold of a prison-ship, the *Altmark*.

All the pale mouths, packed under metal rafters,
Will break into soundless cheers, delivered to air,
The boxroom floating loose on the dusky waters,
Glory catching at dust, and the door ajar –
And the house waiting to take me into the garden.

Taking the Paper to Mr Elvis

Toes and fingers touch a perfect circle,
The sun drops gently into outstretched hands,
The blue sky fits the garden like a hat.

God is idle up there, watching the sparrows,
Which never fall; summer a huge clock,
Its heartbeat steadying the unstruck hours.

The gardener's barrow rooted to the earth,
The croquet balls left fruiting on the lawn –
This is the seventh day, on which He rested.

I cross the world, watched by my old familiars,
Clutching yesterday's paper, neatly folded:
News from nowhere, which must be handed on.

The tangled hedge butts sheer against my path,
Quickly, I slip the paper past its teeth.
Someone I do not want to know will come there,

An Otherness, to pry with ancient fingers,
Picking through leaves for my propitiation,
A name as awkward as a foreign country,

At home with different birds, the different green
Of vegetable-things glimpsed between crevices.
I watch my steps back for our preservation,

Counting a held breath, feeling my skin cool,
The sun twisting the light to disbelief,
The garden breaking round me like a glass.

Reading the News

In the long summer light, before bed, when the rooks
Caw, caw, caw over the huge elms,
In a time of kitchen rituals, closing flowers

And the putting away of childish things,
Two old men sit down side by side,
Benched with other, older justicers:

Sibs and gossips who are weatherwise,
Who know the worth and market price of things,
Familiar with their worlds, flesh and devils.

My grandfather adjusts his gold spectacles.
He has made notes on the six o'clock news
Which he reads carefully to the gardener,

Halting his way through acres of grey water,
Deserts and snows, distance upon distance,
Where armies grope and falter, turned away

From old red bricks, green lawns and hedges
Soaked in a generous and golden light.
The sofa-back is cool; I am in church,

Idle at evening service, when large matters
Are turned over in words black as this earth:
Lincolnshire loam. *Caw, caw,* say the rooks.

A Handful of Cards

You, gone under ground, speak kindly
    Out of lost seasons.
They made their round: flower, seed-head, flower;
    Your box hedges

Still fringe their different garden,
    Down sudden alleys
Say what they once meant: hour, day, hour,
    Time for the taking.

In a handful of cards you come to light,
    Your fingers shaping
The simplest words: love, kisses, love,
    'Bother old Hitler!'

Letters to post: your walnut bureau,
 The blotter's mirror,
Closed on the ghosts of our affection.
 Over our shoulders

Time is sacking all red-letter days,
 Blurred postmarks,
His push-bike ticking love, kisses, love.
 The inks are drying

Where the light plays on pale honeysuckle,
 Michaelmas daisies,
A Christmas rose: hour, day, hour,
 The first snowdrops.

'When are you coming?' A handful of cards
 Asks its one question.
Here, bees are homing: flower, seed-head, flower,
 The scent of box leaves.

Blackpool, by Night

'This is a real photograph.' Above,
The lemon moon swings through a gloss of brown
And spangly wings are just this kind of blue
In *Fairy Wedding Tableau No. 2*
When star-tipped wands light up the bridal gown.
'One more for your album. Lots of love.'
This is a real photograph. The sun
Is creasing shadows in my garden hat
And flattening my lifted drawing-book
Which tells your watching Brownie how to look
At Blackpool: bold, and stary-white, and flat.
But loops of wild illumination run
 Out of that glass and paintbox, flowing free
 From pasteboard filmed and cloudy as the sea.

Sincere Wishes on Your Birthday

Yes, they were happy as I must have been,
Those model children *Bright as Sunny Hours*
In Fair Isle pullovers and buttoned shoes,
Dandling a bi-plane, reading Mother Goose,
Flashing a wrist-watch – *Gifts in Welcome Showers* –
Each arm as fawn and smooth as Ovaltine.
Such lucky charmers, stuck in lands of then,
Who promised sunbeams, joy and trellised bowers
In which the future might be comforted.
Their noble collie rears a sager head
To swags of buttered stuff; the garden flowers
Prink out their sharp cerise, viridian,
  Re-touch the birthdays: all that brown cortège
  Which travels backwards on the album's page.

Bigness on the Side of Good

I slip down alleys to our other house,
Where Granny Puff jollies us into laughter
And a million snails live in the wet ditches.
I swing on walls there, crouch in a Ford's skeleton
Bunkered by long grass, while all about me
Striped cinnabars are munching up the ragwort.
My Uncle keeps a monstrous pig, an airship,
As pink as Churchill woofling in his den,
All chubby-chopped, rooting for Victory.
My Uncle Tommy is a man you must look up to –
A Captain Flint, the proper size for uncles.
His broad back can take a deck of cousins
Giggling and swaying through a summer day;
Churchill gives his famous vulgar V,
Swelling his voice into a buttery grumble.
I take his name apart: the rich grey church
Set heavily upon its smooth green hill.
My Uncle's pig smells rich and rotten-ripe
As I drape its backside with a Union Jack

While cousins fall about with lunacy,
Shelved on the wall like Beatrix Potter's kittens.
Later, we find the flag gone very missing,
Marked, gorged upon, and inwardly digested;
Our stomachs have to swell with pride or tighten.
The pig died, surfeited by patriotism:
John Bull and the pig, wrapped in the flag or round it.
My Grandad is reciting 'Barbara Frietchie'.
'Shoot, if you must, this old grey head,
But spare your country's flag!' she said.
A pig, of course, would not care to respect it.
My Uncle is the most famous man in Rasen;
He does not know that I have killed his pig.
Everyone greets him as we walk together
To the Observer Post out on the Racecourse
Where German bombers in black hang from the ceiling.
Having fought right through the First World War
He'd know the right way up to run a flag,
How to cure hams, how to bring home the bacon.

Jigsaw

'Off Valparaiso': the full-rigged clipper
Dances out of the dark, her box of sails
Catching the sun upon a difficult sea,
Jimp waves that will not flow, but break stiffly
Against odd patches of this cold sea-bed
Which is the floor of the tray, floor of the table
Where awkward, absent things go back to brown
Out of white wings and glamorous ancientries.
My lead ships tumble from the black playbox;
Greyly, in yellowish light, they gather names:
Ajax, Achilles, Exeter – floating out
Between the headlines and the photographs
Of battle-damage and the cheering dock-side.
Bronzed and fit on my Lusitania medal
A bony Death staffs the ticket-office,
Sending the idle rich to watery graves,
And snug in the glass-fronted bookcase
Boy Cornwell crouches by his dying gun.

Off Valparaiso. I pick up chunks of ocean,
Twisting the sandy plywood to blue water,
Hunting a skyline, picking at horizons,
Popping the bladderwrack between my fingers,
Sniffing green slimes on a sunk breakwater.
The beach is staked and spiked: a scroll of wire
Rubs its sharp back up against the clouds
Sliding its box of sails over the coast,
Off Sutton, Mablethorpe, and Valparaiso.

The Salamander

They were right to wake me, right as Cellini's father
Who saw a salamander dancing in the fire
And boxed young Benvenuto's ears to sharpen memory.
My father can declaim Jean Ingelow
With all the little deaths that live in cadence:
    'Cusha! Cusha! Cusha!' calling,
    Ere the early dews were falling ...
For when it is High Tide on the Coast of Lincolnshire
The sea goes cusha cusha in my ears,
Pouring slowly through the bungalow curtains.
That night, they woke me. The grey murmur
That sleeps in dry shells on a mantelpiece
Had grown to a mad zoo of tangled furies,
So I was wrapped up, carried to the Prom,
And while the salt air spun my dreams away
Watched slabs of ocean shudder into concrete,
Toss their exploding puffballs at the stars
As all the winds and waters of the world
Sang with the dark, and with the strangeness
Of being the wrong thing at the wrong time and place.
On other nights they could have drawn the curtains,
Opened my bedroom windows to the sky
And shown me live things dancing in the flames,
But, saved from memory by an inch of sleep,
The wafer of a door, a paper blackout,
Those little sands of time that slouch in sandbags,
They let the room throb to its dull migraine,
Things blind and restless roam beyond the pale.

That flow strewed wrecks about the grass,
That ebbe swept out the flocks to sea …
The poem, too, was something to remember.
I hang upon the last note of the siren,
Feel the last bomber snoring into silence
Till only my blood sings on its one pure note,
Though I hold the room to my ear like a cold shell.

Woodlands, 7 Kilnwell Road, Market Rasen

You carry yourself away: a freight of silence
Closed by the settling dust, the curtains' slow, calm fall
Across your bent glass and the deep lustres,
The phlox, the hot paths and the cherry wall.

Your gas lamps burn on, pressing their yellow blurs,
Their soft snake-hiss against the swarming night,
Your furniture is mirrors, dark smells, lairs;
Lawns level off, your trees twist out of sight –

And all is Lemuria: a family of ghosts.
Manes exite paterni – and thrice again to make up nine.
At any midnight, hands washed, spitting the black beans,
How should I conjure to redeem myself and mine,

Cleanse your barrow of bricks, that scatter of years
Which holds the otherness of once familiar things?
No placation can ease my head, or yours,
Of the dead we knew, and are: the uncrossable rings

Draw tight about us. There, inviolable,
Childhood is sealed off in its rock tomb,
Valley of Kings, rose-red city, long trouble
Of gold masks, love, lost stuff heaped in a locked room.

Blackout

Surely the light from the house must stay at the glass
And pull itself back, into the room again?
For the light is ribbons, faces; it cannot pass
Out into the loose garden, and the rain
Which scrats at the pane with absent, occasional fingers.

And all our drapes, curtains, tackings of cloth
Closed on these glances, glimmers, openings,
Where the cold glass sticks tight to the hung moth
Quivering its white thorax and plumed wings –
How brief they are, how pale those lookers-in –

Are teaching the light it has nowhere else to go
But round the angles of things, filling the square
Where a sofa thickens its back, the bookshelf row
Scatters in flakes of gold, the arm of a chair
Wobbles where shine slinks off, and into the corner.

I slip round the door and the years, into the dark,
My feet risking the gravel, the wind and wet
Slight on my face, but the house is shut: an ark
Where no parting or pinhole eases to let
My eyes build back the room where I am sitting,

Curled on a cushion, dragging the hours to bed,
As I stand outside in the heaviness of the night,
The child in the chair in the room turning his head
To the out that is bonded out from his cage of light.
I am hunting still for a way to return his glances,

For the house is a black cloud stopping the lawn
From sheering off into further wastes of grey;
But the child inside knows well that the blinds are drawn
Not to keep the light in, but the dark away –
And the future, its blind head nuzzled against the window.

Good Flying Days

Good flying days: the kites kite-shaped
Stirring restlessly in children's fingers.
That urgent, papery flap of trapped insects,
Light laths crossed on whispering cellophane,
And wind bowling over the hard ribs
Where the low-tide forest bares its teeth
Out of the old coal-measures.
Under the gallantries of a flying circus
The usual dog eats up enormous nowheres,
Malcolm Campbell on the Bonneville salt-flats,
And little shrieks bob ankle-deep in foam.
Out of our canvas roll we build a bird,
The crush of silk tightened, polished cane
Slipped into brass ferrules. O monstrous crow,
Hawk of the World, outface, outsoar
The low-sky gaggle, lime and lemon dancers
Tossing their heads, fluttering Chinese pigtails.
As afternoon is polished off to grey
I send my twist of paper up the line
To bring the dark wings down, dismantle summer.
Only air whirring in cloth, sea hissing,
And all the shadows pitching in the grass.
New tides of light bleach out our markers,
Those jaunty signs that we were there, yes, there,
Holding the brief sun on a dipping leash
While water cleaned our footprints from the world.

Going Out: Lancasters, 1944

'They're going out,' she said.
  Together we watch them go,
The dark crossed on the dusk,
  The slow slide overhead

And the garden growing cold,
  Flowers bent into grey,
The fields of earth and sky
  Losing their strength to hold

The common lights of day
  Which warm our faces still.
Feet in the rustling grass
  We watch them pass away,

The heavy web of sound
  Catching at her throat.
We stand there hand-in-hand,
  Our steady, shifting ground

Spreading itself to sand,
  The crisp and shining sea.
Wave upon wave they go,
  And we stand hand-in-hand,

The slow slide overhead,
  Stitched on a roll of air,
As if they knew the way,
  As if they were not dead.

Pathfinder

Night-riders gather, and all skies look east.
The stars are steady in their tight formations,
Crossing with light this grind of troubled air.
The house is softening its velvet textures,
Buoyed to its moorings by a bombers' moon.
Its charts record only the stretch of wood
Which gives, misgives, at the sleepwalker's touch,
And stranger-faces turn from watery mirrors.
Outside, the beaten grass is lost and grey
Where levelled meadows launch their thunders out,
Over the shining waters into Europe.
The house is dreaming little flocks of questions:
Fidgets of dark glass tripping in the frame,
Easings of tread and riser at the stair.
The cows at dusk spoke only country matters
As daylight sank behind the window-bars,
And no pathfinder drops his marker-flares
Upon this crouching city of bad dreams.
Over the leaded grate, farmer and dog
Exchange their painted sentiments of loss
As the old home comes underneath the hammer.
The night dies on till all the tides are turned,
And though the ebb was deeper than the full,
From this, our common ground, we cannot single
That diminution in the homing waves
Which speaks of tears, which speaks of tears and flame.

The Loss

Broken out of cold sea, warmish land,
   These tremendous holds of smoky water:
A mackerel sky splaying its bobbles after
   A lather of cumulus; somewhere else a hand
Patching a Dutchman's trousers, just enough blue
   Is showing through

To let me take these hours into a meadow,
   The amber sun floating upon my back,
Prickling small sweat. Turning the other cheek,
   I can hold light enough to cast a shadow
And watch the slight scars travelling overhead:
   The complex dead

In Heaven, where angels high, from rose clouds
   Someone falls the full height of his ambition,
And great fleets, softly plumed, in tight echelon,
   Pass and re-pass: harsh migrant birds,
The grass quivering under their glanced wings.
   Through all their vapourings,

Their strainings at the leash, I pass them on,
   Follow close their dull score of sound.
Manna: the frost of shrapnel on the ground;
   Magnificat in a butterfly-bomb, incendiary fin.
And out of sight, the loss: the children downed
   In the black playground,

The dead reckoning – stars in loose formations
   Taking each bomber up, the iced wings wheeling
Over and out, the slow climb past the ceiling,
   The crew stiff at their seven stations.
Arcturus, Vega: a far field thick with light,
   And the unleavened night.

Jacob's Ladder

When searching cones of light
   Transfix you at your station,
And the radiance foretells
   How night will claw you down
Into a soundless glow,

Who do you see on Jacob's ladder
   When the rungs are blazing,
The children rise in ash,
   Sifting the dark with faces?
Non Angli, sed Angeli,

Pitched from seas of flame
    Into such absences,
Tossed as Dante's lovers
    In cyclones of desire:
Brands plucked from the burning

Quenched in a great cold.
    For flesh packed in cellars,
Bonded, swollen, molten,
    Shrunken out of substance,
Whose hands make cradles?

When the air is full of names
    Blowing in the slipstream,
The city lies in cinders,
    The moon, immaculate,
Crooks her sharpest horn,

Who do you pass on Jacob's ladder
    When the rungs are blazing?
What traffic have the dead,
    Tongues burned, eyes blinded,
As the squadrons turn for home?

Searchlights

God, who struck open skies, unleashed his fingers,
    Making a stab at justice; violet light
Fused the low cloud to his scorched-earth policies.
    I watched him at his random bolts and fireballs,
Then saw, under the skies that had healed over,
    Layering dark upon dark, dark upon dark,
Such towers of white air leaning against the stars,
    That rational light, as pure as gospel-truth,
Seemed to make a clean break for its freedom,
    And whirled over soft ribs of glass
A host of moths, dry silver, Christmas dust,
    Glittered in their endless, quiet fury.

Here, the generator hums the night to sleep
    In a small field, damp with shadows,
But splayed out by a canal in Germany
    Those quiet rods, angling in black water,
Gather to lash a cockpit into radiance
    And wings crumple under their instruction.
'I'm afraid we've had it. I shall have to leave you now.
    Baling out. Good luck, everybody.'
Metals and flesh falling, flakes of ash
    Sifting their way into a later harvest,
His words hang in the increasing silence,
    Uncancelled by those ministers of fire.

A Parachute

    Not flying, but floating
As if to land lightly, seed oneself, rise again:
    A sycamore key twisting
    Into its grass nest, life run
        To all that brown

    Under all that blue, breeding
Its ash leaves, tufts of grey light, thistledown,
    Each spider laddering
    Its perdurable cord, sun
        Still burning down

    These flowers, their heads breaking
Out into blue wings, white wings, pinks flapped
    From a grey bed, silks taking
    Each skirl of wind: dropped,
        The catch slipped.

    And a parachute is falling:
A scallop of pale flesh, open-eyed, rose of death –
    Crete, Arnheim. Baling
    Out, out, under the flight-path
        Goes the ghost of a moth,

Ghost-moth, a soul visiting
The mansions of the dead, loss, a dark habitation?
    Only a child's handkerchief, twirling
    String on a dull stone,
        Or lead man

    Finding his feet, slipping
Quickly through garden green, against cloud, caught
    On a plum-branch, dropping
    A little further into night,
        The crumpled sheets

    Where a child sleeping
Free-falls his limbs, landscapes, his here and there;
    Takes his bearing
    By dream and star,
        And chooses air

    As one unharnessed, leaping,
Span from his plane through night, forest, snowfalls,
    Passed out and through, spidering
    His unsupported miles,
        And woke with men, not angels.

German Bricks

The children's German bricks are boxed up tight
With all their paper citizens. 'Sleep tight.'
A thinnish moon will give the night its head,
Cities and dreams composed under a lid

Of scattered cloud, small hours and the high cold
Whose passengers work hand in glove with cold.
A garden closes on its quiet places;
A boy and girl set out their palaces

Where light chops at water, windows open
On darkish rooms as flowers, faces open,
Fingers lock in fingers over wet sand.
The longest journey starts at the day's end.

And Montaigne reads in his tower; below, the garden.
Night and its cupboard loves confirm the garden:
That dream and harvest eager to placate
The crooked coastline and the bloody mart

Where common things, children, bricks, boxes, tell
The common secrets that they always tell.
A slow cascade of marker-flares goes down;
Clouds of black angels dance upon a pin.

And not a column, brick or spire is lost;
The picture still confirms it: none is lost.
Where Jacob Schutz sheltered, a child cried endlessly
Jesus, my Jesus, Mercy, Mercy.

Service

Hearing the organ stray,
Wambling slow time away
In sit and stand,
A candle-bracket cold to hand,

Watching the shadows pass
Under this burning-glass:
One bright eye
Of lapis lazuli

Over an old saint's head,
A running maze of lead.
Robes of blood,
And little understood

But the high lancet's blue
Which makes the whole tale true
And is definite,
Shifting its weight of light

As afternoon lies dying,
The trebles following,
Stone gone dim,
God down to his last hymn.

And Little Wars

We fought the war through
    In small back gardens,
Set on our cloths of gold
    Each makeshift squadron,

Into action-stations
    By the German bricks
Sent our kilted Scots
    With bayonets fixed,

Pressed into service
    Busbied Guardsmen,
Stretcher-case, bearer,
    Machine-gun section,

Dinky half-tracks,
    Churchill, Sherman,
Red-cross nurses,
    Men and half-men,

Searchlight battery,
    Plastic airmen,
Life Guards on horses,
    Crimean cannon.

But too much marching
    With arms shouldered,
Too many sentries
    With arms grounded:

Non-combatants all,
    Swinging their lead
Into our slow-march
    Victory Parade.

War Games

The armies are parading on the carpet.
Spilled from their call-up papers, coloured boxes,
They master dressings, drill-books, about-faces.
Peace was Christmas ribbons, *light wing'd toys;*
War a sad teddy-bear who feeds on dust
And fixes bayonet eyes upon the soldiers.

When I inspect the long files of my soldiers,
As lined and threadbare as this rag of carpet
Whose corners fold themselves upon the dust,
I cannot see into those empty boxes,
These antique fables nor these fairy toys,
But search for something missing in their faces

And search again, for all familiar faces
Are blotted out by rank on rank of soldiers
And icy winds which cry *All is but toys,*
Lifting the corners of the playroom carpet
To show me in the boxroom with the boxes,
Watching the tiny parachutes of dust

Marching a leaden army through that dust
Towards an enemy with equal faces
As dull as mile on mile of cardboard boxes.
Love glitters on the lances of my soldiers,
My carpet knights who dye into the carpet,
Whose brief Commander knows that *dreams are toys.*

Host upon host; *silence you airy toys,*
Wasting through trenches, mountains, into dust.
Somewhere beyond the fringes of the carpet
The tin men put new flesh upon their faces
And swing down bitter streets, playing at soldiers,
Where money rattles in collection boxes.

Nest upon nest of empty Chinese boxes:
Triumphs for nothing and lamenting toys –
Such knowledge fills the nodding skulls of soldiers
On their brief march from ashes into dust.
The past is only what their future faces
Across moth-eaten rolls of shabby carpet.

The coffin-boxes close on precious dust,
And all our toys have names and special faces.
The soldiers are the figure in my carpet.

The Stain

As the stain spreads, working itself coarsely
Into the grain, I watch the colours run,
The fabric weaken, an inky cloudscape loosely
Darken the white cloths and dowse the sun,
Put all the flowers out, fold up the butterflies.

Out in the dead garden I feel it seeping
Through rough grass; the ladybird on her stalk
Knows her house is on fire, neighbours are shaping
Zeros of sound – those bibles of careless talk
Which cost a lifetime to close on their revelations.

It is reaching nearer and further: a salt tongue lapping
The first beach head of sleep; a ghost of grey
Is nibbling at paint, finding our level, keeping
Our small world company, stretching out each day,
Hunting like a bad smell for an unused corner.

The sky absorbs it: the earth, the stripped hedges,
The cold playground, the shiny bedroom floor,
A game of Lexicon, a sampler of brass badges.
In the beginning was the word; the word was war,
And when the word peeled off, skin shrank from air.

A slow recovery, as if a restless sickroom
Left leaves and faces caught in a long half-light.
The time-bomb ticking away under house and home,
I will them back, sealing them under night,
Blacking their eyes and setting their bricks trembling

Under the siren's call, the mumbled anger;
The handfuls of metal rain on a dark street
Whose crackling tarmac fissures into danger,
And all this later sunlight will not make sweet
An ambivalent sky crouched over the new, bright strangers.

Countries

The countries that we made lived in the gardens,
And sat out in the rain, and went to nothing.
The sentries dropped their guard, and watched in silence
As little creatures ate there, and were eaten.
Such countries grew more blurry than the mazes.

Our mazes lived with careful maps of islands,
Their names more fanciful, their space less peopled.
They sprouted palaces on torn-out pages
Which lived and died in schoolrooms: cells of boredom –
As boring, nearly, as a Hampshire barracks.

The barracks, later, where I played at soldiers,
Had nothing much to say about the gardens.
The metal lockers, tall and green, seemed coffins
In which all childhood was dead and buried,
Although its chapter-house comes in the story.

The story I am telling is of landscape:
A landscape words feel moderately at ease in,
As grave as Poussin, or as Auden's limestone,
A pastoral with tombs, and somewhere, soldiers.
The scenery is flat, and grass, and sentries,

Though sentries now are bits of brick and rubble:
The straight and crumbly edges of a jigsaw,
They stand by hangars stamped with blackish numbers.
I drive more slowly when I pass the flatlands,
These uncompleted circles, Nissen shelters.

These shelters hold a scruff of straw and fert-bags,
Puddles of cold and rather oily water.
I try to make out faces in the darkness
And follow gleams of light I think are truthful,
Talking fitfully of wings and runways.

The runways veer across the maps and mazes;
The by-roads break them. By the gates of farmers,
Or where a slab of names, a stuck propeller,
Cries 'Halt!' with the abrasion of a sentry,
I stand and watch the criss and cross of grasses

Which blow, of course, to mirage: green and silver.
Still, if I have a mirage, that is something,
And a big sky holds room enough to write on,
To say that I invent what I remember
Then touch down lightly on this patch of concrete:

Concrete which shivers into cracks and sparkles,
Something left over, out at night, forgotten,
The runways weathered into desert islands
Which suffer the erosion of their coastlines –
Countries over which I stand as sentry.

7 Newton Road, Harston, Cambridge

Your corners jab out at the wind
Punching across dark, levelled land,
A spill of couch-grass, twitch and vetch
Choking the runnels of the ditch
Which pins your garden to a field
Sullen, cloddish, brown and bald.
Your tingling fence-wire clips the sun,
Drying its nets against a pen
Of hens, dull layabouts, who itch
Feathers and grass to a bare patch.
You live with ribbing: knitted clay
And con-trails laid against a sky
Blown out and scuffed until the blue
Rubs off to nothing showing through.
As Doodlebugs come popping on
You work our fingers to your bone,
Your skins grown callous to the hand
In endless making-do and mend:
Eggs drowned in buckets, dusty coal,
A punctured push-bike's ticking wheel.
Perched on the edge of here or there
You stay unhealing: red and raw.
The village runs you out of life
But the harsh air won't scrape you off
Your patch of sand, or make them go,
The sad and mad who neighbour you

And slew you sideways on their pain:
Cold, obdurate, quotidian.
I lie in bed and hear the groan
Of a green pump still working on,
Hauling the overflowing cess
Out of its pit down scrawny grass:
The sour brown gulps, the biting wind,
Dragging you back into the land.

Neighbour

She stands at the fence and calls me till I come,
Mouthing a message for the wind to lip-read;
Only my name stands in the air between us.
A slattern house, reeking of dirt and music,
A compound of long grass, drawn round with wire,
A summer sky, aching with Cambridge blue –
These are the substance of her misery
Which forces through our bonded bricks and mortar.
Her son comes home on leave; the sobbing furies
Thicken at night. Our lives become a part
Of that insistent voice, those wavering grasses.
Her garden burns, the red rim eating out
A heart of black which blows to feathery ash.
Low overhead the puddering doodlebugs
Comb the cold air, each weight of random pain
Clenched tight – these trivial ganglions on the nerves
Of a slow-dying war. My mother's love
Betrays her to the ambulance, and asylum.
All the doors close, but in the silences
Her message stays. There is no way to read it.

Doodlebug (Kirschkern): 1944

Kirschkern, cherry-stone,
  On a blind date,
Counting it out
  To the rim of the plate.

Cherry-ripe, cherry-ripe,
  Ripe I cry,
Who plays at cherry-pit,
  Eats cherry-pie?

Black Heart, Smoky Heart,
  Leaves yellowing,
Sunken cankers, cracked bark,
  A late withering.

One sour Morello
  At the garden wall:
Earth raked over
  Where the silence fell.

Cherry-pip, Kirschkern,
  The plate licked clean.
Who asked for bread?
  Who got a stone?

'Ich hatte einen Kameraden'

'Ich hatte einen Kameraden ...' – the class shuffles;
A tune rises and falls. What did you do?
Went out, looked at the days, clocks handing us on,
And blowing about our heads that grey and blue
Turning to cold, biting through worn gloves.
Kicked at hushes of leaves by a long wall,
Picked up bits of the world and put them down,
Pulled the trees about to make shadows fall,
Drew our bows at a venture from Drift to Lane,
From Quarry to Field, from there to back again.

And then? Begged at the door, lay out on the lawn
Feeling the eager differences of green,
Watched stick-insects doing nothing, slowly,
Picked the circling bones of the seasons clean.
Went in, cutting wet rind from our shoes,
Fingers fondling Trudi the dachshund's head;
Lit by diamond panes and painted china,
Salted the butter softly on to the bread.
Set out the glories, the servitudes of war
In close formations on a cockled floor.

And what did you say? Nothing, nothing at all.
The wind and the rain have scrambled our words deep
Into a huge silence. Our mouths opened;
Secrets were exchanged. They are kept, and keep
For ever, ever. Do you want a name?
It is the name of your own once-special friend.
'Einen besser'n find'st du nicht' the class wails on,
Locked in iron-bound desks till the song must end,
Till the scrape and blur, the chattering out of sight –
Our faces garbled, strange, swung out of the light.

The Old Gang

The Reichsmarschal is pouring through the window,
Puff-pastry, lardy-cake: his tunic creases
The crazy-paving on the shroud of milk
Hung out to dry upon my bedtime mug.
His breeches swell with meat, his polished jackboots
Suck their black liquorice up against his thighs.
He puckers his face into a little smile,
Tricking love-crinkles from his currant eyes
And littering the night with iron crosses.
O wicked uncle in your fancy-dress,
Tinkling a cataract of cold regalia,
I know you have the shadows for your meiny.
Their liquefaction stiffens to salute;
You break your jewelled baton into music,
The taratantara of Roman trumpets
Banging my head against a moving staircase

Of light and thunder. Now, in his night-school,
Old Gob comes at me with his wooden face,
His long cane swishing at my flying heels,
His long gown scrumpled over secret fire.
The Honour boards glister in heavy gold:
Famous forgotten names floating on oil.
The fat man and the thin man meld their hungers
In one enticing and protracted smile.
The Reichsmarschal smacks his buttered lips;
Old Gob mounts the dais, holds his rally down.
The dream roars, and all the hands fly up:
Hurrah, hurrah! *Sieg heil, Sieg heil!*
The bedroom window has three iron bars
On which I know my knuckles clench and whiten,
Suffering again this tongueless lashing,
Vaulting the wooden nightmares in their stables.

The Wooden-heads

I am learning nothing at incredible speed,
Weltering in ink: a blotted copy-book,
My nibs and fingers crossed unhopefully.
Crumbled from the soft pages of a library book,
The wooden-heads are punishing my daydreams.
Zombie-skittles, they run rings round you;
The circle closed, the victim vanishes.
Having cleared London, they will start on Cambridge.
Ropes and wall-bars offer no escape-routes;
Matched at bantam-weight, I bob and weave,
My gloved hands pummelling the air.
They have caught Hodges; by the cycle racks
I saw him, red-faced, simple, yellow-haired:
Now empty, strangled in his father's toolshed.
The foul-mouthed kapos of the middle school
Are doing a roaring trade in small extinctions,
Trawling a dragnet for us small-fry.
The game is gas chambers. Into the labs with you,
Heads pressed hard against the bunsen burners
Whispering you to sleep. We lurk in crevices,
Closed by dark wood, secrets, grey flannel,

A master with one eye like a scorched Cyclops,
And feel our little strategies go down,
Slipping through all the circles of the underworld.
The gowns and blazers form their broken ring;
There is a gap still I can wriggle through
If I can only purge away my scraps
Of dog-Latin, wrong notes, false equations.
Best to go to ground in the reeking bogs:
Unbolted stalls, chads, pig-troughs of urine.
The wooden-heads are out looking for minds to bend,
My satchel of trash blocked up in their beast-world.
I see Hodges swinging behind a door,
His childhood flushed away, his bright blue eyes
Still laughing at me over his knotted throat.

His Face

His face is everywhere: a slab of paste,
Dabbed forelock, hot pale eyes. His lair
Is a wild nest of burnt metal, shadows,
But I know a good-luck works between my fingers
In Granny's brooch, the soft red-leather Kipling
Where his black-magic cross stands gold and upright
Or swings its level arms over its shoulders.
Its firework cartwheels on his wooden sleeve
Into the pages of a million schoolbooks
As he strikes air rigid with his quivering fingers,
Brooding impossible rages with a tongue
That skids unbraking over the crackled ether.
His flat hand launches out his throbbing arrows,
Flung through classroom dust and the long nights
When scuttle helmets bob in rows before him,
The banners dip, the oily torches flare,
The high goose-steppers kick the air aside.
Tiring, he twists his fingers in his mouth,
Blows out his brains, dowses himself in petrol,
Blazes himself away, runs wild with Eva, Blondi,
All the cold wolves who stuck to him like glue
And slavered to pull down the sun and moon.
Now, he shrinks to a well-practised doodle,

A dead thing which thrills my poking fingers.
When I peer at the cracks between the clouds
I know his fleets will rise to his command,
Their crushed bones hauled and straightened from the tomb,
The cowlicked skulls perched in their greenhouse cabins
Blinding their way across the sulky ocean.
In the School Dining Hall I take my Spam
And cut it to a neat, pink swastika.
I eat it slowly; it is his communion.

The Finger

It is the accusing finger, always saying:
'I denounce, and you are guilty, guilty
Of having eyes, a nose, of being you.'
The grey-haired Hausfrau clutches at her chair,
Her elbows bent; Herr Nobody is crouched,
His face a blank space where the room writes fear.
Between the two of them, a wireless-set
Crunches the moment up between its teeth,
Babbling its careless talk, costing their lives,
And at the door, their child, a bantam rooster,
Perched, like me, on the edge of double-figures,
Stands blazing: damned and righteous
In little shorts, an armband, open shirt.
Behind his finger the Gestapo tower,
Putting on their high hats, drawing guns.
                                    I know him:
This little swimmer into cleanness leaping,
Hiker, boxer, dipped by his brown heels
Into that lake whose baptism will wash
Blonder than blond, whose duty is betrayal.
I look long at his eyes, his accusation
Where all dark sulks, feet kicking at stones,
Pounding fists, tears in cold bedrooms
Flower into self-possession. I too accuse
The cat, the flowers, and the foolish clock
Ticking itself away in dwindling circles.
Blood-brother, wait for me, and I will bring
My cub-cap, toggle, green garter-flashes,

Walk with you, horrid friend, make a stick-camp,
Swap stories and insignia: gleefully
Explore the boundaries of our pride and shame.

The Shiny Pictures

The shiny pictures go straight through my eyes,
But nothing in them adds up to a view.
I feel that I must push those leaves away,
That if I stare enough I'll come to know
The secrets of the road, the blurry trees

And that small figure staring straight ahead,
Dressed in the black and white of photograph,
Walking quite briskly; nothing in his face
To tell me what on earth he's thinking of.
Tin-helmeted and holstered at his side

Two soldiers elbow him like special friends,
The kind who chew gum, warn you out of harm.
I watch them lead him to the proper place
Then level off their rifles, take their aim
And squeeze their gentle triggers with big hands.

His body loose, cords crossed upon his chest,
Earth gazing greyly at his nodded head,
His blindfold white, his jacket creased on blood –
This is how people go to being dead:
Their glasses taken off, backed-up to posts.

Quisling, Fifth-Columnist … the sense of it
Is hidden in what papers always say;
But that's not much about the bits of cloud,
The nothingness, cold happenings, more sky.
I turn back to the start, and let the flat

And boring ground, the figures, trees and road
Go sliding by to their appointed ends,
Which are no ends, but dark re-surfacings
Of eyes, and guns, and gentle-seeming hands
From thick old pages, heaviness like lead.

The Word: 1945

The word is a word stuck behind closed lips.
I take these pictures carefully to bed,

Finger my skull, shape the familiar room
Into some kind of space: a yard, huts.

I can make no sense of these deep pits,
Branches of flesh and bone, once green and quick,

This guesswork of smudged breasts and genitalia
Speaking greyly of guilt in classroom whispers.

I lie there with the word the house won't say;
The pictures move about inside my head.

I cannot fit the word into the war.
I look down quietly at my striped pyjamas.

Souvenirs

Something enormous, with a molten core
Of huge delight: here is a bit of shell,
A whorl of light I picked out of the gutter
Where last night's gunfire did its giant leap,
Stumbled and fell in thousands on the city.
Brass cartridge-cases wild as buttercups,
A bomb snug in long grass under blossom,
Strips of tinfoil stuck on eastern hedgerows –
Autolycus could stuff his ditty-bag
With all these little deaths of shot and shell.
Granny tacks up my shoulder-flashes, chevrons:
A reliquary cased in brass and velvet
Where regiments glow fiercely in my bedroom –
Spiced, musty fragments dedicate to Mars,
Sparkling with war, war, war – a word
As dark and rich as last year's postage stamps
Heavy in orange, red and cobalt-blue.

Old nights grow thick as blackness cramped in boxes,
Kept for something, hoarded; briefly opened
Into cloud split and sharpened by pale sunlight,
Days bright and stiff with names and battle-honours.
The souvenirs lie truthfully in their box,
Cold-hearted now, and most inscrutable,
Dead as John Dee's obsidian scrying-stone.
I know unguessable things are stirring there,
Troubling with their fumes and cloudiness
A past as deep and shrouded as the future,
Where planes fly backward onto broken runways
And stamps released from dried and creaky hinges
Fly round the jarring world with urgent letters
Addressed to strangers, crooked heaps of rubble.
I watch my ghosts stand to their glowing anvils,
Beating their ploughshares back to swords again.

The Field Transmitter

The Field Transmitter, heavy in its box,
Uncurls its oily braids and hanks of wire,
Stuck by a green corrosion to brass terminals.
The knurled knob taps and stutters dit and dah,
Its V for Victory: 'For you, the war is over.
Come in, my children, from the echoing green,
The city street as yet unlicked by paint;
Climb from the bunkers in your sad back-gardens,
Yesterday's foxholes: iron, sacking, iron.
Hand in your outsize helmets, bits of perspex,
Your bomb-fins and that treasured German arm-band;
Dismiss those leaden armies to the dust
Which settles into what you will call memory.
Crouched for the last time on the garage floor,
Let my headset's hard constriction tighten
Till all your war becomes a new, strange tinnitus,
The bombers climbing through your cloudy brain-cells,
Gaining their altitude and levelling off
In as much sky as spreads from ear to ear.
This band of gunfire bouncing off your skull
Makes the thick sound of other children dying,

Out of your reach, beyond your messages,
Who played their war-games, heard the sirens glow
Hot silver filaments in miles of night,
Till gathering babel took them to its arms
And held them still, and held them very still.'

V. E. Day

Carpamus dulcia: nostrum est
Quod vivis: cinis, et manes, et fabula fies.
Persius: Satire V

Noticing oddly how flags had been rubbed thin,
Bleaching in shut drawers, now unrolled
In blues, reds, their creases of old skin
Tacked on brown lances, headed with soft gold.
    Clothes-lines of bunting,

And light fresh at the front door, May
Switching the sky with stray bits of green,
The road levelling off; the day much like a day
Others could be, and others might have been.
    A woman laughing,

Sewing threadbare cotton to windy air,
The house open: hands, curtains leaning out
To the same gravel, the same anywhere, everywhere.
Birds remain birds, cats cats, messing about
    In the back garden.

And a table-land of toys to be put away,
To wither and shrivel back to Homeric names.
Scraps gathering myth and rust, the special day
Moving to its special close: columnar flames
    Down to a village bonfire

In which things seasoned and unseasoned burn
Through their black storeys, and the mild night
Fuels the same fires with the same unconcern:
Dresden, Ilium, London: the witch-light
    Bright on a ring of children.

Night, and the huge bombers lying cold to touch,
The bomb-bays empty under the perspex skull.
The pyres chill, that ate so fiercely, and so much,
The flags out heavily: the stripes charcoal, dull.
    Ashes, ghosts, fables.

The Other Side of the Hill

Who is it mooning about in his half-lit room,
Sharing my name, the set of my bones: a boy
Hung in my chains of words, puzzling it out
Under suspended judgements, gagged and blind
While Time poisons him cloudily under the door.
What are these thoughts I badger him into thinking,
These possible routes I map for him, joining the dots,
Holding his secret writing up to my fire?
Oh, he is poor Jim Jay, stuck fast in Yesterday,
With his party tricks, the clumsy deck of snapshots
He shuffles, cuts and deals, those blind fingers
For what I have dropped and lost on his bedroom floor.
I would like him to put our heads together, confer
About old hedges, pavements, the dazzling film
Which is racing out of sync with its dusty soundtrack.
Perhaps, though, all he can say is 'I was there',
As if 'there' were a special place, or a right of way,
Not a sentence shared with the other prisoners:
The sad Italians behind the bulldog gate
In the flat, unhurried fields, who turn and wave,
Ridiculous in their Commedia diamonds, moons,
Our next-door neighbour, jabbering lost Polish,
The bitter stench of her house dark in our nostrils.
She paces for ever behind her shining fence-wires
Which sing as I pluck them: the Chekhovian sound
Of a nerve thrilling under a huge dull wound.
Absorbed, at home in this peculiar country,
He leans from my Tower of Babel, anxious to help me,
Then settles back again into his thousands,
Swinging his satchel, counting his souvenirs,
Reading the signs on the other side of the hill.
For old time's sake I offer him this future:

Another chance to make things up. After all,
I am the victim in his puzzle-picture;
He is the child that I go looking for.

Under the Barrage

Schlafe, mein Kind
In your mother's bed
Under the barrage.
The soon to be dead

Will pass you over;
It's not your turn.
The sheets are warm
But they will not burn.

In your half-dream
Sirens will sing
Lullay, lullay,
Lullay my liking

A saucer of water
For candlestick:
The night-light steadies
A crumpled wick

In a house of cards
In a ring of flame;
The wind is addressed
With a different name.

Schlafe, mein Kind
In your mother's bed.
Under the barrage
The soon to be dead

Lie as you lie,
And will lie on
When the dream, the flame
And the night are gone.

Watching the Perseids

The Good Thing

Will the good thing come, laired in its wet hedgerow,
Grown sick and shy in the rank smell of elder
And June's half-light, dangling its carapace
Over the less-than-wind, these loaded branches?
Sighing flower-heads, bushed inclinations,
Make their pale gestures to my outstretched hands
Scorched brown from holding out unchancy gifts.
What is it that these shades are fostering
In all their awkwardness, their nods and shakings
Pushing about this stillness of close air,
A mess of stony earth and broken feathers?
Will the good thing come to these unbudding fingers
Barking their skins against a nest of shadows?
Unreadable, the scribbling of the leaves,
And for all the wisdom they lay up in green
The trees can only answer yes, and no.

White Things, Blue Things

White things, blue things, their stalks tenuous,
The green pale where it moved to root-life;
Brought home, which was not their home,
Although they made it feel more like home
Than all that furniture: forests of dried sap
Creaking dry boughs where the lost wind
Sharpened to a draught cornering the room.

And, of course, though not asking to be,
Picked by the wayside; not asking anything
But dumb life, set in its green confusion,
Drawn always out of what lies hidden.
Plenty left to litter Spring and Summer,
Leaving each other about to be uncounted
Or seed themselves to sleep when time said so.

Crossing themselves in glasses, hung untended
Against a window-pane, out of their element,
Their gauzes drawn between us and the sun,
They look back out of memory and snapshots
Adding their lustres to 'Do you remember?'
Their heads calm, unshaken, when we ask
Our other question: 'Will they last in water?'

Paradise Gardens

I remember them inching gingerly into the past,
Testing their thoughts against the shine of clay:
A woman propped in a high-back chair, a prim sharp face,
Her dress the black shadow of her near-century –
The sand poised in my glass, hers running fast.

Old heads are heavy with dull wonders they cannot share,
The strength of root-life, tales told out of school.
They see the dead, warm and unwrinkled, walking
Down Paradise Gardens, up the Line, keeping still
To their careful patches of rain or sunlight, air

Which blackens roughly out. They know the closest names
Of those who tease them with sudden laughter, tears,
Forcing dreams with their passwords, tripping on birthdays;
We arrange the past years as neatly as cut flowers
But kisses burn and scald. There are live coals, flames

Before the exposure of ash, the short years before
We too must pass beyond the last visible ghost
To a time when all we wanted to say, or said,
Will be, like Etruscan or Linear A, quite lost,
As opaque as those banks of love on which we draw,

Which are buried so deeply behind our clouding faces.
The post is blankly angled by the lost tennis-lawn;
The invisible net catches nothing over and over.
There are faces adrift in all the window-panes
Mooning at rain, which is twisting their garden grasses

With tides of air which have no use for the dead
But to blow them back into graveyards and out again.
I stand, scraping green lichen from a tall family stone,
Allow cut names to shine, and all that I learn
Is how the signposts stood by roads down which I am led.

Familiars

You have grown terrible to me in your love,
Who did not ask to be forgotten, leave the lawn,
The careless signature, lit breathing-space
And courtesies of your good neighbourhood
For wind ruffling the stillness of those acres
Where you keep sullen house under spent flowers.
You are my dream-walkers, absent-minded ones
Pressing my head close to your fussy wardrobe,
Lost scents of flesh ageing their creature comforts.
I trust myself to your light-fingeredness,
Caught between kindly skin, the skeins of bone;
And, when I speak to you, my dear familiars,
I only take three simple words back home
Which wandered, lost, between your deaths and mine,
Chancing 'I love you' – which you knew already,
Turning from scribbled lawns and signatures
With half-smiles quite untroubled by such truths
As these words carry down my whispering gallery.
Oh, you slight ghosts, grown frail as all ghosts must,
More luminous, sustain me from your shadows
On these late errands, posting your dead letters,
Your small-change bright against my spendthrift hand.

A Red Ribbon

for my Aunt, Marjorie Wallis

The long passage is a climb of wet ice:
Cocytus, river of mourning, where all tears meet
And starry antechambers hold in place
Those whose eyes have fallen out of our light,
Wandering where memory yellows at the corners.

Shadowed in creamy white she lies in wait,
Touching and feather-brained as an old song,
This great girl: her hair fined to a plait
In a blossom of red ribbon, her traipsing tongue
Picking her brains, telling untidy lockers

That this is a prison, warded by sheets and bars,
To which, picked up stunned from her bungalow floor,
She has been sentenced for living beyond her years:
The best hotel – room-service. For here,
All are booked in; need make no reservations.

How good of me then to come for the last time,
And share in those happy nevers we must have had,
Whoever she is, whoever I was, or am,
Watching a red ribbon dancing over the bed,
The usual flowers draining their glass of water,

And how much she wants me to know, lost for a name,
Puzzling me out her son, her nephew, brother,
That she is much loved, lucky to be loved by them:
Those who have seen her so far, will see her further
Through ice, Cocytus, the sealing of all orifices.

The Master Builder

for my Uncle, Tommy Scupham

On leave, he must have slung his British Warm
Across this chair, hugged, kissed, and joshed them all –
That fire still warms the corners of the room.

His cap-badge showed the way the land could lie
For one more tommy coming home for good:
The Gunners' wheel above its *Ubique.*

He found the House that Jack built tumbling down
About their ears: the devil left to pay.
He picked things up; his ropes could take the strain.

He squared the family circle, found a skill
For throwing sky-hooks up against the clouds;
With blood for mortar raised the roof and wall

That set his brother and his sisters free.
They packed their cases, off to pack their brains
By ways that he had made. They made their way.

And where he grew, the little Market Town
Spun at his finger-tips: that tarnished wheel
Flashed out its golden spokes; became the sun.

A Monumental Mason. Near and wide
He played the jester, but they knew him king,
Bone-shaking off to Charlestons in his Ford,

Hanging one-handed, striking down a grin
From church-clock high: a monkey on a stick,
Or banging aces at some farmer's lawn.

He stood in his foundations, making clear
His rule, his measure. Children trooped the Yard,
The House that Jack built now set fair and square.

And still the family ghosts go whispering,
Whatever houses they inhabit now:
'You owe your brother Tommy everything.'

Teasing me still, he strolls the garden where
His old Victoria Plum nods in the wind,
And *Ubique:* his hands build everywhere.

The Photographer

Their fancy dress is penny plain. *The Stork*
simpers from blowing serge and ribboned straw,
The Sea Nymph, back from Flanders,
his one-piece swimming costume nipple-tight,
bathes in the North Sea's developing solution

and *Robert the Nut* puts on his 'don't ya know',
with arms akimbo, and a cockerel strut.
Tweedledum and Tweedledee mock Tenniel,
with languid cries-cross and a drape of hands,
Types of Lincolnshire Beauty stare at the sun,

as if, by burning out their eyes, they might
see further than the summer of 1920.
Across backyards, plots and corners
shadows play at lengthening the lifelines
of *Swank, Dog-frightener, Supercilious One.*

As for names, why, the whole town knows them.
The Four Just Men, gowned, authoritative,
register them daily. In this roguish gallery,
only the rabbit: hugged, silent and quickly mortal,
must, for somebody's sake, be known as *Brownie.*

One landscape. *Tealby. The Sounding Cataract.*
Some five or six brown feet of plash and tangle,
a puff of falling water. Then he's back,
the builder and monumental mason's son, sighting
for a last, uncaptioned snapshot. In the yard

they have cut the last name (which liveth for evermore)
of those now in their younger brothers' keeping.
Nettleship, Starbuck, Topliss. Whelpton ...
Look into the eyes of *The Boss,* his old headmaster –
There's hardly a tree in leaf in the whole album.

The Map Maker

The sound of the paper – surely that's the same?
Open it out. Sprung on my finger-ends
the resistance is purposive, a clean flip.
On the obverse, four spots of glue hold nothing, tightly,
their ochres caked and crystalline. He spreads it out
as I spread it now, smoothing its awkward lie.
Folds guide small rivulets of shade, flats cream
under gaslight or whiten in the profligate sun.

This is how he sees it. Rather, how what he sees
in the beck, the lane, the heat-haze over the wolds
can be dried and certified, held like the moths
in his killing-bottle. Catlike, he marks his journey.
Ink runs thinly, darkens. He sows words broadcast,
dips the scratch-pen, straight-edges the railway
as, outside, hot verges coarsen with umbellifers.
Lineside. Tiger beetles, flowers. Lepidoptera in general.

His head adrift with flutterings, sheen and texture,
he pushes his way through millions of green and brown,
holding tight to a spinning signpost of names.
His tracks race off the paper through *Nova Scotia.*
J. Scupham July 9, 1916. In brightest Lincolnshire
my twelve-year-old father carefully encodes
Hill, Clearing, Viper's Bugloss, Yellow Underwings,
ransacks *America* for its *Heaths* and *Tigers* –

the Large Heath *(Epinephele Tithonus),*
the Scarlet Tiger *(Callimorpha Dominula)* –
this Midsummer, his 'Prize for Nature Study'
is Furneaux' *British Butterflies and Moths.*
With bruised laurel, cyanide of potassium,
the countryside may be coaxed into your trap
and, later, secured by silver, black or gilded pins.
Be sure the poison does not merely stupefy,

leaving you horrified, when your box is opened,
'by the sight of the poor victim struggling to free itself',
a teeming landscape unwilling to lie down.
I refold his paper, packed with nests and burrows
thickets of skin and fur. Ink and copy-pencil
shine briefly against my lamp, keep the dry glaze
lost by close on a hundred years of eyes.
The dead rustle back to nest with a stir of wings;

the annular rings thicken and simplify.
I could stand there still, lost in a no-man's land,
holding his childhood's trench-map, think of his brother
laying his gun-sights somewhere on the Somme,
consider how folds of dead ground foster rivulets,
hedges whiten to blackthorn, cream to hawthorn.
As he dies, I ask how he spends his time,
bedbound. 'Oh, just go for walks,' he answers.

Eldorado

Remembering Francis Norman, Bookseller

And so, no Saturday door to be angled through
    And find you again,
Puzzling about our latter-day quids and quidnuncs,
    Your Proust, Montaigne,
While Heath Street under a patchy cloudscape suffers
    A water-stain,

Or shuffling in, your keep-net a Sotheby's bag,
    (The catch indifferent today),
With quiz and chaffer and chat, with news of the ones
    That got away.
They settle to lighter dust on my patchwork shelves,
    Your Dryden, Gray.

A Professorial Chair, the spoils of Time
    Brown at your feet,
Babel: her grammars and guides in curling vellum,
    Collated, complete,
Long to be pickled in drowsy Academe's
    Cool winding sheet,

The learned Doctors, Johnson and Eustace Chesser,
　　Ephemeris, Folio,
Cities of Dreadful Night and Beautiful Nonsense
　　At criss-cross row –
And crumbs of learning tossed from your bread and cheese;
　　In a sunset glow

Here then lay Eldorado, blocked in gold,
　　Our Box of Delights,
The smoky torches of knowledge guttering down
　　From Ancient Lights –
And a pinch of your salt still left for us to savour
　　On Attic Nights.

A couple of rooms, all sects and centuries
　　In broken run,
And your late courtesies, your text and gloss
　　Victorian.
Now, the catalogue checked, and back to the printer:
　　Finis, and Colophon.

The Christmas Moon

Cry for the wrinkled moon,
Pale face, box of tears;
Sharp-set on its line,
Pegged out by brittle stars.

Prop your dream-ladder; hang
Your head in miles of air
Frosting the topmost rung,
While the whole cirque d'hiver,

That feral zodiac
With blue and glittering eyes,
Fixes you in its lock,
Brings you to your knees.

Ask the cross-hatched night,
The brooches of cold flame,
That ghost in silver plate
Crossing your outstretched palm,

For this one night the marred
Changeling to be gone;
The stolen child restored,
Slipped back in your skin.

*

Something you asked for,
And it wasn't given:
Light from a lucky star,
Pennies from heaven?

The whole house lit
By grace and favour,
Doors on the out shut,
The bad dreams over?

Just what you didn't want:
Your face caught in the glass,
As innocent as paint,
Gift-wrapped on its loss.

*

The wishing moons fall:
A clutch of silver
Down a dark well.
The nights cloud over,

The hour-hands move,
Blurring orb and cusp:
Faces of love, of love –
Just out of grasp,

Each soft nimbus,
Unhealing bruise,
Setting your compass
Twirling its rose.

Travel by ancient light
Glanced from the dead
As it grows so late
On the beast road.

Lantern, dog, thorn-bush
Will see you home:
Silver dragged from ash
Spell out your proper name.

Levels

By shivering easels
The Old Dutchmen
Drew the days in,

Muttered to their sables
About clogs to clogs
In three generations,

How they stamp clay down
To the dull as ditchwater
Of life's quotidian.

Not enough blue here
To patch their trousers;
Just winter, water,

Finding their own levels
As the heart does,
As the leaves do,

Leaving a chink
For starved fingers
To keep time from freezing.

Young Ghost

for my Mother, Dorothy Scupham, 1904–1987

1 Arriving

Whose are these faces clinging to the gate
That seem to have been left out in too much rain,
Blown-back leaves shimmered on a bent pane,
Which soften, work loose, fall? It is getting late

As I swing round on shoals of small stone
Crowded with damp air, skirmishing about
With blocks of shadow, this whole house wishing
It had been somewhere else. Here is where alone

Is growing visible, spreading its mesh wide,
Easing itself always between things left and taken.
The car is drenched with mud, dance-tunes shaken
Out of the past's throat as I drove where the trees died

Along the Roman road; from each tall going-down
The sap dried, a December night half-healing
The struck sets of bone, the growth-rings wheeling
From the young sapling to the full tree: crown

Crushed out, roots loose to the stars. I am there,
Where something fragile as blur on the warm windscreen
Hangs to old furniture, the once, the might-have-been
Of things. The faces rustle to the wind, asking me where

They must take themselves, being creatures of blossom, gleam,
Shifts of nothing much on brick, the interlace
Of black waxes, thickets of lost green: the wrong place
Gathers the ghosts of love into its own right dream.

2 Moving Round the House

Moving round the house, watching the shade
    Weaving loss into the Norfolk light
Blowing from rusted petals, closing the wide
    Places in afternoon which smells of night,
And hung with trees keeping their branches crossed –

I see things out of the corners of their eyes
    Glancing away from the huddle of the bed,
Staining the carpet, making their armistice,
    Drawing a late sun down from that overhead
Where God re-works his face from the cloud-scatterings,

Pulling the sheets, oh, slowly over the house
    Until that hugeness mixing its whites to grey
Coaxes the room to its own absent-mindedness –
    All the long nothings we have left to say
Lost in the dark that anchors the winter-garden.

3 The Fence

The garden had not much to say
Except that that was where stuff grew
By paths which ground themselves away.
Obedient to the names you knew,
It could not help those names to fit,
Although it made the best of it,

And putting on the usual show,
Brought all its flowers out of bed
In tetherings of to and fro;
In sun that brought things to a head.
Some other garden held your eyes;
This could not take you by surprise,

But studied your indifference
In blurs of white, or brown and green,
Beyond the dark, unyielding fence
That you had set so high between
The spaces you were moving to;
The garden only passing through.

4 *This Evening*

I watch you turning into memory,
Becoming something far too sharp, and clear.
You dwindle on the bed, and make a space
As small as Alice, waiting far from here

In rooms the size of photographs, on sands
By seas whose waters could not brim a cup;
Dressed in an inch or two of brilliant light:
Profound, and serious, and un-grownup.

As if you spend this evening trying on
The proper size to slip into a head,
Knowing how small the clothes are that must fit
That plain and simple hugeness: being dead.

5 *Old Hands*

Old hands, burnt out, the sap fallen: talons,
And a gold ring cutting closer to the bone –
The hands of children leaped across to meet them.

Always something left to do, undone,
Before the huge refusals of the world:
Those awkward women sitting in sad kitchens,

Fretting for stuff the years had dropped and broken.
Her green fingers worked best in the cold,
Dead-heading their autumnal gardens,

While her own border flourished its white spires,
Glooms where her stray cat, *Sawdust My Love,*
Crouched with bleak eyes, pads locked on tiny claws.

6 Christmas 1987

Once more I cover this nakedness which is my own,
Beyond shame, wasting, wanting; soon to be ash,
Pulling her nightdress down over the sharp bone
Which bites through the shocked absences of flesh.
    I hold viburnum up to her face; it is the Host,
    The offer of wax to wax – I am becoming a ghost

As I fuss for the damp sheets rucking across the bed,
My breath crossed upon hers when the choked sighs come
And spoons of morphine swim to the propped head.
It is time to die in this house which was never home.
    Rough winter flowers grow slack against the light;
    The days are another way of spelling the night

In this molten place where a silver photograph-frame
Runs like mercury, shifting its beads about,
Rocking her once again in my father's dream.
In the long-ago garden, holding the summer out,
    Her eyes laugh for his love: the ridiculous, wide
    Hat over dark hair, the white dress poured into shade,

This house burning away in my arms: the flowers,
The pictures loose with their huge and radiant trees,
Their cornfields crushed and rippling to faraway spires,
The cards blurred with angels and unpacked memories,
    A letter alert for the quick ply, the thresh of life –
    I am cut between glittering knife and glittering knife,

All honed by dangerous love. I drift through signs,
Defenceless, for there is nothing left here to defend
But the wrapped gifts helpless in their tinsel chains.
Somewhere Christ has been born; here, the promised end
    Thirsts for that promise kept: her one desire
    The pure trouble of fire, and what will become of fire.

7 At the Gate

By something about his air I knew he had seen me.
I had thought him left on the bed where a woman had died,
Lying in wait for his box and his gift-wrapped flowers,
The fire by which he had asked to be purified.

But there he was at the gate, juggling the sunshine,
Propping his cloudy windows against the view
Which kept the bricks and the grass in their usual places,
Leaving it up to his light to see things through,

As if those sharp-cut leaves, the restless traffic,
The blossoms bobbing about in their scuds of rain,
Were long breaths drawn and held in a foreign country:
A language cut on the cross, and nothing plain.

I knew the intransigent way he tugged at the world:
The rucked-up gravel, sun split by quartering trees.
He rubbed the skin of the day between his fingers;
Worked himself up into broken surfaces.

And this I should have foreseen; fostered, reminded
By what the dissolving landscape had come to prove,
Of how, by a different gate, from a different bedside,
He had broken the daylight in. His name was love.

8 Blessing

We are giggling about like girls in the Registry Office
As I hold her death in my hand. Can I spell its name
For the stunned typewriter, jolting its bones together,
The circumlocution of walls, where the nineteen-forties
Wobble their ghosts in blisters of cream and green,
Sigh in these box-files and the scraps of drugget?
Oh, what is hatched from these matches and despatches
When the mountainous Registrar takes a flower from his drawer
And swims like a seal through this wedding, where no impediment
Stands between bridegroom, all his astonishing hair
A wave of peroxide, tumbling to sharp lurex,
And bride, whipped like cream, scenting the flowers
Which twirl in the gloom and dazzle her nervous fingers?

The whole room buckles to life, swells with napery:
Handkerchiefs, tips of icebergs: a watch-chain's anchor
Sliding deep into billows of navy. Voices roll
Out of the broadest of acres; their brasses jingle
Under the crisp rosettes pinned against flesh –
We are flooded with Eastern light, and there in my hand
I hold my mother – a small, excited child
In her plaits, her buttoned boots, her Edwardian trimmings.
About us, the high parade of a Hiring Fair,
The plash of dirt-straw under the wedged beasts,
The huge teams dancing on their feathered feet,
Dancing away with love, as I consign her
Back to the files, back to the cradling dust,
With all these blessings, warmed by the fires of those
Who bless without knowing how, or whom, they bless.

9 *Childish Things*

I stand, my mother's weight upon my arm,
My clothes as serious as the future hid
Among the coffin-brasses, all this calm
Of lilies, granny's face beneath the lid.
    We move through scents, and she is at my side,
    Lips moving now: fast falls the eventide.

The house falls too: perched on a coldish spring
It waits in silence for the knacker's yard –
The clocks, the cups, the bits of everything
Dim out their lights; they too are dying hard,
    Losing that gloss I'd shimmered on their skins,
    Whirling away to strangers, widdershins,

For childish things grow dust, and go away;
That four-years' absence on a double-bed
Shrinks to the compass of an April day.
I had not thought how much goes with the dead,
    Nor yet how different my face could be.
    I pass the baked meats, and the funeral tea.

Again, the family faces gather round.
Suiting their darknesses to what they know
Must come: church flowers, cut sandwiches, the sound
Of huge words and small echoes. As we go
　　I hear my father drily say: 'Your mother
　　Would not have thought you out of character' –

These casual clothes – the stuff she could call *me*
If I had come in by a different gate
In different light. The bearers move, and she
Rides on their neutral arms. I take that weight
　　Searching me out, and through. Past shine and blur
　　Her mother's coffin-trestles wait for her.

10 *Young Ghost*

Oh, the young ghost, her long hair coursing
Down to her shoulders: dark hair, the heat of the day
Sunk deep under those tucks and scents, drowsing
At the neck's nape – she looks so far away,
Though love twinned in her eyes has slipped its blindfold –

And really she glances across to him for ever,
His shutter chocking the light back into the box,
Snapping the catch on a purse of unchanged silver.
Under those seven seals and the seven locks
She is safe now from growing with what is growing,

And safe, too, from dying with what is dying,
Though her solemn flowers unpick themselves from her hands,
The dress rustles to moth-wings; her sweet flesh fraying
Out into knots and wrinkles and low-tide sands.
The hat is only a basket for thoughtless dust.

And she stands there lost in a smile in a black garden:
A white quotation floating away from its book.
Will it be silver, gold, or the plain-truth leaden?
But the camera chirps like a cricket, dies – and look,
She floats away light as ash in its tiny casket.

11 Dancing Shoes

At Time's *Excuse-me,* how could you refuse
A Quickstep on his wind-up gramophone?
How long since you wore out your dancing shoes,

Or his vest-pocket Kodak framed the views
In which you never found yourself alone?
At times, excuse me, how could you refuse

His Roaring Twenties, stepping out in twos,
Love singing in his lightest baritone?
How long since you wore out your dancing shoes

And shut away that music, hid the clues
By tennis courts long rank and overgrown?
At times, excuse me, how could you refuse

To say his choice was just what you would choose,
Although he spun your fingers to the bone.
How long since you wore out your dancing shoes?

The Charleston and the Foxtrot and the Blues –
The records end in blur and monotone.
At Time's *Excuse-me* – how could you refuse?
How long since you wore out your dancing shoes?

12 1946

Our ghostly neighbours, walking their wounded rooms,
Dun her with stillbirth, madness: fierce dues,
And she must pay them out of an empty pocket.
Now, being chosen, how can she refuse?

Her black goodness blows to smuts on the wind;
Her dull sobbing sinks to the kitchen floor.
She fears cancer, being dissolved from us all
Into a nothing, a burnt offering, a for-ever-more

Of the cold stuff looked-out for on winter evenings
When we children press our noses to the pane,
Smelling dead light, worrying the road bare,
Lost on the trail of the late car and the last train.

She slams the door, slams her darks on the dark;
The house drops through the night like a black stone:
Her thoughts the jostle of rain in a loose cloud,
Her love bright as a child's fever, clenched as bone.

13 *The Fire*

The things they left unsaid
        Were less than air:
Shifts of an autumn sun
        From here to there.

There was the fire's low rush,
        That daring sibilance.
Its beads of steady light
        In the near distance

Drew all their secrets in,
        Each turn and glance –
Such hunger to consume
        Irrelevance.

As if the endless hour
        Of memories, names,
Was building a new dark
        From the old flames,

Feeding the chimney-stack,
        Whose sooty love
Posted what they had kept
        To things above:

Just a cold fold of tiles,
        Sugared by rain,
The spaces between the stars
        Clouded again.

14 *The Finished Life*

The finished life. And so it floats away
In rest and syncopation – an old song
As rough as breath, quotidian as the day,

To join the host of quick, completed things:
That clematis pinned back against the wall,
Those daisy-heads, adrift and thickening

Because the month has turned again to May.
I balance her upon my open page
As if she had become a holiday

As warm as sea expected to be cold,
Whose lights run out against a childish sun.
Here, she is nothing young, and nothing old,

But takes her chances from a sleight of mind
And, castled in her unrecorded hours,
Must lend herself to what the words can find:

A strip of ribbon burred across the skin,
Unstitched from choices worn to ravellings;
A spool of dark exposures winding in

Cups, conversations, an unfocused sky
Looking so clearly at the myriad grass –
And all we greet each time we say 'Goodbye'.

15 The Stair

I stop on the stair, look up to the lucky landing
       Where frosted sky
Aches apart on the early dead and the last.
Caught in the crook of the turn, my body bending
       To let you by,

I try once more to allay this trouble of faces;
       With double sight
Angling the dark for the truth of yesterday's ghost.
As the living slip to the sun, the dead to their houses
       Bricked out of night,

In a dusk retreat where much has been taken, given,
       I question air,
And under my feet that shuffle of ash and dust.
About you the tricksy shadows might have been woven
       From greyish hair.

As the hands from the dead-sea shore crowd an upstairs window
       Spliced by the moon,
I think of the places which keep the things I have lost,
And – tremor cordis – what I must do, undo,
       Knowing how soon

The ice in the bone will harden the outstretched fingers,
       How flesh, unmade,
Will scatter its tracings out on the lands of the past,
Into the haunts of the once-familiar strangers,
       My own ghost laid

Under this ladder of shades, the stair-rods ruling
       Their glancing bars
Across the climb of the night: still unconfessed,
Our share in that love which steadies the sky from falling,
       And lights the stars.

16 Birthday

Flesh touched, as if today
Something crosses a grave,
A poem, whose words carry
To anyone listening

Her sampler, silk house
Gardened by stitches;
Her box of Swiss music
Dancing on silverpoints.

Closed, she opens like the roses
Blown early in a dry summer
And lazy with girls' names.
She would have known them,

But speaks under the wind's breath
In twists of birdsong
Whose course she followed
Through woods, gardens,

Hidden in such green.
As June leafs over
The wish is a question:
'Happy Birthday?'

The Christmas Midnight

I

The day slams down: the dark, the smell blocked thick;
I climb again up into the loaded car.
Thousands of miles are jumbled against the clock.
Black straps go tight on my electric chair.
The Sergeant-Major barks: 'I will run you in
So fast your little wheels won't touch the ground.
I'll spring you over the feathers, the bleeding skin,
The cliffs and the groan of sea at your land's end.
Shaking a forest of grass in your wind-machine
You'll be driven hard; at every straight and bend
Metal will duck from metal, the stars come clean.
As urgent and unpunctual as air
You will be somewhere. You will not be there.'

II

I do not think I am understood tonight
By things my head breeds language to understand:
Cold dials, green with a fishy light,
Cats' eyes glazing out from the swooped bend,
Those things which cross themselves, as if for luck,
And wave their hands to my vanishing curve of glass,
The wheel whose skin sticks to my fingers, the trick
Of shadows tossing me stuff I could hit or miss.
I play with loaded springs, my hands and feet
Dancing slow in close and musical air
As the engine drags and worries me out of sight,
The clutch slipped; time changing its gear,
Telling me how it will bring me safe out of harm:
Whinnying, trembling – my hand on the bonnet warm.

III

Tonight is black and white and go and come,
Is left and right – all swung antinomies.
The needle will not stick; it has to climb.
How many miles an hour to reach the skies?
I play with swings and roundabouts: a road
Where all these bits of driving, being driven,
Could make soft shadow, cloud, a being dead,
Floating for ever between Hell and Heaven.
I watch my ghosts whirl their excited hands;
They haul me through this pounding, heavy stuff
Whose cabs lean down: star-ships with clear-cut ends,
Their constellated lights a sliding graph.
I brush the road, light as a stolen kiss.
This is what I have come to. What is this?

IV

I come to myself, come home to chills of wind
In anchored trees, here, on this little hill.
My hands are shaking. It is at an end.
Light cracks and metals cool. An owl must call.
The car's thoughts settle, iron out its pain;
It snugs itself against the kindly frost,
Shrouds of light ice, ribs, webs of hardened rain,
Things ticking over, and things getting lost.
My cenotaph, my palace of black glass,
I lock your heart out with a silver key
As bright as moonshine. You shall be the place
Where I keep safe the absences of me.
In bed and open-eyed, with whips and goads
I drive you down my bright arterial roads.

V

I strap an image down. It bursts the seam.
My roof-rack thrums its cold Aeolian harp,
Chafing the stars, the wind – things as they come –
To burning elegiacs. Floating up
Between the night, the screen, his young-old face
A half-worked manuscript: intelligence
Wormed-out by maggot life, an empty house,
The Beardsley pull, the drink, his bright, intense
Low fires of loneliness, the phone that stretched
A spider-thread of thought to miles of pain,
The self-inflicted words, the silence. Wretch,
Find in his shadow your Samaritan
And clench your thought upon the girl who said
The living have the choice to be the dead.

VI

As dead as those who live: struck silences
Who dress themselves to meet themselves each day,
Floating like us in whispers, darknesses,
Lights dipped against the strangeness of the way.
The service-stations hospital the night,
Snapping the wind round coloured bits of tin;
Drugged by injection, music, chocolate,
We flicker back into our lives again
Dreaming of home: the dolls' house on the tip,
Warm chamberings for badger and for mole,
Honeymoon Lane – the shack on Smoky Top
Where someone's arms could try to hug us whole –
Scarecrows, lions, tin-men, all that crowd
Dancing round pot-holes on a witch-lit road.

VII

To trace the fault? With skill, with time, with love.
That alien murmur from the wear and tear,
Glossed-over, taped, roars into overdrive.
The lever frozen fast in second-gear,
What relay service comes to get you home,
After the crying, while the sobs go on?
Your plotted journey blown to Kingdom Come,
The more who pass, the more you are alone,
Pacing dull yards of tarmac, aching head
Full of cracked ice and pity for your sins:
Commissions and omissions. Down the wide
Careering freeway of the clean machines
The flash of orange beacon-lights – or blue –
Might steady climbing tumult; hunt you through.

VIII

Is to be young to wish the close of day,
Shiver at nightfall by the sway and hum
Holding your placard, letters rubbed away,
Watching the unrevealing headlights come,
So quickly go, leaving the dark unblessed?
Though the intelligent hitch-hiker's guide
Is out of print this year, and early frost
Picks at the fingers bumming for a ride,
Not only Spring-heeled Jack the Ripper stops
His reeking car; insinuates, cajoles,
With eyes as black as buttons, Bluebeard chops
And secret chambers for the cure of souls.
By luck, by fate, the good lifts come; the road
Smooths out a little underneath the load.

IX

The days are drawing in, are drawing down;
Their linen folds and blinds curtail the stars.
I start from cold; switch my ignition on:
That punctual red alert which disappears
Into its image. Advent. Stupefied
For some deliverance, I ease the brake
And slip into the habit of the road.
She will die soon. How long does dying take?
How many crossroads meet upon that bed
Where loaded years dismantle into love?
Pubs fairy-light their cypresses. Ahead,
The night is creeping skin; a shimmered glove
Whose blindfold sockets pull me to their ends:
Cradlings of bone, and layings-on of hands.

X

In this, the Christmas midnight of the year,
Viburnum flowers against the rain and cold.
I pitch my tent beneath its waxen star;
It is my myrrh, my frankincense, my gold.
In the huge shadows which are swarming her
She feels the scent cross miles I cannot cross;
Mothers me with a word. 'Lovely.' I hold the power
Of winter and its hidden promises.
There are no tears. Kneeling beside the bed,
We nurse her gently, under discipline.
I hold her far away, as far as God;
I wear her closely as a second skin.
We are as fluid as refusing air
That will not strip those sheets and pillows bare.

XI

The doctor stares, untongued. We shut the door.
Threads draw to breaking-point. I sleep alone.
He wakes me up into some darkness hour.
We look into the rags of time. 'She's gone.'
Hours he has spent beside her cooling flesh,
The *Holy Sonnets'* groundswell in his head,
Testing their weight, bare to each balm and lash.
There are some words to check. From out his shroud
Donne strikes lament and triumph: a dark bell
Whose golden tongue waits on the quick and dead.
I take his press of syllables, the spell
Of that communion, that wine and bread.
Truth at the well's foot. Our St Lucie's Night.
We sit in darkness reaching for the light.

XII

Always the Morello, its gouts darkening
Over a dream of white flowers, drifted sticks.
The end of a garden: a huge wall, light quickening
To slips riding on purples and soft blacks;
Always the Crab-Apple, and its painted gourds
Tumbled starrily on sweet-scented ground:
This down by a gate where I stand lost for words
Except those words I lost, which make no sound.
And quick on my lips the taste of bitter-sweets,
Of hard and soft found wanting, and found good,
Their sustenance weightless as these driven nights,
The bright fruit fresh and sour as my own blood.
I pluck them, pick them, press them against my tongue:
Savours which stay for ever, will not last long.

XIII

'Look in your mirror.' Look in it for luck.
It is packed with obfuscation, and with rain:
The past heaving about, its greasy slick,
Unharboured lights, things laid upon the line,
The sharp, unhooded eyes which fail to see
How close the dead are riding on my back,
Or how, beyond this bend, the land will lie
And how the road is about to break its neck
Where a string of lanterns keeps the narrow and straight.
His white beams locked on my dancing points of red,
I will lead him through a grimpen of mist and night;
I will guide him to something I might have understood,
Throttling the engine down to its beast-purr,
The moon as sharp as a hook in a velvet paw.

XIV

Ah, these blue undertakers in the rain,
Tender to wave me on or flag me down,
Comforting sick metal once again.
Sockets drip glass – how very much alone
These mortal houses with their painted skin,
Slewed on the verge of being what they were:
Between the sadness of what might have been,
The craning necks that cannot leave them there.
Banks carry flowers for them; a slow cortège
Winds awkwardly about these hats-off cones.
Can you see ghosts? There at the busy edge
Sits one released from his broken flesh and bones,
Drying his wings in sunlight: an ash look
Fixed on the pages of his judgement-book.

XV

Here's this, your ginger man, who does not know
I smell of death, but knows my engine's purr.
His simple tricks are magical as snow,
Boxing the compass by a sleight of paw.
He, too, has journeys he is bound to make,
Holds conversations with the night and rain:
Our speaking likeness that will never speak,
The great good cat, the looked-for thing, the sign,
A feral innocence with power to break
The human heart – supply his place again
With life that looks like love, like love can take
That puzzling something off that we call pain,
Ebbing away in furs which warm and sheathe
A quick-step pulse-beat and a sighing breath.

XVI

The scraped-out nerves of things will come to fledge
And even signposts learn to tell the way,
Old christening-robes of blossom dress the hedge.
Light could hold longer if it comes to May
When giddy people eat their cakes and cream
But that's a distance yet. If it's inclined
To take me through a mirage to a dream,
A dream to the substantive and defined
I'd bless the road; would fit it like the glove
That fits my hand that fits the steering-wheel,
Keep a blue weather-eye on what's above
And out of reach; what I must bring to heel:
The smell of burning, and a ski-track skid,
A footing lost, a scorched and greasy road.

XVII

Oh, Sunday drivers, harnessed to your ease,
To blue-rinse bobbing head, upholstered lane,
May you, like flocks of sheep, most safely graze
The uncut verge, and Ambrose or Jack Payne
Put cream in coffee, pennies in small rain.
May water-lights from naked glass and chrome
Spring off to fuse with an embracing sun,
Your pad-nags turn their simple heads for home.
And you? My shadow, censor, *vrai semblable,*
Reined in by meadow-sweet or salt-licked sea,
Loose to the air my teeming courts of babel.
Clock up good miles. Let instruments agree,
And black horse, white horse, chariot, charioteer,
Drive four-in-hand the slip-roads of the year.

XVIII

Sometimes a light grows up to window-space,
A window-space to door. That light must know
How much it shares the nature of a star.
Would only fools or wise men think it so,
Stooping for miracles? Your scented tree
Has blossomed lustres all this Christmas-tide;
I picked a bunch of shadows, could not see
One candle burning for the flesh that died.
She holds me tight – as tight as I hold you,
Our winter-hands alert for quickening
Your garden, where Demeter dressed in dew
Holds out an urn to conjure with the Spring.
Tonight must hold us all, it is so wide –
Love born, love resurrected: crucified.

The Musical Box

The musical box has faded, as book-spines fade,
Taking the weight of the sun as the days come:
The key-hole out of key, the notes faltered,
The curry-comb gat-toothed on the spiked drum.

My gift, in lieu of that box in wartime Cambridge,
Going for a song, when songs were few, and dear.
In the half-lit house he opens it, posts his verses.
It is love: for her, for me. She is very near.

Memories? Let them rest in their quiet chambers,
The timeless gifts of time, forever ours,
But the one who is last to walk in the sunlit garden
Must watch for us both the play of the living powers,

The emerald lace-wing fly on the kitchen window,
The mating frogs with their hoarse and urgent voice,
The drift of long-tailed tits through the high box-elders
And the missal-thrush that sings for us both, Rejoice.

It is an age-old tune for a penny whistle,
Not for the pomps and stratagems of art:
It is a quiet tune that needs no playing
For us, who have the melody by heart.

He has two years left. When gifts return to the giver,
I take the box; find, read, and let it play,
This tune that needs no playing: a quiet chamber,
A coffin of silent sound and blurred inlay.

I crank it up, and under the ribboned glass
Let the jimp teeth flicker up on the rusting comb,
Sing of short turns about the sunlit garden,
Plantations, the Swanee River: old folks at home.

Dying

for my Father, John Scupham, 1904–1990

1 *November 24th, 1989*

My sister and brother-in-law think I should come
To see my father, who lies on his marriage-bed
Considering the seven ages of man,
Opening the windows on his Advent Calendar.
The books and pictures of his conversation
Place themselves calmly round about the room
For air to shelve and frame them.
Time slips its moorings. He eats little,
Sleeps to dream, and is pleased to see me.
His head is hoar-frost in a mild winter;
His eyes are smoke-blue. They do not waver.
It is time to mother and father his childhood,
Fetch and carry, ease him out of tangles.
Once he told me he wanted to be a poet
But decided that Yeats could do it better.
I would like to do justice to this mild, distinguished man
Who can handle seasons, flowers, the affairs of men,
Whose loosening mind keeps the Arnoldian touchstones
For sentinel on this, his longest journey.
He carries light. Dark will not hurt him greatly.
His veins are heavy plaits under a skin
Wearing its tenderness against the bone.
As muscle wastes, his tongue supports his weight,
Shaping, with all the clarity of reticence,
Sketches for the poems he never wrote
And would not have called poems if he had.
There is collusion. Each has his alibi.

2 *'I have lived in a world which makes intelligible certain older worlds …'*

'The things my mother made I'll never see again:
Potted beef, Lincolnshire fashion, flavoured with mace.
Food of the Gods. Melted butter on it. Marvellous.
Give all the pâtés in the world for it.

My mother was super-marvellous.
She came from a refined and educated home
And found herself married to a man who was neither.
She said: "Every one of these children
Is going as far up the educational ladder as they can go,"
And pushed them till they did.

By Scholarship, County Scholarship, County Major Scholarship,
We shall raise the wind –
Even if it comes out of savings – winter coats.

My father became an acute alcoholic.
Very serious indeed.
I spent morning after morning trailing him,
Deterring him from going into pubs.
Oh, it was a rum time.
He got money, and used to hide it in the garden,
But always knew how to bring half-pound slabs
Of butterscotch home for the children.
Broke it up with little hammers.

Mother's kind of heroism.
When she was quite old – her eighties –
Tommy arranged for her to go to classes,
University Extension Classes – poetry.
She wrote an account of a local bazaar
In heroic couplets.
She took vast pleasure in this.
She said: "I shall give this up.
Roger would understand me going to Bridge Parties;
He would not understand this."

I learnt two things:
To discount nine-tenths of what I read
About the ills of women in bygone days,
And that you could have a family at the mercy
Of mortal illness and bankruptcy,
And, given the right people and the right spirit,
It could be gorgeously happy.
And she was rewarded.
The children turned out diligent, and clever.

Her sisters all married professional men.
One of them said:
"Kate is the only one of us who's got nothing,
And the only one of us who has everything."

I know that the answer was the simple word "Love".'

3 'Oh dear, strange and long life is.'

'I would like to have been able to call myself a Victorian.
Of such small vanities ...

I think I am that vacuum-cleaner,
And I sweep up gold-dust – very precious.

My ambition at the BBC – this sounds like vanity
But it has some truth in it –
My organization put out vast masses
Of simple biology, physics, geography, natural history –
My ambition was to be able to talk
To the producer of each specialism
In his own language and on his own wavelength.

Consequence was I met a lot of very surprising chaps:
Attlee, Herbert Morrison, Crossman – star turns –
Sutherland, Michael Ayrton ...
The best minds of the day walked into my parlour.
Ronnie Knox – very agreeable.

"Man is but a reed, but he is a thinking reed."
That's Pascal.

I have a natural desire
To make myself more important and interesting
Than I really am. Of course, of course.

My ambition would have been to live a long life
With no events in it, and grow a great beard.

My aim now is to sit in a dressing-gown all day
Thinking disciplined, high thoughts.
I wish no part of the Contemporary Theatre.'

4 'Look in the next room ...'

The books in the house are numbered
As carefully as the hairs on an old head.
Books behind books. There is a master-plan.
The building is the Celestial City.

'G. M. Young's dictum: read till you can hear people talking.
Not only what Wellington said to Creevey at breakfast
But Jacques le Bon to the grocer –
Behind the generals and the generalities.
Get me *The People's Armies,* by Richard Cobb –
Chap who lived in a fossilized watering-place.

If it were not for *The Children's Encyclopedia*
How should I know about *The King of the Golden River?*
How should I know about *Barbara Frietchie,*
Not to mention *Hiawatha?*'

He takes *La Rochefoucauld,* holds it upside down,
And reads the footnotes to his memory.

'I can do you the first hundred lines of *The Prelude,*
Or *A Toccata of Gallupi's.*

Fetch me Hallam's *Tennyson* – the second volume.
And if you see a book that's not worth reading,
Pass it to me, and I won't read it.

Even if it costs the earth
I want you to get me *Buried for Pleasure,*
Or *The Pleasure of Being Buried*
By Edmund Crispin.

As for those books from Waterstone's,
You could take them straight to Heaven and read them there.
I think the seating-arrangements would be better.'

He knows that Christmas is somewhere round a corner.
We have put out his cards, read them to him,
Hung the odd picture with a twist of tinsel.
It is time for one of his favourite quotations:
'The feast of reason, and the flow of soul',
When the world perches on chairs, hands Chinese figs,
Sips the liqueurs he offers us by proxy.
It is Boxing Day, late afternoon. We bring the crib.
Virgin and Child suffer their nativity,
Doubled in his dressing-table mirror.
He has put an occasion together in his head,
And, at some far, unguessable cost, watches
A candle in a lantern, swinging softly.
'The Holly and the Ivy, when they are both full-grown ...'
And, please, he would like Dorothy's favourite carol:
'He came all so still where his mother was ...'
We eat, drink, and are merry. For company,
He nibbles air in front of a petit-four,
Asks and answers a little of the *Spectator* quiz.
For an hour, he is the Master of all Ceremonies,
Asking formal advice for 'friends who live next door' –
My sister's family – would we please suggest
A Place of Significance where they could spend
The three-weeks' holiday he would like to give them.
There is a quotation. Something to do with
'Breathes there a man ...' and 'plains of Marathon' –
I cannot see things clearly enough to find it,
And he would like each member of the company
To suggest a print, an etching he could buy,
Supposing he had that princely sum, a hundred pounds to spend.
It is not easy to put names to all the faces.
He is very tired now. He has managed it quite beautifully.
When the door shuts on voices, love and manners,
'Well,' I say, 'you had your Christmas.'

'It was lovely.'

At three in the morning he calls for me,
His candle bright in its darkening lantern.
'Is it Christmas? Happy Christmas.'

'Happy Christmas.'

6 'Who do you say you are?'

'Life's difficult. How do you know you're not me?
You say you're Peter.
Do you want to persist in this claim?
You'll have a job to prove it,
Unless your documents are in very good order.

You were born in Bootle?
You couldn't say "a fine city"
At the entrance to Bootle.

Anyway, who would want to be a poet?
Poets are rarely millionaires.

Tennyson had a dubious sense of his own identity,
And when he found himself alone, would murmur
"Far, far away, far, far away".

I might deceive you about myself,
But I wouldn't deceive you about Tennyson.

I feel like a vacuum in an empty space.
Vacuums in empty space
Are very much at a loose end.
Now Blake wasn't at a loose end.

You know too much.
You claim you're Peter?
There are certain sorts of knowledge that are forbidden
And there's only one source they can come from,
And that's the Devil.

Are you the Devil?'

7 *'The Scuphams are steadfast, inclined, you might say, to obstinacy ...'*

He demands a doctor, now, at two in the morning.
Threadbare, I lose control, shamefully, and say:
'Quite the little autocrat, aren't we?' – stumble to bed.
A little later he calls me softly.
'Would you like to hear the History of the Scuphams?
In epic verse. There are lyrics,
But they aren't all written yet.'

'That's much better. Yes, please.'

'I speak for the Scuphams, the Scuphams of Scupham Hall –
At least God knows if I really speak for them all.
But only the younger line, the older, trusting to belt and braces,
Having left no sons and heirs, and very few traces.

When the old confronted the new, face to face,
The Scuphams stepped right out of the Pilgrimage of Grace,
But I can tell you, in 1215,
The Scuphams were on the right side – you know what I mean.

Magna Carta, you fool!

The Scuphams never yielded to men nor beasts,
Neither to red-headed kings nor gay Francophile priests.

There's truth there – though I may exaggerate
The power of the Scuphams.

I have invented a deviant, weaker Scupham line.
Soon I shall come to Darwin, Newman and Pope Pius the Tenth –
When you get the intransigent stuff.
It is the business of the Scuphams
To stand up against French free-thinkers.

Scuphams show common sense, and a general scepticism
About foreigners and their intentions.

But I fear some of the younger Scuphams
Are showing traces of the *Heneage Beard* –
As long as your whole body.'

As long as an unfinished epic.

8 'What time is it?'

'Twenty to five? It can't be.
Do you mean twenty to five yesterday?'

The hours are pillows, propping us together.
I would call it night, the huge small hours.
I enter his space-time continuum.

'For God's sake. This is *urgent.*'

We must work hard, form a committee of absence
To sort out the affairs of Zing and Bing.
How can these villages get their washing done?
Land must be purchased, a machine installed,
Power-lines laid, teachers and clerics assembled.
On Sundays the washing can be blessed out to dry.

He restores the King, the Red Kite, in Wales,
Foils the egg-and-feather gangs,
Brings the lost thing home again.

On Smith's farm he works the harvest —
Six sheaves to a stook —
'Long, tall bones and magpies.'

And, waking on the floor in a twist of bedclothes,
Falls 'into the hands of a remote Scottish Clan
Of unbelievable barbarity, who fed me on porridge.'
We struggle with the dead weight of the living.

'I am all right, aren't I?
I have woken up in my own world,
Not in some nightmare system of pipes and sewers?

What have I been?
I thought I was some sort of animal in the night.
I want to wake up and be a man now.

You say it's ten,
But by the amount of experience that's gone into it
It must be at least half-past four.'

For six weeks we have listened to our whispers,
Read signs and omens, taken our parts
In this play of seven ages. 'I've no doubt my nurses
Are good men and women, which only goes to show
Good men and women can be very tedious.'
He has lived beyond the possibilities of living,
His body sewn together by threads of thought,
The flesh pale, scarred, flimsy as a chicken-carcass.
He cannot speak. His eyes are constant, open.
The Doctor is interested. 'Uraemic frosting.
I would like my student to see this.'
In the night I read to him from *The Prelude*,
Celebrate a Midnight Mass for him
And the communion of his faithful ghosts:
The country child, damming the beck, skating,
At home in Legsby or in Willingham Woods,
Prospecting for gold-dust hidden in small flowers,
The Scholarship Boy, the Cambridge double-first,
The tennis-player with the kicking serve ...

'Dust as we are, the immortal spirit grows
Like harmony in music; there is a dark
Inscrutable workmanship that reconciles
Discordant elements, makes them cling together
In one society.'

At three o'clock in the afternoon, he dies.

Cause of death
   1a Uraemia
   1b Carcinoma duodenum
   1c Diabetes
   1d Myocardial infarct

'We live by admiration, hope and love –
As someone said – it must have been Wordsworth.'

I glance to where he is quizzing his *Times* obituary.
Quietly, we continue our conversation.

Clearing

Four years ago, the house was waiting for them,
As cool and as convenient as light,
And each had eighty years to pack, unpack there,
    To get things right,

As right as trivets, blackbirds, briar-roses,
Millennial stones and letters from old friends,
The winnowed books in which the past had printed
    Beginnings, ends.

And from the sunroom window, looking inwards,
An eighteenth-century landscape on the wall
Showed trees whose leaves grew calm by a brown gradation,
    But could not fall.

The days drew in; the days grew longer, deeper,
Made living-room for the tiresome, loving dead
Who shared their dreams, their food; who told them stories,
    Left things unsaid.

The difficult chapters come to a kind of end.
The books rewrite themselves as fiction. Things
Fall easily into our hands as if they believed them:
    Withdrawals, offerings,

As the dark stuff in its album strips away,
Leaving the house ghost-naked, white as a sheet –
The convenient light pausing at wall and window
    For its heart to beat.

Watching the Perseids: Remembering the Dead

The Perseids go riding softly down:
Hair-streak moths, brushing with faint wings
This audience of stars with sharp, young faces,
Staring our eyes out with such charming brilliance:
Life, set in its ways and constellations,
Which knows its magnitude, its name and status.

These, though, are whispered ones, looked for in August
Or when we trip on dead and dying birthdays,
Drinking a quiet toast at some green Christmas
To those, who, fallen from space and height
No longer reach us with their smoky fingers
Or touch this sheet of water under no moon.

They are the comet's tail we all must pass through
Dreamed out into a trail of Jack O'Lanterns,
A shattered windscreen on the road to nowhere.
We stand in this late dark-room, watch the Master
Swing his light-pencil, tentative yet certain,
As if calligraphy could tease out meaning,

And, between a huge water, huger sky,
Glimmers of something on the jimp horizon,
There might be pictures, might be conversations.
We wait for last words, ease the rites of passage,
The cold night hung in chains about our questions,
Our black ark swinging lightly to its mooring.

Calendarium

Ianuarius

I saw the cloudy genie burst his wine-skin
And blab large promises. On the dead ground
New gifts lay wrapped: a calendar of days
Unspent and unremarked. The wind idled.
At last I turned, and saw beyond the door
Resolutions thaw in the brief sunlight.
'I'll cook your goose.' The goose was cooked and eaten.
Under the Christmas trees I watched the children
Search for a brief kindness in the snow.

Februarius

Fur sits by the hearth, yawning a red yawn,
Easing his claws. The year has turned,
But the dull acres lie all senseless,
Rain, dark and rain guessing at their contours.
Undo this button, set the chair closer
And thorns under the pot: a fool's laughter
Raising the roof-tree to the clouded stars.
It is a comfort to write long letters,
Urge frozen fingers to a little piece-work,
Stare at the nothings bobbing in the fire.

Martius

Much can be seeded from a stiff yard-broom,
A duster shaken from an upstairs window.
Room now for the look of things to clear,
The pliant heart to suffer some excision.
It is medicinal to graft and prune
Under these wayward gusts, flecked by birds.
Set your house in order. Make a start.

Aprilis

All that you know, all that you thought you knew
Ploughs under as the share deals it.
Resurrection is in the air, the sky loose
In quick clouds, bold Easter wings.
Luck lies in a horseshoe; at the field's edge
I picked one out of shining clay, iron
Struck from a sweating team the years had harnessed.

Maius

Meet on the field-path, at the kissing-gate,
And read in love's fine print, still dancing
Its old measures in this press of leaves.
Untie the daisies; your sharp nails will bleed them,
Slit the pale stalks to die against her throat.

Iunius

In this cloudless weather, where reflections hang
Under the substance of their woods and cities.
Nothing is sweeter. Make hay while the sun shines.
In the white spaces of the longest day,
Urgent against the shades as yet undarkened,
Siren voices plague the drying grass.

Iulius

In between moving to and moving from,
Unfolding green, disclosing darker green,
Lie deep fields, cornered by the eye of childhood.
In between moving up and moving down
Uncut plaits of wheat bend to the land's lie.
Space between then and now. Sleep, and good dreams.

Augustus

As you sow, so shall you reap. The bags packed,
Umbers and gold swollen between the purse-strings,
Getaway cars nose on a hot scent.
Under striped canvas the patrons gather,
Staring at blue, incorrigible seas.
The stubble burns a hole in summer's pocket;
Upon the baked crust of their world, the mice
Scatter their ashes to the harvest moon.

September

Sun lingers out the senses; shawls of light
Ease the eye into fullness, and late suns
Polish our gourds. There, at the orchard gate,
The God deals out the first-fruits of the season,
Equates desire with his huge performance.
Much promise lies in apples, and in flagons.
Blue, though, is the colour of enchantment;
Enter the hooded skyline, leave the windfall
Ravished and puckered on the cooling lawn.

October

Off with these lendings. An Indian summer
Cracks every seed-head under rising wind.
Time now to cauterize by fire
Outscourings from crooked corners:
Barren leaves, the sack of libraries
Enfolding in their Dead Sea scrolls
Runes whose ancient salt has lost its savour.

November

Night and the laurels hang their sad shields
Over parades of gravel by the lych gate.
Victory and defeat are out to grass,
Each known unto God by name and number:
Muck upon mould, caught between wind and water.
Blind scatterings, poppies of oblivion,
Ember days, uncalendared: the mists down further.
Remember. But what shall we remember?

December

Daylight shortens; your anticipation
Eases the candle-flame towards its end.
Cassiopeia swings above the fir-trees,
Embraces night. Between such diagrams
Manger and child float down the centuries,
Brilliants nursed on soft cloth. Time is now:
Each life an altar where the Mystery
Repeats its dream of gift and sacrifice.

St Madron's Well

They might have crooked their fingers, turned things over,
Paring the fleshed moment down to bone.
In the silence of their silence something hung
As hopeful as an unglassed crescent moon,
As rough and brilliant as lost love, love lost
Where twigs cracked cold wishbones underfoot.

It was, perhaps, the hope to find a place
Where moonbeams could be lightly packed in jars,
And thought, half-thoughts, blurring to images,
Could rest their small-change on the shelving darkness.
Here, at the Saint's Well, where the strips of rag
Pinned such brave hopes to briars and unfledged elders,

They saw these things, and kept their own counsel,
As if each wish had not been wished before
By those, who, dead and human, only saw
Spring trying to prove that something could come true
In makeshift green; the salt of centuries
Thrown over their left shoulders by the wind.
The Saint standing in his ruined Baptistry
Turned towards them in a dress of leaves,
His hands, bleached to sea-air, blessing them
In the brown habit of his crinkled water,
And cold light crossed itself in holes and corners
As if there was something one could take for granted.

Last Offices

Smoked glass flares in the sun: a host of wafers
Posing a juggler's waterfall of cards,
A palace where the functionaries of process
Encode their black or beatific vision
And liverish house plants infiltrate slow tendrils
Between rolled shirtsleeves, scents and after-shave.

The untidy street works up to semaphore,
Feeding the tilted panes with talk of clouds
And silent traffic cutting the light's corners.
Glass runs like tears, and holds in its suspension
Each stroller and his object of desire.
They blossom to a cool millefiori,

As if the sky, stonewalling us with blue,
Was only something to prop up our windows.
Here, a Christmas hexagon, sealing snow
And every leafless garden of the heart,
Dies through half a century of frost-flowers.
Your nail scratches the ice to a white powder

And there are your sickroom ghosts; the hot glass
Waves to itself in a swirl of yellow curtains,
Leaves brush the sky as bedclothes brush the flesh
Beyond an endurance which must be endured.
The street walkers are lost in a crowd of rooks
Flocking their ash wings down to the falling elms,

And someone, pausing, a something in the city
Is crossed with a gardener and a slatted barrow
Stashed with brown leaves. A cat, as dead as Egypt,
Washes its face, primps, summering itself
Where faces ripen like a crowd of apples
Hung on the past, the far Hesperides.

Last Offices: a Grand Messe des Morts.
The stained glass burnishes its road to Calvary
And the low plain-song from lost terminals
Asks you its fitful questions. Search, recall
Your own curriculum vitae passing through
These rainbow filters, palindromes of light,

Before the nights draw in, this magic lantern
Projects itself as pure geometry,
And secretaries of dream redress the files,
Puzzle over petals, minutes of lost meetings
Or lift their heads from scents of grasses, roses,
To new moons rising, cold and thin as luck.

The Ark

The Ark

The boy on the floor is putting his ark to bed
To the sound of a sea which is blood, and sings at his ear
Of how it could ruck the carpet-fringes to weed
But leave those ochres and buffs unwatered, bare.
The blue of the ark is as blue as all he could wish for.

I watch the way he is watching his bridge of fingers
Walk hand-in-hand in the air with whatever comes.
A hold of promises, the ark grows stronger,
Hoarding its bitten features and spindled limbs.
It is hugger-mugger in there, a must of darkness,

And the rain is cats and dogs in a green outside
As the clouds and curtains crease into sudden skin
With sweats, curls, aprons, kisses: the moil and crowd
Of shadows aching for home or a clasp of sun,
A chirping of birds, a puzzle of half-built faces.

The kindly Ones and the Furies calm the air
To the faded browns of an always afternoon.
The mahogany table swells its feet, each claw
Anchoring sand. But now the rip-tides run
Till his fingers are only the flickering ghosts of fingers

Aching for rainbows, caught on the shoals of light
Swollen from uncleaned silver and blurs of glass,
The ark of his skull trepanned on the restless freight
That he must steer to its safe and certain loss
Through pulsing water, the long salt silences.

Less than the Truth

The rough dark goes solid. Trees come first.
Elm, oak, beech? They grow to the dream's height.
Fields tilt their hectares into camouflage.
November, teatime: cold quick in the nostrils,
Frost lacing foreground mud between the goalposts.

It would be good to be certain of this, to tell you
How a woman walks a dog on a slack lead.
That will not do, any more than I can show
The freckled captain with trailing laces.
That seat is real enough in its fluted irons:
Le vieux parc, invitations of ghost-life.

No. One must be content with less.
Nameless trees, fields, white posts
Gibbeting the air, mist coming down or rising.
I am sure of sodden leaves, but that is different.
They must be there, but they are not the truth,
Though, since they must be there, perhaps they hide it,
And why this feeling of panic, the encumbered soul?

Somewhere, trackers: the wet, dilated nostrils
Full of a coat-smell, hunting for half-dressed flesh,
A bandit, bent over the purr of his detector,
Out for the buried torque, a girl whose hazel-twig
Can leap nonsensically over the life of water.
Things here are so gone, unthreaded beads or needles,
Perhaps they should look by the trees? Look, not hope,
For the press of a split hoof, a clean feather.

Accident

1

Dear reader, I'm writing this to tell you
How a small freckled girl walked by the verge
With a white dog and her grandfather. Can we take this further?
You are dear to me, my lucky, astonishing friend.
We make rapprochement on the lip of sleep,
And though I shut my eyes, you keep yours open.
We do not read much at night in the blowing libraries,
But now, I like to think, her page lies open,
Slipping its catch between your beings and doings,
Tempting you to a view through its white window.
Here, then, is the girl, closed on her own meaning
As she walks from a glimpse to an image. Now,
She should be eating her dinner. 'Reader' is easy.
If I give you another line, will she be a sonnet?

But have you taken this in? There could be a problem.
In this line, perhaps one of cadence, that *amour de voyage*:
A girl and a dog, and her grandfather; yesterday's roadside
Blurred by the tune of a late-Victorian metric.
And how should a line like this hold your span of attention?
How was she dressed? Shall I tell you? How would you dress her?
Oh, folderols, bright flows of things. Blue jeans?
Look, you know when you're in the front passenger-seat
And the driver brakes without warning, almost too late,
You swing, weightless and out of your assumptions
With a 'What the hell are you doing?' Well, glance in
The mirror. What's there? A clumsy line break,
A repeated 'white' in the first section?
What's happened?

Let's start again. Were you given this book? Did you buy it?
As yet I can't see its cover, or where it's lying,
Least of all, where I shall be when you read it.
What hubris, trusting us to have this future
In which to make a special sense of nonsense.
Let's get back to the business in my hand
And strip away those qualifiers: white, small, freckled.
Combined, they call to me with a tender disgust
As if I'm talking of a mouse in a laboratory.
And was the man her grandfather? Please forget them.
But though your limbo file is full of adjectives,
Remember the man who kept his treasure safe
By one condition. Whoever dug it up
Must not think of a white badger while he dug for it.

I'm telling you the truth. Because we *share,*
(Each is the Red King in the other's dream),
And each of us has space and time, can spare
A little of ourselves upon this theme,
It is important that we learn to trust,
If not each other, girl and road and man.
Do not believe the useful rhyme of 'dust',
Believe that I can make a sonnet scan.
A neat container: what then is contained?
A stopped frame from a film that's running free,
A coarse and grainy stuff that's not explained
By titling it in bold **'Life'**, **'Memory'**,
'Gone with the Wind', or subbing out the text
With flickering cartouches of 'What comes next'.

5

For what comes next is something we can make
Only in easy half-light and the half-rhymes:
Bright, broken things, the seductive lilt of the dark
Patting about with words at the old names –
August, with a fly-blown ache of sky,
Smelling of war and slow holiday,
With its Panama hat and a dolly-twist of straw,
Rough pasture, and a half-blind terrier,
A gravelled voice, pacing words slowly
And throat-stopped now for half a century,
A brass ferrule poked in a molehill,
The sag of wires from pole to pole
Black with birds and silver with sound,
The held hand lost in the holding hand.

6

How can I count her losses as they pass?
I cannot count my own. Each loss must be
Particular and endless. Does the dry grass,
At summer's end, whisper 'Remember me'?
There is a blur of dry and green, a car
Spacing itself to where the day begins –
They're something still, but were not what they are,
Such particles have glimmered from their skins,
Each photon stuck and hinged inside a head,
Probing the space-time of the zodiac
Or lying down, pretending to be dead,
Beyond the spooky half-life of its track –
Reader, what do you see? Let's play 'I-Spy',
Scrambling the skylights of a single eye.

7

Let's take a sodden castle, in a rain
Which mizzles blue and unremembered hills.
Stand on the magic carpet. Count each pane
Of puzzled glass. The rocky landscape fills
That crazy paving with the ghosts of trees
Which meet the ghosts of chiffoniers and clocks
And offer up their crystal truancies
To light which greets the window, and unlocks
A living space: one bright, and real, and so,
Where loll-tongue dog and man and chattering girl
Can meet in fiction's radio-active glow,
Conspire to make our head and heartaches whirl.
Outside and in don't match. A missing room
Hides dust and lanthorns, mémoires d'outre-tombe.

8

Is it Lot 93, or 92?
The sharp-nosed auctioneer, two lots a minute.
'What am I bid?' No provenance, no signature.
A rural scene. Amateur, but not a print.
The gangling man in leathers, the holiday-makers
In from the rain, and Mrs Moore, dealer in bric-à-brac,
Are silent. Everything must belong somewhere,
Be at home in a finite series of numbers.
It's a rotten likeness of something, but still a likeness,
And will grow lovely if you grow to love it:
An old man blurred enough to make an ancestor,
The dog and child whose trust, fidelity,
Is all you feel, and all you feel you've lost,
The frame waving goodbye as they walk towards you.

9

There is merriment and puzzle in Cookham Churchyard
At the moment of resurrection, when all discover
The relief of realizing they need no adjectives,
Or need them only in the Pickwickian sense,
As nuns own maiden-names, or rosaries.
No one says 'What a funny hat you're wearing!'
'That walking-stick was Jim's.' There are no brand-names
For brands plucked from the burning, the saints and martyrs
That we have dignified to be our votive images.
And if the Panama hat, the aertex shirt belong,
They must belong as prayers and flames belong,
Clothing the lost majesty of Proper Names,
Which, at their most proper, become as common
As man and girl, as dog, as road.

The underwriters tell me I should tell you
About this accident, this impact. I drove within my limits.
There was no tyre-squealing; there were no skid-marks.
All that humming cage remained responsive;
Just a catch in the engine's throat, a change in the fine-tuning.
I pulled the car in carefully to the verge
And remembered the hazard-warning indicators.
A bit too late. I realized I'd gone clean through them,
But the sun picked them up in its own good time,
Walking no more, and no less carefully.
I think the girl might have been carrying flowers.
What do you think, dear reader? You're the only one
Who has some cause to make a claim against me.
Is our cover comprehensive? Shall we call it knock for knock?

What do you Believe?

The voice of the dying man spoke from the marriage-bed,
His head lit by the lamp closed on its dark wick.
He spoke, dying, between the rock and the dead light
From a hard place, where the blackness had no seam,
No rivulet along which there was movement,
Or space in which one seed of time could grow,
As if that lamp, in its going out, could speak
From sand, countless; from disinheritance,
Sending the stir, the shock and bloom of things,
To beg its way from flesh to memory,
From memory to image; then to nothing more
Than the one question: 'What do you believe?'

Someone there at the bed's foot, spoke to the sheets,
To the pale eyes wide open on the dark
And all that sand and disinheritance
Of woods and waters, closed on their glittering,
As if there were words to answer those four words,
The lamp could be trimmed to burn with its small flame
And make more luminous one serious thing;
Picked up a book, and read to those wide eyes
Words by a dead man, in which the inconsolable dead
Had looked for consolation. The wasted hand
Which could not move stirred for the lamp's key;
Set the globe leaping with a clouded light.

Spoon River

'It's Spoon River,' he said, looking past things
At refractions of marble, swinging in chains of light.
'And if I could tell you, what could I tell you?'
Best to say nothing, as they were saying nothing;
Do nothing, but look at him looking:
A head worn into patience, a kind of godhead

Hunting for space between judgement and mercy.
We turned away from the heat of the graves
Where his mother and father lay, his brother,
In a dark dream of grass, brightening
In a late sun, in a time before time to go
From this clock-stopped time of gold and edges.

Was it playing God? Each to his own omniscience,
Which was denied. Did he call for resurrection,
His head a stoneyard where a lid thrown back
Set Billy Brumpton harnessing his mare again,
With wisps of hay and cooking-smells at corners,
The sound of old money arguing at market?

But Spoon River, with its hanging judges
And women taken in adultery?
He had nothing to say to this town in its water-lights,
Its blobbed flowers dying in handfuls.
'If I told you their stories, it would only be lies.
We shall leave all that for the Recording Angel.'

No locks on the gates. As I turned back with him
The light grew confident, then magisterial.
What could be said? To whom could we say it?
Their lives reached for his keeping; his unmoved eyes
Gathered their names as a child gathers in secrets,
To hold something in trust for the trusted silence.

The Pond

The sheep hangs on the surface of the pond,
A porridge of bobbled flesh; the trees are still,
As still as anything. We stand there, and look down.

I had day-dreamed this moment, showing them off
That clear dark eye; the fence of thorny stuff
And all the careful crookedness of paths

Leading to where I had only asked a place
To be itself, and keep my kind of secret:
Lit water, holding itself against the rim.

This was the place, refusing to come clean,
The sky, spreading its headache over the dip
Where zig-zag lights and weary filaments

Picked at the ragged edges of the leaves,
The natural day scorched by their dirty brilliance;
The secret, turning its insides out for us.

Long snows, these winters. The packed cold
Mulled by black boots into rot and grey,
Yellow animal piss in steaming holes,

And, overhead, the nursery rhymes go on:
A cloud like Mary's lamb, led to the slaughter,
Snow-goose feathers, plucked from something dying,

Which pass and settle, settle and pass again,
As I pick my way, eager, the lost leader,
Towards the ambush and the long way home.

Night slides off the Umbrian hills
And fireflies come out in Luigi's garden:
Smoke-dark, high-lit, the shallow stream
Trips under the bridge to feed moonlight;
The sky ripples, on the edge of lightning,
At the dull thud, twang of his music-system.
But the Mills Brothers, with fur-lined voices,
Try to fit them to the Glow-worm Song,
Dazing Linnaeus with close harmony,
These lampyrids, elaterids,
Not to be confused with Lampyris noctiluca,
That heavy girl crouched in long English grass
Giving the green light to her blacked-out mate
From an abdomen of uric acid crystals.
'Thou aeronautical boll-weevil,
Illuminate yon woods primaeval' –
Enough of nature-notes and country comets:
Each shiner is the other's metaphor,
And as for 'lighting tapers at the fiery glow-worm's eyes …!'

The *Dream* again? Yes, the performance,
As always, wrong in its open-air production.
This summer, every night's a first night,
And, perhaps, the backdrop crinkled paper,
The bridge a merely operatic construct
Strayed in from *Cavaliera Rusticana*.
Max Reinhardt strings his fairy-lights
Across the insubstantial gauze of evening,
And now that Micky Rooney has stopped kidding
We can put a few lost lines together,
As if the play were a charred manuscript
And all that can be read is 'Night and silence',
What night-rule here about this haunted grove?
Merely the wand of darkness tipped with stars,
A twist of proper names. Titania's power
Diminishes to the chime of Tinker Bell
As these faint pulsars navigate the dell
And we give audience, who know
The best in this kind are but shadows.

As all our lights are only shadows
Of the one 'Fiat lux' that it is necessary
To put our faith in. So, in this other country,
In the shade of an old mill which grinds nothing
But a handful of dreams and idle summers
Back to the chaff and grain of memory,
We stand and watch, without really watching,
These macula, indifferent particles,
Scraps of glitz, wisps whose will
Wanders free from our determination.
The music off, the house-lights down,
Out of the hush, their stammered off-and-on,
They fly as tributaries to our parables,
Remind us of our singled affirmations:
Smiles for strangers, reassuring hands,
The small courtesies of a meant 'Good morning',
Civilities of the sick-bed, gifts out of season
Making a dance where windless hills incline
To one small festival in Luigi's garden.

Fête Champêtre

How to welcome the advent of remarkable things?
The King in his double-dyed-in-the-wool wig
Steps out with a mobled Queen, ripe in full fig
Walking as if on water, arms akimbo – swans' wings,
   The hissing stifled; the beaks pointed, poised,
   The lake stage-struck by rain, and all amazed

At the tenor miming his love in a dark gondola;
His flab abeat with an impossible desire,
The Tannoy going Oyez, Oyez, mad as a Town Crier.
We sit it out on a wet night at the opera,
   Watch the sweet nothings, listen to whispering grass.
   The rain has brought things to a pretty pass

As each damp dryad twirls in a daisy-chain
Across ridiculous trees; a summer frost
Of limelight crisps the edges of all things lost,
Drowned and unchancy: plane across rainy plane
    Whose greens cannot be followed a thought further.
    What could, in this velvet hour and this weather?

You can see through the clung dresses down to the bone,
And through the bone to the marrow of the night,
Whose rich pith shines by sizzling sticks of light
Planted in mire, guttering, dying alone
    As each cold courtier must. Let tender rain
    Fall softly, softly on all our Castles in Spain

As the rockets kiss goodbye to cars in echelon
Hull-down in mist under each slow, red rose
Of stars ripping the dark with their oh-so O's
Until the last crackles of silver rain are gone
    Which lit the hampering hampers, the watered wine,
    Leaving us leaving, leaving things left again,

And nothing more extraordinary here but rain
Building its tarnished scaffolding as close air
Swells, adrift with tears, brooding on where
Those gay umbrella-segments bobbed over real pain
    Which knows its place, has given a long slip
    To this littered ground, which looks like clearing-up.

Cat on a Turkey Plate

It is a fine thing, and a sufficient thing,
To see a great cat of weight, some fifteen pounds,
Hoisted, in season, onto a turkey plate,
Quickset with holly, lord of his own grounds

Ancestral, with a flame to burn behind him:
A cat of amber, with full and electric fur,
His eyes open, but not with the wax greens
That light red candles, and to hear the great cat purr.

Such a calm breath, such comfortable stance,
And all around the small sighs of applause
At the Christmas Cat in his scallops of old china,
The needles working from the slow flex of his paws.

Homage to him, in the deep pile of his carpeting,
His bend wavy, though not sinister.
He waits for hands, and the paper-chains of love
To minister unto him, as he does minister.

And though the wicked knife and fork in the half-light
Can see things clearly, and can see them plain,
In his benevolence he dreams of making
Umbrellas for mice, to keep them from God's rain.

It is a fine thing, and a sufficient thing,
To see him at ease, large and admirable,
In a room powered by his own true carolling:
It is a grace before meat. It is seasonable.

Monet's Garden

The old man stepped out of his studio,
Ridiculous tin car, unfinishings,
Leaving some dignity of beards and ladies
To keep the past and its bucolic engines
For those to whom black is a favourite colour,
Who drain themselves back into photographs.

He asked if we had come to see some flowers,
He'd tidied up the kitchen, scorched it yellow,
Invited Hokusai and Hiroshige
To climb like cats on every wall and stairway,
And told his pictures how to turn themselves
Into the sizes that would fit our pockets.

His flowers rippled gently in the sunlight.
He sat in the green boat he called the garden
And rocked it softly. Crumbly at the edges,
The shadows whispered in a foreign language,
And all the flowers we picked and pressed in childhood
Were there for us to pick and press, in camera,

As white and bridal as our mothers' trousseaux,
As pink and blue as an Edwardian nursery.
The lily-heads came floating up at us
Out of that tumbler full of painting water
In which we used to dip our sable brushes
In long and hot imaginary summers.

He waited for us under hoops, down alleys,
In a pink house pinned up with open shutters.
What could we say to him, to Monsieur Monet,
Except we thought it pretty as a picture?
He thanked us, out of radiance and silver;
A ghost can make white light out of a rainbow.

The Web

A broken web is hung about with rain,
It could be perfect, but the perfect hour
Hangs in the gallery of God knows where.
Things pause, and stay a bit. Wet stone, white flower

Make no alas for that, but being so,
Catch at an eye that does not look for them,
And presidential in the morning light,
A quick-still spider, cloaked in diadem,

Threadbare, indifferent till spinning-time
To those lost finishings which looked like art,
On props enough for its own truth of things
Holds the tight epicentre of its part

Where lust and hunger fuming into green
Become a garden: that menagerie
Of pick and unpick, hot and wet and wings,
As right as rain, as sun, as things could be

Which batten on the borders of backyard
Where nothing seems to fit; just lies about –
That mountain-bike with rusty handle-bars –
And nobody much in, and no one out,

Or someone's landscape cooled by balustrade,
With stencilled cows at munch among the rough
And lawns and lawns, parterres, and lawns and lawns,
A bowl of Chinese fidgets – all that stuff.

Clouds come, clouds go. They never look much wrong.
The fly gets framed, gets trussed. If there's a soul
The web is hung how something wants it hung
And would not be more perfect were it whole.

Half-Hours in the Green Lanes

Half-Hours in the Green Lanes, by J. E. Taylor.
'The first book that I ever bought with my own money.'
Birds, whose sharp cries relieve lanes of their loneliness,
The feathery tribes, the pleasing recollections –

'If you want my autobiography
Read Wordsworth, Traherne, Vaughan.
As Donne says, 'There is not so poor a creature
But may be thy glasse to see God in … '

And, in his commonplace book,
This litany of conscience:
'Bird: A Penitence. (Et Ego)
A Blue Tit, A New Air Gun.'

John Woolman, who killed a robin with a stone
Then killed her brood, who had no dam to nourish them.
'The tender mercies of the wicked are cruel.'
Bewick's bullfinch, his little Matthew Martin.

Frank Kendon's catapult, the shrilling wren
Whose entrails lay shining in the hot sun;
De la Mare with David's sling, a sparrow for Goliath,
'And the hot, pallid, grinding shame of it.'

Charles Tennyson Turner: a swallow,
Its fallen head huddled in highway dust:
'I would not have thy airy spirit laid,
I seem to love the little ghost I made.'

Taylor: 'Their movements create an animation
Whose absence we can hardly realize.'
I remember his childhood's case of butterflies,
Dead freshets, rusted pins and crumbled thorax.

Annunciations

1

After siesta, the promenade, the passeggiata,
And Gabriele looking for Maria:
That easy body-language, shoulder-shrug,
Flexing of the parti-coloured wings,
Plumage stroked down by light
Which runs like water off the oiled feathers

Still warm from such a golden plummeting –
Heaven's courts into the quattrocento.
They're making notes: Piero della Francesca,
Spinello Aretino, Beato Angelico –
A whole host of them who paint like angels,
Can draw celestial circles freehand

And fix the pair into their double-curve,
Balance his pinions on her reticence.
And should she laugh, throw her pretty hands down,
Would they catch the rattle of his lift-off,
The hand slammed on the hand of a fellow-angel –
'She wouldn't listen' – the drifting primary?

2

Wind rose to its full height.
When I asked for a sign
The dead leaves hissed
In their cold plumage.

'Whose child is this
I was born to be?'
From a blue-rimmed saucer
The tea-leaves answered

In dreary twists:
'Of chance and happenstance.
Their long bickering,
Unfeatured faces.

They have entertained you
Without entertainment
And unawares.' Then the shiver
Ran down my shoulders

As if the want of wings
Could grow them;
There was a message
For me to deliver.

3

And these interludes? Angel-visits,
Few, considering how great the hosts;
Far between, as interstellar spaces.

He flew in from the sun, grass brightened.
There was clover, there was speedwell.
Hundreds of names lay scattered broadside

And yours was there, and yours, and yours.
There was neither promise nor recollection,
He stood there on the unbent flowering

And someone took a photograph.
Such a whirl of shadows; the cold
Chipping away at toes and fingers.

Here it is: a perfect tabula rasa.
Was it the happiness that wrote so whitely,
Was it the deep illusion's perfect zero?

4

I knew him straight away, my guardian angel,
I counted on him in my hour of need
To be my friend, my mentor, show me how
To make a blood-bond with our Saviour,
Redeem the promise of my white election.

I saw by inner light how bright his eyes,
And how like mine: that north sea chill.
We guessed our thoughts out by each other's whispers;
Spilled each other's tears upon the streets,
His vice-grip tightening my virtue.

The blood-beat thick in my anointed temple,
I felt his halo burning sulphur-yellow,
His keen wings a jostle of bright knives.
I plucked a pinion with a razor's edge
And set about to purify the city.

5

It was drifting about the woods all day
In desperation. The birds mobbed it
Through thickets of 'Halloo' and snapped branches.

Perhaps it came from fields of light so bright
Our half-light dazed it. Someone drew a bead on it
And watched it fall back into fallen nature.

Pulled out into a roughish crucifix
It hangs now in the gamekeeper's larder:
You might just think it touched by evening sunlight

But the gold is real enough; rubs off like pollen
On the plain skins of those accompanying thieves:
The magpie and the stoat, who swee there, drying.

And that so-human head. Does the wind turn it?
What maggot-life gives those lips a credence
As if they had a message: urgent, undeliverable?

6

She bent over him as he lay there,
Wasted to androgyne, the drip feeding
Its pure elixir into impurity.
Time on the clock-face ran
Past absent numerals.

Then sat, her worked fingers
A light cross borne on blue
Which opened onto sky and summer.
His heart paused at a familiar door,
Then, with quick patterings,

Crossed the green lino to the bed
And waited for her.
'Lullay, lullay, my little tiny child ...'
There was a cold as snow and soft as feathers.
Smiles lit the rooms

Whose eight walls folded into four,
To the run of curtains.
The clock spelled nothing,
Spelled it clearly:
Only a face kissed by hands,

7

Azrael, whose wings are of a muffled sable
And undistinguished by the life of stars,
Is attentive at the last bedside.
History has not been kind to him,

Who has cloned himself so often,
Wearily uncloaked his case of opiates.
A Phoenix, whose eyes are benignant tumours,
He rises now for the last time

To make an end of suffering;
To lead those cooling and transfigured hands
Through curtains of black velvet
Onto the morning pavement.

With a wave of his hand,
He stares into the forbidden light,
Waits for the second trump of the Archangel,
The uneased accomplishment

Of his mortality, the wings
Blown leaf-dry, moth-dry,
The dust of his passage
Sun motes dancing over New Jerusalem.

Foliate Head

Deep in, the unintelligence of things:
Coarse lines, underscored,
Knit rust: no hold, vantage.
But the painter perches en plein air,
Smooths into light his gratified desires
Of wandering mothers, bonneted children,
Whose flesh is drenched in rose-shade.

Air sweetens his glancing brush:
Twist of sabled sunlight
Gold fan in a blue-veined hand,
Poised as the light poised on a lace-wing.
Today the woods are nothing more
Than the cool end of a spectrum
Where trespassers must be prosecuted

By what's at home in ambuscade:
Branches at their trammelled coronation
Of a face simple as a wicker skep,
Natural as the whip and thong of bramble.
Out of those intricacies, features
Fly into place as tesserae fly to a wall,
Patching fired fragments into sainthood.

This is not sainthood. From the selva oscura
He watches the artist pack his keep-nets
Loose with smiles, fleece-grass, featherings;
Rooted in metamorphosis,
Would take those hands, work the nails to buds,
A transplant made, a sharp graft taken,
His heart of darkness centring the light.

Stone Head

The tower so clearly made of light,
The loneliness of light, from lonely money
Sighed away on a late medieval death-day.
And the pretty names: mouchettes, sound-holes,
Double stepped battlements with pinnacles –
One of God's fairy things

To sway with clouds, but pinned
Into the illusion of a high motion, lift-off,
Setting four devils at their platform angles
Reaching for Heaven, crop-winged
For fear of flying: saturnine,
Staring themselves out of countenance.

Till slam. After so much star and cloud
A thunderbolt of wind cracked off the corner
And flung this one poor clone of Lucifer
Headlong. Picked from couch-grass,
His down-to-earth bone-glare
Domesticated in a red-brick alcove,

He has put off the smell of brimstone:
One of the Foliots, Lares, Genii,
'That kinde of Devils conversing in the earth',
As James puts it in his *Demonologie*.
Lop-eared, crook-mouthed, cheek-chapped,
Kissing-cousin to Meg Merilees.

The Longaevi, the fallen angels:
One down, and three to go,
To suffer jolt and jar or slow erosion.
Look in the grass; find his bolted feet
Still clawing for a toehold
On a flawed block of consecrated stone.

Nacht und Nebel

for George Szirtes

1

It seems, at first, as if the eyes of the dead
Are sleepy with sadness at being first to go.
What was wanted, not wanted, doesn't matter much.
The muscles of life become involuntary;
Leave the eyes as open as that window
Traipsed by cloud. It has been met now,
Whatever *it* is: mist, night or radiance,
Those words we choose to make a special nothing
Of nothing special. Flesh pared to childhood,
A parting gift from things unparcelling?
That I didn't see. Childhood was in the tears
Cried lately, late. As night comes tidying up
A face begins its pilgrimage of mist,
The loosening features bandaged into memory

And love: that word with its intolerant echo,
Loud as the gibberish racing off sprung-concrete
As the coach leans into the tunnel's curve
Stripping the hunted rails clean of silver
And grimy windows fill with passengers.

The family-faces drift in fuzzy light;
Turn towards you as you turn towards them.
There is a weakness in such inflammation,
Arms loose, heart shaking in its cage of bone.
To love the dead? That is cloud and nocturne,
A yes that is the negative of no, a bouncing bomb
To breach the dam set at the valley's head:
Landscape fills to an eye, headlamps under water
Racing for out, the drowned rising.

2

Clocks are the unblinking eyes of time,
Cyclopean: eternity must blind them.
Hours are numbered carefully, forgotten,
But, in time, every clock will cover
Its white face with its hands.

Here is George's painted wooden one:
Mors, Virgo; Death and the Maiden.
He takes her liltingly from behind.
Soon, her bones will penetrate her skin;
Now, her hair flames to a furious sky.

Between the starry floor, the watery shore,
Reds and ochres talk of Bosch and Breughel.
Saturn, roughest of luck, tosses his head back,
Mumbles a child's head with hot tonguing,
Another kicks lightly from his idling hand.

If there were trees here, as in Tacitus,
A centurion and his rape of soldiers,
Numbed by the silence of the Schwarzwald,
Could watch dead legions hanging on live branches,
Their arms grounded, the earth souring.

In such an accoutred landscape,
Taylor, the Water-Poet, saw the hangman
'Burst his chin and jaws to mammockes,
Then he tooke the broken, mangled corps
And spreade it on the wheele'.

Let the meal of suffering be garnished,
The pangs of wit soften a deathbed.
Pastiche, rococo, petal that dark motto:
'Timor Mortis Conturbat Me.'
The clock's brazen heart beats faster, faster ...

3

Iritis: an inflammation of the iris.
Take a single eye, swollen, under pressure,
Meat-red. In the absence of atropine,
Bella donna, the lady of alleviations
To dilate, fix and school her eager pupil,
The eye rages for a draught of night,
Hungry for mourning, sables, cold velvet,
To be buried alive, out of sight and mind.
The visions are tolerable; they are of nothing.
Sleep? Your corded eye, a giant bladder
Will not admit you. A pure and endless darkness
Is the one unsure promise you want kept.
Let there not be light: one splinter of white glass
To break the spell of your blind date with pain.

Old Street for Moorfields: all those patient backs
And turbaned faces. On the optician's card
The crownèd A is quite recoverable
Over small anagrams of Amor Vincit Omnia.
It is good to bring things into focus
And grow accustomed to mere double-vision,
To find Blake's old man crouching in a thistle,
His guinea disc a host of dancing angels.
There is the natural pick and mix of metaphor:
A festival of clouds chants *'God si love'*.
While Dr Aziz flashes his instrument,
Looking for secrets in Miss Quested's eyes.
An ambulance breaks the lights in mounting panic;
Newsprint feeds the famine of the gutters.

Dying is so much, so many of it all,
Each pair of eyes that opens, looks and dims,
Making its lie of sense, its lie of nonsense;
Guiding a pair of hands to tug the world
To the same difference, a tongue to cry 'I love you'.
It is as much, as many as being born;
The one perfection is that equipoise.

I met Lazarus; his name was on the Menin Gate.
The Last Post had been blown for him so often
That all his tales lacked credence. He had come back
From that obscurity which is the Kingdom of Error,
And all he could tell me was that he was dead.
Now, at the end of April, not far from Easter,
Something has come again to make you shiver,

To set your teeth against anticipation.
It would be nice if things went swimmingly in heaven
For kings in pyramids, our common clay,
But who could bear an eternity of memories?
Someone's up there, schoolmasterly, round-spectacled,
Telling the Schützstaffel how to mark all papers:
'Nacht und Nebel – night and fog.'

5

Pencil and film: our two recording angels.
In a quiet hall high in the Pompidou Centre
Ghosts from the death-camps lie on ghost-paper,
Expose themselves to gentle, special light;
But the old photographer is a spool of bones,
His camera's lung is punctured, its eye clouded,
Shuttered down on a host of negatives.
In the houses of the dead reversals of light
Char flesh, burn off the frocks and jackets,
Chalk out a court of shadow on grass
Cut to a level killing-field. What remains?
These tricks of camouflage, arguments of ash,
A child's case packed in an Auschwitz warehouse:
'Jungkind, geboren 1933'. My year.

And how about some bricks for that child to play with?
In my grammar of architecture, alphabet,
Things were spelled out in black and white,
The white lie making its grey bridge between them.
Allow his bricks their little absolutes,
Coded as we code devils, rats and snowdrops.
Black, grey are safe: fear the presence of white
Which is a little too much like the radiance
Of lightning, bomb-burst, bone and sacrifice.
The child sings, building its fragile city
Out of the neutral tones of a dead war-film;
When things are put to sack, the tower-blocks fallen,
There are always crying women, shawled in black,
A white arm skewed from the pit, grey rubble.

First Things, Last Things

And it was first, after the mess and straining,
Runs of hot water, new-bread smells of linen,
Ripples of light, and I think there would be flowers,
To bring, from throat and loosened tongue
The urgent vocables of love and fear,

Which might be only the ungiven names
For what was warm, cold. The night, the night,
A face pressed against the press of milk,
And, under a smile stretched from her smiling,
The suck and sob of things …

In between, the long brocade of lies,
Truths, half-truths, webs of such distinction
That every face he knew could grow to fit them,
Though there were flowers with a myriad names
Dying easily on dying grasses.

And it was last, and the retreat of words
Drained from the bed, as Matthew Arnold's sea
Drained, still drains over the smoothened shingle.
Again, flowers: the new-bread smells of linen,
The urgent vocables of love and fear

When hands that never touched were quick to touch,
Touched to the quick. There were no names for things,
Because, in that communion of shades
Which sang in paradox with angel-voices
The dark was entered easily as the light.

Your Troubled Chambers

It's there, in a flash, a fist crouched on its anger,
A dark blush stumbling the cheek of a lover
Caught again in the toils of his recognition.
You were there. What happened? Time may tell.
He tells lies easily: white lies at a garden door,
Darker lies which breed like rats in a coven,

Their blind eyes nuzzling for truth in a crowded well.
Go to the weird sob-sisters. They might help you,
Chancing their witchy crystals on kitchen tables,
Teasing out lifelines, measuring you for a shroud,
Snipping strength from your hair, gabbling in dreams –
Blank verse which stings like soap in a child's eyes?

What works, works in the dark. Things wait their event.
The child in the netted pram smiles at her killer;
A nuclear trigger clicks on a bare-ribbed plain,
Its giant camera snapping the troopers' bones
And fingerless halt babies wait to be born,
Crying softly from the other side of nowhere.

Back in this community of the faithless
A schizophrene hoods his eyes on the pain of light;
A surgeon bleeds through his gloves and instruments,
Signing a death on the horoscope by your bed
And something sings 'Have you no ghost-room for me,
To let me second-chance your troubled chambers,

No room, perhaps, for a drifting chromosome,
A patch of drying blood and spun-glass hair
Once pasted on a wind-swept yard of tarmac,
An uncle whose sweet caresses touched the quick,
Or such slight ectoplasm as a wagging beard,
The wrong light on the dust in the right room?'

No doubt, the room could hear what was going on,
Or, rather, sounds could pretend themselves at home
Without disturbing a leaf in the jardinière.
There were lilies there, which neither toiled nor spun,
And roses worked to the stems in silk, for time
Was a bunch of immortelles; had enough to spare

Of itself to web, delay those messengers
Whose messages, unforgotten, remained unread.
Those *Four Just Men* and *Girls of the Limberlost,*
Safe behind glass, looked strange as any strangers;
A cast-iron Norman fireplace burned the dead
With invisible fire as hard and pure as frost.

And everything there knew it must be for best
To be still multiples of their quiet selves,
Consuming air, as the votive candles do
In a cool temenos where God is lost
In his own dark shawls of wonder, the salves
Of a dying silence let something through

Which was not the sound of children on ricketing stairs,
But the rustle of painted leaves on a balustrade
Of painted cloth, where the Passchendaele soldier stood
Waiting for Charon to ferry him down the years,
The spick shroud crimped for the mantelpiece parade
And all kept safe under the veil, the hood,

While the net-curtains eased shadows about the light
As a green screen parts, unparts, over a glade
Littered with tiny icons of skull and bone
Where the dry moss pads about on its mild grey feet
And the uninvited bomber scrawls overhead;
And all the desires are here, and are clean gone.

White Lies

Is it the saying, for something must be said
As a livre de présence, an enunciation?
Rather, for her, an annunciation: the words
Tucked loose in the dove's ring, the good tidings
To let the tired leaves know how green they are,
Her calls consoling as the lightest rain
And that good-earth smell of transfigured dust.

What does she see as she follows the garden-path?
Flowers at a ticker-tape welcome, the whole panjandrum
Alight with sun and unspooled messages.
The cat, that good thief, told he's a good cat,
Cries over spilt milk in pure delight,
Trembling a dark purr. And then the pleasure
Of greeting them all again, those terrible visitors

Who have borrowed the habits of annealing shade,
Their hopes as dull and thick as furniture.
How well they look, and how each colour suits them.
She must offer them a summer of Christmas cards,
A winter of wings beating the butterfly bush.
What more can she do, to make more beautiful
Their faces lined with plain, unvarnished truths?

But ask them to come again to this house of wishes
And read their welcome lurking in the tea-leaves,
Their lucky fortunes in her crumble-cookies,
Or, lost on the doorstep, look up to the bedroom
Where the suspicious curtains draw their secrets,
And hear, as she lies there crying on her pillow,
'I'm afraid she's just gone out': an occluded star.

The Clock and the Orange

In the living-room, the dead room, full of anger,
The two of them stand, each to each stranger
Than when they first looked, each at each, closely.
Wondering. They have filled it quietly, furiously
With choice and argument: rug, chair and book,
The wedding-present of a careful clock.

He swings it head-high, lets time drop,
Cower on the floor in its time-slip.
Will he throw the clock which is poised there
With its delicate wheels which have come so far,
Which has kept something in some sort of order,
As if a clock could draw the line at murder?

She stands there facing the light, the light facing
Up to their faces, squaring up to the amazing
Thing which can't happen, is about to happen.
She grips a foolish orange, her eyes open
As a hung mouth. You can just see the light
Which is dead-still, and can't get out,

Glazing the clock, so brown and circular,
Its reasonable tick trimming the wild air;
The passionate fruit with its tawny rind
Locking its love-juice round and round:
All wet with tears, a closed bubble,
A marriage stupefied to lies and parable.

Light Frozen on the Oaks

Light frozen on the oaks: a long time without wind,
And nothing much to mark this morning, except time
Hung in gold letters on the spines of books,
Dust-motes claiming title, a long-case clock
Stopped at the hour past the eleventh hour,
Its hands surrendered to some noon or midnight,
Struck among roses and unflurried birds.

The sky, in all its graduals and ordinaries,
Promises no more than a midwinter pallor,
A reach of spirit to a shelf of silence
Where memory has arranged its broken secrets.
Even the dead must hold their breath today,
Their texts a commonplace, their strength of purpose
Caught in an act which breeds no consequence:

Johnson, the axe of some deep sentencing
Swung to no fell; the table-talk of Coleridge
Stopped as a fountain in the heart's wasteland.
Today is a garden of dried flowers, their scent
Far colder than that reach of pink and blue
Unrustled in its china cabinet.
Are you eager to watch grass grow, light move

In answer? But the shadowing of the sun,
Delays its fingers on the skin of things,
Sleeps in the cracks between was-once and will-be;
And the clock, chained to conspiracies of wheels,
Is birds and flowers programmed without memory,
Without hope; as the wind, when it comes again,
Will deliver its empty mouth up to our sighs.

The Provisional Thing

And again, the provisional thing
As everything is, provisional –
In default of that Arcadian wind
Which could cut flower or skin without such sneaping
As this, from the East,

Which works over the ground
Without promise, without adjective,
And has no bargains to make with us.
There might be time, if time is of the essence,
To fill the wind in,

Provide it with a season,
A change of direction,
The blobs and runnels of a loaded brush
Blurring the contours of a simple landscape
In a simple book.

For now, it will have to do.
It must know its way about
After four hundred years of hole-and-corner work,
Fossicking at brick, falling down, sobbing
With the hurt of it,

Borrowing the pain
Of all things loose, discarnate,
That have borrowed our incomprehension,
That sing for the space, provisional,
The house is in default of.

A Habitat

1 All Roads Lead to it

There is always a guide, a golden bough of keys
Loose change in his hand. Leaning on the car,
He looks at netted thatch, close brickwork,
The plywood lids nailed across the eyes.
In a cold foyer Virgil waits for Dante,
Looks at his watch. 'Shall we go in?'

And what will you learn, when you find your survey
Was 'conducted in virtual darkness'.
There are, as usual, major areas of instability,
Widespread infestation, structural distress;
The seven standard requirements have not been achieved.
'I am not fearful of major collapse in the short term.'

Though, perhaps, one should be, thinking it over.
Who bewildered those floors to sand,
Tumbled the tumbled brickwork? Who attended
To the long marriage of queen strut, king post,
Set swimming in the porch's pediment
A merman and a mermaid of white stucco

Who swing their lovely, rough-cut tails apart
And stare with chapped eyes at the east?
Who sing, as lorelei from their high storeys,
Over lost time, over all loss and time:
'We have this brilliant magic: to command,
Cheat dirty seas, and raise the drowned we drown.'

2 Out of Season Harvest

A cock-eyed house, beset by open fields
And too much wind. Each evening,
Light, undressing, makes itself a ghost,
Slips through chipped hands, looks dull,
Pores over unfaced brick and threads of lime.
In these worked-out seams, poor stuff:
Nettle-rash, and casts of brown iron,
Small saws of grass to cut, and come again.

Spring, in all its brutal innocence,
Webs it about with marker, stake and claim.
Is there a garden for those teeth to bare,
Disclosed, but secret, all its petal-shells
Rehearsing rumours from a summer sea,
A child, blood-sucking from a slashing blade,
Blown into rags of travelling light and dark
By the same wind, though swollen with lost voices?

There is forgiveness here; not much forgotten.
A simple, careless weight of young and green
Saps ill-seasoned wood on its chewed hinges.
Across the empty spaces you can hear it,
The old lie of the land: 'I do my level best',
And feel the farm hands, calloused, broken-in,
Unclog the shreds of yellow binder-twine,
Leave used-up life to dry out in the sun

For you to glean; an out-of-season harvest.
Then, bent-backed, feel the house hang loose,
Flag in the wind, flock of substantive shadows
Punished by echo and the ghost of echo,
The need for ardour and an arduous love.
What can you do but take it to your arms,
Undress its walls back to the mother-naked:
Each worn to ravellings, locked face-to-face.

They have put brick on brick,
Those headers and stretchers,
Hands mapped, wrinkled
With white scar-tissue.

Houses, common as dirt,
As moonlight, sunlight,
Slide their counters
From lean horizons.

And much sweet-talk
Of bevel, chamfer,
Letting bugger, bastard,
Take the strain.

As for this thick air
Harried from post to pillar,
Those shadows inching
As cats unfurl their claws,

This worry of light
Struggling weakly,
The house takes it in:
A bustle of photons

Countless as death
In its courts of grass,
Millions of everything
Signifying nothing

But 'Keep your balance.
When poles dip
You need a blindfold
To cross clenched water,

To twist a handle
To turn the corner
From then to now
And what comes after.'

4 *Love it. Choose it*

Love it. Choose it. Whatever the words mean
Hauled from the moil, the tumult in the head
And heart. Walls will obey
The flock of paper thoughts you hang on them,
Curtains ring and skirr on runs of ice,
Glass let you in and out to watch
The green things growing with a steady violence
In what you call your garden, this room
Switch its cushions and its books about,
Light, insidious as a lover,
Lisp its morning catalogue of lies:
'This is for you. You make me what I am.
I was a dead thing till you quickened me.'

Now look: How rich I grow in your possessing,
Dreamy as a child with a button-box,
Showing you *you* in a cup splashed with flowers,
Dandyprats who prance a biscuit-tin,
A cat whose whiskers blacken at the root.
So much finery, Arabian stuff,
Caught in the prisms of your kitchen-sink
Where crumpled bubbles tear themselves to nothing
With the sound of a small fire in another room.
As you leave, the wicked light slips under
A carpet sewn with buttercups and clover,
And all is, as the rose in the desert, beautiful,
Though the door shuts, conversation becomes voices.

The house, gathering its mass, says:
'Sursum corda.'

'But we have no hearts to lift. What are we?
Broken glass at night, and no glass broken,
Smells of warm fur at sleep's corner,
Crackle of bones in a grey floorboard.

In the high thrill of blood in a stranger's ear
We talk of what life once remembered
Which is not life. We are long ago,
And ride in dreams to the crop's firing.'

Beneath let and hindrance, in the leat
Where time flows: a scribble of dust-water,
Coccytus, conduit of tears, flux of pain:
Over the roof-tree, stars.

The house commands: 'Ite, missa est.'

'Where should we go? We are the faces
Annealed in glass at January's window,
A curtain slithering into costume,
The chance of blessing.

You are the root of our conspiracy,
House of Atreus, in which the hands of life
Wear unseen rings of marriage, and of mourning.
There is no dismissal for the wind.'

Painted hounds, leashed on a limed wall,
Each mouth unslaked, look to their quarry.
A crucifixion of withered nails,
The strained flesh dust,

The house groans:
'Asperge me, Domini, hyssopo,
Et mundabor.'

'There is no cleansing.'

6 *Where is the Key?*

Perhaps the house is full of awkward questions,
As if all questions weren't awkward:
A voice raised as the roof is raised,
Instinct with a question's anger.
Each stone interrogation
Cuts a blood-shape to the mark of Cain,
Each steady, single vowel lobs a grenade.
When the house was born, did it cry in the first wind
For its delivery from stone and clay,
Shaken, unhinged, gathering its baubles
To be the playthings of its own dark future?
When the stomach sickens, the gorge rises,
What is placated by this mess of sweetmeats?

Living here will be enough and more
To turn the hair white with grief.
Where is the key, the key to this parade
Of drawers and wardrobes. It is thinner now,
Though it always was a skeleton; unlocks
Life with a fluency you could despair of,
Knows the cosy terror of the habitual
The saved and sloughed-off skins
Which keep the curious shape of yesterday;
That walk to La Courante in driving snow,
The field of flax which opened a powdery eye.
When the key clicks, tugs, what is unlocked?
A coffin for the memory of memories.

7 *This Room, that Room*

This room is a hold of chattering teeth,
Split-pins shaken in a dry tumbler,
Light plugging your silhouette with flat knives
In the Cirque d'Hiver, the cold, the cold.
Washing hangs barbed on front-line wire
And air jolts to the high, explosive words
Tracked by the huge scream of their arrival.

That room is dense with a dead thing,
The surfaces are coffin-lids come off
And with them come the sticky skins of faces
Which might be where the flowers have had enough
And sent their candles drowning into wax.
The words? A Tennysonian murmuring:
Oh, oh, alas, alas, was, was.

This room believes in the belief of moths
And shows by the dark how to betrothe darkness
To the space where wing-chair and carpet sing
In their dull brilliance about gone sun.
I think the onset of Alzheimer's
Is making the words run in and out of their colours.
Quite charming, this prattle and confusion.

That room is locked black and sobbing.
The walls are dry bread and the floor is water
Where Alice wept when she was sent to bed.
When you touch wood, it turns to iron;
When you touch iron, the cold scalds you.
Listen. The words are kicking hard
At both sides of the door. Which is echo?

This room is where they put the other rooms.
Chekhov would have known the servants' names
Who pulled the rug from under the feet of time
And spread it out, a great big dirty dustsheet.
Light is loose-limbed over mottled marble
And words are tic-tac, miching-mallecho,
The chirping of dead mice from the underworld.

That room? Ah, that room is the last room,
The doorway swung on a brass fanfare of light,
The dustsheet flicked to a conjuror's hanky.
And here they are, so many he's and she's,
And all as pretty in their love and ugliness
As any thousand pictures. And the words
Are quite unnecessary.

8 *Numen Inest*

Ah, numen inest. At first, clouded,
They are always there, shapes of nothing:
A genie aching for the flanks of his bottle,
The stoppered stillness. From brush and deadwood,
A greenfield site with goalposts floating
In curious fog, a quick train's lazy rattle,
Come voices which insist on being missing,
Belonging out, but wanting in and blessing.

They need you, fly from you, the passers-by
At work in frost or green grazing:
A sharp retort in the copse, gruff talk
Lost in the hung stuff between earth and sky,
The burr and wobble of a plane pausing,
The trouble of branches going cark, crake.
Sound upon sound, adept for the long haul,
Easing its substance through the strongest wall

Until the crammed air's thick with frequencies:
Your mother preaching from her photograph,
Books at close argument, a singing cat
Jouncing its flap. All well-worn distances
Dissolve. The past unseals its epitaph
And that is this which certainly was that.
You feel the whole house brewing up a soul,
Choked on some filmy substance: a black hole

Where lives cook up a starry-gazy pie
And then are gone, dragging into its maw
Bruises and smiles, arpeggios and flowers.
It has a vampire's hunger, and an eye
That's unappeasable. It asks for *more,*
And gets it, as the tin parade of hours
Hastens its virgin tribute. What do days *do?*
They make a radioactive wraith of you.

9 *Let Things be Nice*

Let things be nice. Get out of bed the right side.
The floor is paved with sunflakes
Washing the floor and scraps of tissue clean.
It is that old-gold image, quattrocento.
Look into light: incursions into haloes
Make runes, mandalas, alphabets of time
Spent in a good place, with a good heart.
Today, the broken figurine can dance,
The clock purr, the chipped plate
Brim to its full circle. Under the willows
There is no danger on the unburnt bridge,
No parting of lovers, unstrung instruments.
It is time for a picnic on the far shores of your garden,
For loving Miss Bates, fostering the small endearments.

Now, add the colours of pastness to the proper names:
Madame Carrière, Saxifrage, Rosa Rubrifolia,
Obedient to that multiplicity of laws
By which invisible things flesh into substance.
Possession. Dispossession. What do you incubate
When a thorn drives deep, the heart grows callous?
Today, the windows of the house
Are all alive with the dark look of water.
The house is cupped for a draught of light,
The rinsing of veils and curtains.
What is reflected, but your own reflections
On the unspoken speech of brick and flowerhead?
Sloughed, dry as your skin;
Immortal as your memory.

10 *Substance to Silence*

Consort of viols, communion of the faithful?
Those handsome words; they work as the hands work,
Alert for lifting a little the dark's corners,
Holding nothing but air, but what does the air hold
Which lets go of nothing but is all union?
Single additions, which make the single full,
The knot of ribbons

Flown from fingers, field-talk, a swung necklace,
The chimney's cowl, the lacing flesh
Under its glittering coverlet of dust.
Sky, what do you purchase, when the pedlar
Unpacks the spectrum of old songs and snatches,
Juggling his feather-lights, his primaries,
Love, Death and Memory

Swung high, higher, caught at their vanishing
Point of departure, which is their arrival,
As, outside the gate the Vauxhall eases down
The box on its tonneau spilling a cornucopia
Of gifts once-given, twice-given, for ever given.
How pleased the dead are to see us, cheeks flushed,
Hands brown, and the names

Flying about like kisses, out into all,
The cat sprawled on its back in its gravelled fur,
A flower on the lawn of winter, each singleton
At the dear heart of all that's circular,
And all completed by what's fugitive
As the past opens its enormous future,
Reads us like a book,

And the oak-tree there, consonant and shapely
Where the stars can sing themselves invisibly
Into the white dark, lives by our whispering,
Cradling the air to one substantial mirage:
The deep, continuous thing on its endless way
From substance to silence. The House dreaming,
The many mansions,

Things living as they must, things that must live
By the light's traverse, holding their hands to it,
Whatever it is, which is light behind light,
And the book? The small print of a summer dress,
A tract of time. Hold out your hands
To the air; let it show you its finest detail,
It will bear your weight.

Faces come thicker at night; a host of stars
Breaks uneven ground to a wild glister,
That different sameness which the cold flays bare
With each close look. Stars, which shine and shine,
Bothered by names and regimental numbers,
Are pesters of fine print against tired eyes.
They wear the look of something thought about
And make their own obedience to the gestural:
A purple codex lit by silver uncials.

In winter, not much need to name the grasses
Pushed through pea-shingle crunchy as packed snow.
What is, lives only in dim crevices,
Burrowed between its accident and substance.
Still, it's something to be startled by Orion,
Listen to a north wind, as Bevis and Mark did,
Pausing under an oak at the top of Home Field.
There are familiars: the dog-star blue with cold,
Pleiads and Hyades clouding into cataract.

We watch them into being, like the dead,
And, like the dead, they find the space too huge
For anything but whispers of forgiveness.
The house, black-backed, swells against open fields,
Hunted down by those long strides of starlight,
Those bright bows drawn at yet another venture.
Quick, throw it open, let its lanterns draw them,
Setting clean squares adrift for all that ghost-life,
This flurry of winter moths against glazed silence

For something in the bite and tang of time,
When moonlight hangs there with a medium's breath
To riddle, sift and screen them. Watching, waiting
Under these frosts, who can you turn from your door,
Such thousands hurry to your long house-warming?
There's Quince, the young white cat, whose corpse
Grinned in the ivy, who sleeps under his quince-tree,
And, dead, sits patient under this bright hood
For doors to open, all things to come home.

Scissors

So random, when people walk out of it like this,
Taking themselves and their flowers off to the cemetery,
Or, as now, lying down with their feet in the kitchen,
Head in the passage. It's a cold suspense.
And where to look? There's a hundred soft things,
Glittery things; they don't know where they are,

And can't be told any more, by the slightest of Angels,
How they came from Reigate, or that loft in Mayo.
Alas for the sepia people, their wits quite gone,
Labelled 'Aunt G at Filey' in such invisible ink.
And everything blue with cold in a crying November,
Especially now, when someone is asking for scissors,

Which after all, have to earn their severance pay,
Are silently, somewhere, whispering; working the dust,
Snipping the web into flyaway patterns of light.
The amputations, the deaths of a thousand cuts
For a daughter, a friend in Croydon, an Oxfam covenant,
A ticket for two for *Much Ado About Nothing*.

It's all so remorseless; they must have come into their own,
Setting about it with pure and bloodless precision.
Every drawer is a drawer for a kind of bridal,
And 'What will happen to me?' sighs the brass fender,
Who came naked into her world, and so must leave it
When the scissors snap each room to echo and footstep.

You can hear them fuss, as blade slips over blade
With a kiss, with a kiss: a life folded over and over,
Grown paper-thin, and the cut sharp on the creases.
Are they moons, are they stars? Look, with a child's wonder
You can hold it up to the light, a white fretted window,
A seamless ribbon she steps through, smiles, and is gone.

It is always pouring itself away.
The scullery tap, when pipes knock and throb,
Wheels its head over a rod of water
With a sugar-stick twist, a cripple's twist,
Which only looks like a stronger, deeper light
Against all the other lights which have wandered
In from the garden.

And under it you can hold your rose of fingers
That have been places – a fistful without memory –
That curled in the womb, that have known
Such crush and pile of stuff, tasks under leaves,
Gestures in rooms where all the talk has run
Far out into yards and yards of blown fabric;
Known running water

Which always runs with a twist, though steady,
Its million beads fused in a shaking rod,
A racing pulse that your weeping hand flows through,
Feeling its lucid weight, the flap of a flame
Through which a finger can pass without much pain.
And still it is pouring itself away,
This trickster's wand

Waved over a tiny, white-lipped cut
Where the blood is rinsed in light, the blood
Which is not thicker than water, and quickly lost,
As if all those hurts which poison the wells
Could be cleansed by something brilliant as this,
Kind, held in a twist, like space, like time,
Which are pouring away.

When the Train Stops

When the train stops, in a mid-afternoon,
And its motion continues, which is soon gone,
And the light stops too, your train of thought
Tripswitched, broken,

There was a house once, which you come from,
And one to visit, which is not quite the same
But will have its claim on you, as of right.
At your sudden waking,

Now, in the middle-distance, a house is there,
Drawn suddenly in stone on heated air.
The breakwater wall runs down to the gate,
There's a girl swinging.

And there it is: the completely known,
Flesh of your flesh, bone of bone,
Your washing blowing on a branching line,
All calling 'Mine',

And its mine is yours: the half-swung door,
Elder and Ash, the slight copse where
Your fingers pick for feather and skull,
The scuffed hill,

The curtains blowing across the dark –
You can read it easily as the book
By your side, which you will not read at all
Till you get there,

Which is not there. With sighs, relinquishings,
The undertow of some black trembling,
The carriage moves. There is nothing at all
To keep you ...

Night Watch

for Margaret

It's Good to Talk

We should have heard less than this,
paid more attention to the lip-service
offered by mile on greying mile
of queasy combers, rufflets of wind
where oak bustles against oak.
Small particulars ebb and flow,

swirl in a shell's black plastic orifice:
that chamber where something died
and a ghost heart murmurs
'But it's good to talk.' Things in orbit,
swung wires, the stunted lattices
whose heads bristle with a light dementia,

pass it all on, pass it all away,
that one long message hung out to dry:
'Am in Wolverhampton. Tell Jinny
I'll be back about nine.' Somewhere, someone
wants *Aïda,* Big Jim Reeves,
news from Serbia and the Cones Hotline

while a cool forest of rain starts
to pack the world with disinformation,
the jumbled code of a Chinese whisper
seeding the air waves
with sound as light, unfocused,
as blood which sang in the ears of the dead ...

A Victorian Way of Death, 1998

Nearly over, this murmuring and plucking,
shuttering of rooms where in great terror
elders and betters ring for servants
to pound the stairs, fetch coats and sticks,
tickets for somewhere

away from this dull provincial town,
Big C, out in the flatlands. Their indecision
seems to be modelled on the first draft
of Act V in a lost Chekhov.
Grandfather, born in 1852,

with his wall eye, blush-pink fingers,
anecdotes of Paris in the siege,
is comforting grandma, pale and flustered,
dressed in that crushed blue
Ellen never liked much.

A long haul and not what they asked for,
a giant step for two Victorians
whose fingers of brilliants, heavy signet ring
almost touched the twenty-first century.
But here they are dining

in the last chance hospice,
hanging on to it all by a stuttering heartbeat,
a 'Steady, old girl' as the headroom rocks
and their shapes and colours
dim to the storm, go out, go out –

Arras: Easter 1998

Ploughed low the dismissed parade lies
undressed, unmarked. By leaves,
by stems which lean, recover
as the wind sidetracks the grass,
they speak in sighs and exhalations –
two hundred thousand armed men breathing
where shallow draughts of mist
stand easy, and stand to
at first light and when late light dwindles.

For the dead die a little faster this weather,
the skies heavy, water-luminous.
Reflections lie about face-down,
those showers which freshened up
the curls of Chaucer's popinjay from Flanders,
drown memory out, continuous
as the opening Arras barrage
when the shells rode a snowstorm.
Today, the past receives an embassy.

Bearers, kin, and one survivor,
must treat with ghosts at observation posts
of emblazoned stone at Monchy-le-Preux,
by flurrying rain and wind made one
with these 'somtyme in chivachye'
who suffered burial and resurrection
to make some boxfuls of old bones
a theme for yet more spit and polishing:
three Fusiliers, two metal dog-tagged,

late, but uncrimed for this last posting;
their taken names and numbers
restored for eighty years good conduct.
One, obstinate in a dumb insolence,
dispersed his syllables about the earth
and, carried in to this assize, must be
sentenced to the usual reprimand –
'A Soldier of the Great War, Known unto God' –
also to Privates King and Anderson.

Midi

Today and every day Monsieur is dead
but rises from the Famille Mortier
to head this half-laid table of grey sparkles
and dawdle in the purgatory of photograph.
His lip and nose eaten away by light,

his ectoplasmic hair reaching wildly
for the high cirrus where the saints float
their immaculate maculae in iris blue,
he has only a small enthusiasm
for his aquarium of clouded flowers

or the familiar similars in his chapped gaze.
In this, our briefest of encounters,
he shows no partiality for Cowper's letters,
or concern for the old Assamese proverb
'To the toothless mouth one slap is hard to bear'

as he waits for night and his poilu sentry-go.
The Stations of the Cross in Sainte Marie
will quiver and jump to violet lightning,
the steeple sharpen up its old 'J'accuse'
through mist-wraiths and mountain-thunders,

but the dead shut up shop these long afternoons,
careless of coarse marguerites, white cattle
dwindling to ghost-selves in the heat-haze,
or the grass sibilant with its long chirpings
of mille regrets, regrets, regrets …

Quick-Quick-Slow

They're lightly wondering 'what's become of Joe',
(The Kit-Cat Band, November '26).
Inside that slatted cabinet
Their hottest notes are pleading, yet,
The spiders' legs and flies' wings just don't know.

Cutting her quick-quick-slow from airless air:
my mother's ghost goes into her routine.
The circling dog from HMV
growls dark and gravelly as the sea
and every chord is asking where, oh where

are all those dancers who have danced off-screen,
the Bradford Pals, the shut-eye doll, the cat,
whose *Wanted* posters on the wall
say will-not-come when you-must-call,
however hard you beat the in-between.

But still she makes her diamanté feet
follow the lead of each burnt-out old flame,
tells all the world that it should not
so quite forget what's quite forgot
and shrouded in the wind on dead-end street.

'Gee, but we were happy, not long ago' –
at least we said we were, and that's the same.
For her, for Mary, Theo, Jill,
the jigging hit-squad warbles still
'I wonder what's become of good old Joe.'

Falling Downstairs

Falling downstairs, further, and still falling,
I passed the good dreams hunting for the light,
but the house was black dust in my staring fingers
and the bad dreams tumbled with me into the night
as the raid went head over heels down the snuffed chimneys.

Dragging their sacks of sound into the Midlands,
the Flying Bombs growled over their blazing tails;
I came to grief where the treaders followed the risers
and things were as soft as rot and as hard as nails.
The floor boards walked in their sleep and groaned for comfort.

Falling downstairs, further, and still falling,
I bounced the candle-flame off the stinking wick;
the yellow lamp-glass ducked its head in a corner,
the dropped light played its simple vanishing trick
and switched the darkness on like a witch's lantern.

Then the dreams got lost in the dark and punched each other,
and the chuckle-headed bombs were having a war,
busy becoming murder and fireside stories.
I hit the bottom rung; love cracked the door
and hauled me through by the hands to the Christmas kitchen.

Falling downstairs, further, and still falling,
I clutch at the lost faces, but in my ear
a throat of shining sound is singing for morning,
rubbing it up like Aladdin's lamp: All Clear,
and the sheets frozen to ghosts in an empty bedroom.

Uncle Walt

for John Mole

On the branch-line, coming back,
my head stuck from the carriage,
I watched us duck for the bridge,
in a pother of steam and smoke,

the engine bent on the rails,
by the signal's clack and go.
From all that hullabaloo,
the hot and clinging shawl,

grows a face fringy as cloud,
benign, watery, lost:
the ghost of the family past
who'll never get out of the wood

as he uncouples the carriage
and sets it up at the back
where bluebells fume and smoke,
old sleepers make a bridge

for summer children to go
to where he's gone off the rails
in his potter-about and shawl:
the blue jay's hullabaloo,

the paints which keep getting lost
in a fringy pipe-smoke cloud
as thin as a beech-tree wood,
the slow train signalled past.

A Slice of Cake

Remembering Evelyn. The Gatehouse, 1942

I watched her sifting shreds of sun,
with soft and sweet into her bowl.
The air was full of harmless love
which slipped her fingers: lights above,
geraniums with their vixen smell
beyond the glass. The past could say

her hair was trimly tied, tell how
the morning flicked its cleansing tongue
about the room – such lemon zest
for licking scraps. It did its best
to make the knives and glasses ring.
I had my cake, and ate it. Now,

my childhood self, too old to learn
new table-manners, ask for more,
I dare not let him out of sight,
matching my hunger, bite for bite,
a day, a week, a month, a year –
he must have known I would return

for these late crumbs of comfort, wait
for grace, the gift of tongues I lost
between her black and silver hair.
A second slice. We break, we share
as if I still could find the taste
to finish up what's on my plate.

Family Reunion

What can I ask them that I never did,
now that they've walked into this puzzling room
and found me here? Those dialogues of the dead
that litter Landor's pages, lighting time
with wordy lanterns – art, god, politics –
wouldn't quite suit, and, anyhow, they know,
if anyone can know, the river Styx
runs brackish with such baggage. Let it go.
There's still a smell of box, the slanting shades
under the window, and, of course, we'll chat
a bit about the journey. 'Don't be too late
in starting back,' I say – 'the late departed.' 'That,'
my father says, 'is tomfoolery, and you know it –
the sort of remark you'd expect from a minor poet.'

He turns to my books, pulls them out and about
'Not quite all gone to the knacker's yet, I see.'
I know he won't take off his overcoat;
I know she can't stay for a cup of tea.
There must be things to buff and dust below
and kissing-comforts for those awkward neighbours,
some who can name each golden bird and bough,
and picnic-traipses to see Cerberus.
My father, far from home, and restless, hums
'He sold the brick to buy a feather –'
turns briefly to the crossword in *The Times*
'– and it blew away in the windy weather.'
To say little enough means quite enough has been said.
Why change the habits of a lifetime because you're dead?

Dead right, of course, for when a black hole yawns
'We needn't go into that now' makes perfect sense.
Why mention Cleopatra's nose? What happens,
happens. The rest is of no importance.
I say I'm glad to see them look so well,
and he 'The change has done wonders for Dorothy.'
It seems a good idea to keep the talk small,
defer, as usual, to their assumed maturity.
They look as if they've chosen how to look,
deep in the prime of a late middle-age –
work to be done, but time for gardens, walks,
gadding off on some petty pilgrimage.
'Peter's books are so much neater than yours were, John.'
'That's because he never reads them.' Chit-chat goes on

as if I'd written it myself. And God?
'An agreeable enough little man,' he says –
his clinch on parleys with the great and good.
'You look yourself more like the Ancient of Days
with hair like that – or the Wild Man of Borneo.'
In this sub-Yeatsian trembling of the veil,
there seems some little distance left to go
before I can divine the immanent will.
Angels? I hazard. 'Optional, if you're C. of E.
Dorothy, look at that ridiculous cat.'
And she? 'I'm a Christian, except for immortality
and the soul. I don't believe in all that.'
As a cloud gathers, no bigger than a man's hand,
I ask her what other excursions they've got planned.

'We're on our way to visit Mother.' Yes,
but who on earth is 'Mother' going to see?
They'll have to change between the acts, confess
grey hairs and wrinkled skin pure mummery;
How are they wanted? Decked in sailor-suits,
a tea-gown, Oxford bags, a little fur
with shining paws ...? I have no doubts,
their dress-codes being what they always were –
'You can't come with me till you've brushed your hair' –
that they can pull such wools across the eyes
as the occasions call for. 'It's not far,'
she says, but this is where he mutinies:
'My dear good woman ...' he starts. Dumbed by déjà-vu,
I feel it's a blessing they're only passing through,

for clearly, there's not much they want to know
except that rose's name, whether the pond
has newts, what I am teaching – time hangs slow
upon the clock. Why lend a helping hand
to my intrusive jigsaw stuffed with holes
whose bits they've always hidden, screwed up tight
in tears and silences, or old wives' tales
of Billy Brumpton, Theo, kissing-gate
or college-court. Then, his defensive quote:
'Deep questioning, that probes to endless dole ...
I think we should leave the touchy-feely bit
to Doubting Thomas.' That old recoil.
Smiling, they turn – are gone. No handshake, kiss for mother;
it's much too late now for seeing through each other.

Parting

'Parting?' Yes, to die, and more than a little:
carry the poetry peculiar to that word
from banks and shores of sunlight –
the shining stuff you thought no slick could foul –
past cloud-hems into – something

For this bed – sweat-stains,
linens falling to the cold sea-floor –
was always what the sunlight led to.
You played in childhood at being dead
and look, it all came true,

learning to hold your breath for ever,
the bed singling itself out
to a drunk boat, a one-man crew
slipping anchor from these ivory coasts
to trawl in depths of ebony,

where, hopelessly in love with shadows,
you racked yourself to the mast
against their strong seductions,
knowing those dead reaches; the dead reaching
across and into you for landfall.

Crossing the Peak

Crossing the Peak, unsingled stars
broke from cloud, hung on the lines
which drew them into gods and heroes.
Saw, low in its laval cauldron,

Manchester threshed to amber,
trapped in shrouds of earth-light:
each voice, each singular, abrupt,
incorrigible voice quite lost.

What broke loose then, could not.
The car-roof was drummed stupid.
Some huge entanglement of wing,
some claw, racked and pinioned,

skating its hooks on cold metal.
Had night stooped to kill,
brought a Fury out of hiding
to ride my shames bareback?

The hours removed themselves
into a deep vow of silence.
West became East again.
North grew to South, slowly.

The Northern Line

END OF LEAVE, 1950S

1 Boarding

Kit in first, I wave to trees and no one,
then take huge gulps of smoke and chill,
my head slung from the window's shoulders.
Things creak and sniff, start monkey-chattering
through low-flying cloud and belts of rain;
metal floors part and greet themselves,
thick up with dog-ends; doors hang about
over piss-pools, trampled paper.
Two fish-cold sleepers, mouths agape,
float in unrinsed light. In Ashwell church
our foolish tribulations are incised in stone:
'A great wind blows through the world,
and only the dregs of the people left.'
Night grows luminous with false perceptions
and up in his yellow cage the signalman
is a silhouette whose arms are strong enough
to haul his lever through a change of tenses,
switch the points the whole shebang must head for.
Night pothers out a film of greasy stars
over chalked-up trucks, the Dickens thing
of big wheels, stovepipe hats and chimneys,
trains 'gliding on like vast weird funerals'
through burning meat-smells in the Welwyn tunnels,
and 'unknown languages in the air, conspiring
in red, green and white characters'.
My shoulder strap cossets my beret, badged
Sua Tela Tonanti – to the thunderer his weapons.

2 Under Way

Some delight, to grin like a gormless thing,
sway, drunk on a fierce night-wind,
skelter down a swung flare-path,
locked in the banshee wail, Joe Miller's jest-book
riddling away at nothing, nothing at all.

'Why is a chicken when it spins?'
'Because one of its legs is both the same.'
The knives flicker, paring back
to the core, the stalk, the longed-for absence.
Khaki rubs at the neck's nape;
the badge catches at light: *Sua Tela Tonanti*,
and a crown which crowns a million skulls.
Under Vimy Ridge mines packed and primed
sap out their Ammonal. In the lit city,
patched by criss-cross feet, scar-tissue,
dark-finned bombs wait with uncrazed skins
who followed their noses into the Roman dark:
bones, oyster-shells, sandal-thongs, brickbats,
shadowy centurions, masons of Mithras,
driving ghosts hard who still can't tell
their sinister from their dextra.
Tucked in far silos, clean-cut missiles doze
under strong enchantments of code and key.
Who will cosset them into nightmare,
help them sing like stars in the glory
of their imperium? I brace myself
against the pull of England, on the curve.

3 *Junction*

Hanamanoosh, hanamanoosh,
all the sixes, clickety-click. Wheels
pound at the cracks, the discontinuities
in these long tricks of shine that tell the night
'Follow the gleam, follow the gleam'
to where the signal's clip-crop stiffens
us into drag, a stuttered run-down,
a dull slide by shelves of puddled concrete.
Jolts. The slam of doors. Then nothing
Only a voice, garbled and rough as God,
denouncing the stations of the cross.
'The steam hissed. Someone cleared his throat.
No one left and no one came' —
except the usual suspects of the time
who drift up in a press of awkward shadows.
How much will each compartment hold:
sixteen moustached poilus, eight horses

cut loose from Mark Gertler's roundabout?
Eccles, Bluebottle and Moriarty
double up under a gigantic doll,
its sallow face cowlicked, toothbrush-tached,
its right and awkward arm saluting nothing.
Anna Neagle, a Cameron Highlander,
head matchstuck on with Harbutt's plasticine,
a corpse-white milkman with a leaden face
balancing his pails like scales of justice –
Then, the long whistle with its sexless thrill.

4 *Off Again*

Doctor and Housewife have done their duty,
turned blind eyes to love's refreshment room,
its white orphanage of cups and saucers
as cold as charity or a shut sunday,
as hoped-for, never-to-be-given kisses. Now
the Guard's flag flicks green for danger
and whoomph, whoomph go thick smoke-beats
as faceless dream-girls wave their hankies,
Gothic windows blub and snivel,
strung lights coagulate. The Stationmaster
raises his baton and the band strikes up:
'Oh we don't want to lose you,
but we think you ought to go …'
What a send-off for the cold war captains
high-staking it in a first-class compartment,
tobacco-wreaths drifting sagacity
about the forehead of each fellow-traveller:
Dulles and Eisenhower play Brinkmanship;
Stalin and Molotov, at Stakes and Leaders,
wash undigested countries down with vodka,
growl of executions, wolves and medals.
Churchill – 'the voice that breathed o'er Eden' –
slumps balefully while his marionette
languidly picks my number from his Homburg,
despatches me to Suez – where I will not go.
'Never mind what they all say, my dear,
but take a return ticket every time the train stops.'

5 Back

Back, back to the land of the midnight sun,
the Hornby loco set for Rockery Junction
and long derailments under the elder
which still holds out its musty memory-clusters
over bright, battered liveries of war,
scattered among marigolds and shrapnel.
Back to the keys which wound the past too tight,
the fizz of clockwork, and the broken spring
Back to the branch-line, Snelland, Wickenby,
the tired old brutes that clanked and puffed
before the Reverend Awdry got at them,
the sentiment of bells, clock-faces, milk churns,
a lattice of sweet-peas blown by light
into a summer coronation.
Back to a melancholia of shut wagons
shunting the bombers' night into the sidings
with a long, sonorous diminuendo.
Back to the Gatehouse.
                    Later, came to a different conclusion.
The smell of steam is for ever the smell of dying.
After that 'first powerful, plain manifesto
The black statement of pistons' – what?
The lament of the birches at Birkenau,
and half a century's epitaph: *Arbeit Macht Frei.*
Back to Derby station, father hunting corpses
under the arc-lights and the rubble smell.
To the thunderer his weapons.

6 St Pancras

The wheels spin backwards, and the train
lurches to terminus. Unstud the window strap,
Let it kick back into the door frame.
Hit the ground running. The engine blows its top.
'Soldier, I'll have you off this square so fast
your feet won't touch the ground'
the Underground. I float past sleepers
wrapped in their shrouds, government issue,
Henry Moore, Mark One. In my kit,
Baudelaire, the *London Book of English Verse,*

sing lightly to the unborn dead
who will not turn their heads to look at me,
trapped in the invisible cloak of uniform
like Chesterton's postman. Somehow –
Farewell, Leicester Square – I must meet
my Waterloo, thread this place of changes
where my hair tingles with prognostication.
A busker flower-powers his guitar –
'Where have all the soldiers gone,
gone to graveyards every one' –
and City gents hurry to strap-hang home
from The Blitz Experience, The London Dungeon,
neatly funereal under Magritte faces.
Celia Johnson, eyes bunged up with tears
hurries past the gangling man with dreadlocks,
and push-me pull-you trains with moony faces
cry 'Follow, follow, follow me'.

7 Underground

'Shun the frumious Bandersnatch'
doped to the eyeballs, unexploded luggage,
the moving staircase, and the sliding door.
'Up and down this world goes round, down.'
Mind the gap. For this, our travelling grave,
the vacuum makes its little sigh of closure,
the Northern Line parts to speed our passing.
No conversations. Only, off the rails,
the scream of Orpheus in the Underground
'A bodiless childfull of life in the gloom,
crying with frog voice, What shall I be?'
I am 22651134, the toybox soldier
twenty-two million, six hundred and fifty-one
thousand, one hundred and thirty-three later
than Private Cain, MM, the oldest sweat of all
who eats the ones like me for breakfast.
I have punched my number into my mess-tin.
It must be true. Here is my hand to prove it.
Someone up in the sky is fond of numbers,
knows how many flying miles and inches
I travel daily from the place called home.
This catacomb grows slippery with skulls

beaten from light, 'Follow the gleam.'
Strip off our foolish clothes, this metal shell-case,
laugh to see us burrowing mother-naked,
bent for sitting, standing with one arm raised
in hope of resurrection, and the life to come.

8 *Waterloo*

Raising their fish-cold faces to the light,
their mouths agape for stony crumbs of comfort
from the *Evening Standard* – Late Night Extra,
the Chronicles and Heralds of stale beer,
the nudes descended must ascend the staircase.
We gaze tremulously at the family portraits
of girls in Berlei bras, gents in Aquascutums
and smarten up those glad-rags handed in
to giant rats in the Quartermaster's Stores,
or given to the daily help, or Oxfam.
I carry myself as luggage to the concourse
and here I am, in *camino del mezzanine,*
feeling a bit shaky, a touch of flu
or of the golden birds, watching what's past
or passing, or, in these glasses dimly,
what's to come. *Sua Tela Tonanti.*
I pat my beret, sharpen up my pleats –
'His smart bearing and efficient manner
have made him an asset to his unit.'
Back to Basic Training, civvies parcelled home,
perhaps from Escort Duty, Embarkation Leave;
who never got to Cyprus, Egypt, Cythera,
glimpsed Naafi nautch-girls throwing flowers
and singing love-songs to the weltering moon,
the calme, the luxe, the whole volupté bit.
Time enough, though, for a lipstuck cup of tea
with Baudelaire and his red-haired beggar-girl.

9 Encounter

'C'est magnifique, mais ce n'est pas la gare' –
Somebody has turned the volume down,
halted the goose-step of my second-hand,
stopped those digits racing into nowhere.
I think of a week in the College Stanislaus
on the Boul' Mich, lectures at the Sorbonne –
Servitude et Grandeur Militaires –
a kiss under the Pont Neuf, strikes on the Metro,
home with my 78's, Claude Luter, Sidney Bechet.
Scribbling in pencil under yellow light,
I lose the poetry in my translation:
'Those begging arms should only pray
some other to your charms' display …'
I'm conscious of that bent, oldish man who looks
as if he'd like to catch my eye. He's *there*
as the first star you cannot see by staring
'*À une Mendiante Rousse.*' What did our father say –
Beware loose girls – you should be so lucky!
The next line you want will go like this –
'and chase his teasing hands away'.
You look dubious? Yes, I was, too.
It's very possible 'we'll meet again,
don't know where, don't know when'.
Hang on to that anthology, that Baudelaire
I've lent you. I'll expect to see them
back on my shelves when I get home.
Goodbye. 'You, that way; we, this way.'

10 South

Stunned, I write the line down without thinking,
watch him weave the concourse, dodge
three German girls with rucksacks, push past
the stripy candyhats filling baguettes,
the Military Police, the chinless wonders
fresh with their Mons or Eaton Hall commissions.
And as for me, stuff's waiting down the line:
a Pompey Coronation Fleet that's all lit up,
more juvenilia torn for their bad verses –
'The soldiers stamp about the square,

Defaulters wait by Majors' Dens,
The dirty offices are filled
With the sad scratch of pay clerks' pens' –
and long night-strolls putting the 'fifties right
with Corporal David Winnick, MP.
Old queens, false knights, young rookies,
and Elvis Presley yowling *Muss i' denn.*
That's all to come. There's my train.
It fills up with the dead, the real soldiers
from Neuve Chapelle, Dunkirk or the Ardennes,
who take up all the room there is and none,
their pallid kit-bags stencilled fiercely
Tommy Atkins, Nobby Clark, Dusty Miller…
back to their squares, the Indian verandahs,
and waxed moustaches of their Sergeant-Majors.
Sua Tela Tonanti. I face the engine's music
in a black Pacific at the tag-end of steam.

11 *Terminus*

'And then there came both mist and snow.'
Up there. Cape Wrath. Ultima Thule.
At Carlisle, below the stumbled wall,
Paul Nash paints a new Totes Meer:
Northern lines, where the dead ride at anchor
and all our loves and partings come to this –
the disjecta membra of clack box, frame stay,
bogie guard and steam chest cover,
whistles handle, sight-feed lubricator –
poor tarnished ivories of the graveyard.
To the thunderer his weapons.
Here, at the crossroads of a century,
arc-welders flense each carcass.
In masks and fountains of white fire,
pull down the Castles, Kings and Cities
into the raw materials of desire.
'Attendant, with many a clank and wrench,
were lumbering cares, dark meditations,
huge dim disappointments, monotonous years.'
Troubles packed up in the old kit-bags
have drifted out through rusty eyelets
and cannot find their ghostly comforters;

the chilled air is blown about with kisses,
dries on the cheek like an unwiped tear-stain,
like rain, drying. 'Thus, at Mugby Junction,
at past three o'clock of a tempestuous morning,
the traveller went where the weather drove him.'

Night Watch

The branch rocks the moon off, on;
animal heat springs out a flare
on steps, concrete, the ribby glass
in the vehicle park. It won't go far,

as light goes, but each bit helps,
as the glimpse of a named thing or star
helps. For heat after blood and treasure,
it's a cold, small day up there,

and squarely cornered by night.
The girl stretched on the calendar
wears out her skin's uniform
slowly, slowly. A chair

squawks. Helmets in Trônes Wood
are holed by rust. Every door
is a question for this bunch of keys
whose wards fail to answer

that slow pulse on the stair,
the pushed-about dust. Easier
to lie unclutched on the table,
look gleamily up at her

as she moves to answer his heat,
short-change their silver,
open herself to the tree, the dark
in blackface and balaclava.

Night Kitchen

Headlamps glancing away from night ahead
glaze the room over, pausing for a moment
in the sheen and hopeful dust which flows from,
sticks to, the pretty cups and their sadness.
Whatever is being searched for, hunted down,
darkness will not be taken for an answer.

Everything which happens happens in passing.
The kitchen drowses in light, that nervous stranger
coasting lost into a place of secrets.
Things here have made love to each other so often,
undressing each other's colours nightly,
that his embarrassment is hardly noticed

as the chair sleeps in the clock's arms,
what has been left out finds itself really in bed,
the cats and spoons grow desolate and cosy.
At the window, a spectral twirl of roses,
and, in the room, something being raised –
which could be yesterday, that ghost of a smile

haunting the lazy plates which will not finish
themselves up, or get down from the table
for this visitor playing at seeing how long
he can hold his pale breath over, under, water;
whose brief composure is carelessly ruffled
by the sink-tap, crying slowly in blobs of sound

which nobody wants to hear. It is all on offer;
appearances cannot be saved. The films unreel
in a flurry of nothing, the fingerprints drift
away from each surface into the hands of a stranger
who paces himself through the dark, his eyes
bent on away, white gloves calming the wheel.

In the Picture

A heavy man holds a frame about his head,
twirling it round in a slow dance while the city
goes about its business of the movements
of its dull clock with no escapement

fractioned in turn, passed glimmeringly on.
There's not really much to choose
between this and great lancets meshed with iron.
The glazier's art specifies nothing but seasons,

that spidery wait for an eye which might appraise
each minute boredom of blue, each belly
of slow-breeding cloud. You could hope
for something more than people, birds or stars

as a heavy man makes a tedious film,
and out of this window the packed greens
in my field of vision wobble with light.
Quickening air takes their converse apart

while Mr and Mrs Andrews wait by a cornfield:
the world's skylights lie flat on their backs
with extraordinary views of nothing at all
reaching its ceiling. The clouds dissolve

and a smudged view stares at the back of a man
framed by a city room, watching a film
of his own slow, insufferable dance:
a heavy man, twirling yesterday's business.

Nothing at All

Nothing at all out there today but a name
that could be 'mist', which is before one's eyes,
or 'fog': too active, swirling about in its chapter,
though the tumbledown house is pushy enough,
riding its angles into the heart of whiteness

as if close-hauled, its wormy timbers braced
against the shock of some darker, whiter hulk
steering itself, steered or anchored
in the over-there drenched and sodden stuff;
fuming or steaming away into that name

which must be 'mist', but not 'love-in-a-mist',
not today, though that is love's habitat,
unless to wait, and see without watching
how a bare chart, a sky which cannot be compassed,
tempt definition, are, possibly, love,

and 'love' is a word, hoping also for definition,
as on the edge, approaching the curfew of mist
is a line of trees, their sprits bare of canvas,
a clean palisade of leaf-pointed, vertical iron,
and beyond, just beyond, those metres of rough

something: dead ground or slack water,
receding, filling, promising nothing at all
but a hardness to hurt, a depth to drown in,
as what can be seen moves out to meet its conclusion
where the bell's clapper is tied, and Cordelia silent.

A Trunk of Letters

Is this the chapter where the treasure-seekers,
flinging the lid back, rinse their hands in gold?
Listen – the gulls. The sky breaks up their voices.
which might have consequential things to say
about snapped wish-bones and a sandy bay,
the cave's ribbed window, attic salt, and cold –

but no, the dropped scraps of such conversations
run out into the bladderwrack and foam.
This sea-chest disappoints: all cling-film faces
and little creepings underneath the skin,
brittle green ribbons and a black-head pin,
a night of family faces coming home

to roost, to babble volumes in, confess
how much they missed each other, what they read
in faces that were not yet photographs.
Their news, as common as the common cold,
as flowers or visits, work, or growing old,
grows rare and nervous just by being dead,

as cursive, itching fingers whisper on
'We mapped this land, charted the deep-sea swell,
and time and tide were in our reckoning.
Not now, not you. See how our crosses mark
heart-burials.' In the November dark
the shaken house keens like a giant shell.

In Camera

They swim in and out of focus, the Campo Santo's
depth of field, the stone exposures of time
in the postcards you bought, and sent abroad,
which was home, to lie for their country,
the snaps you took yourself in the Mezzo del Camin:
those greens, reds, indigos, that little museum
with a wall-eyed dog and paintings by Circa,
the cobbled alley which led you down and on
past boys pirouetting on bikes to a view of the sea

where clouds which are far too white blow over
the lacklustre names of poets and senators.
Today, somebody else, wearing your camera,
takes a picture of difference, and calls it beauty,
though beauty is nothing much to write home about,
especially that view of the sea, chop-chopping away
at a headland stiff with confectionery houses,
trim, childish trees and a church whose gloom
is primped by time-shares in everlasting candles.

In this place your affections must make-believe in,
stay-at-homes shoot lines for the traveller
wild as the musketry of their cherished insurrection,
and haunting the junk-shop window a curling postcard.
shows your mother and father crossing the street
by a huge parked car with white-walled tyres.
They are looking away from the sun-blanked square,
with its flags, shoulder-straps and floral lamp-posts
for a last view of the sea on the way to the station,

three trains and a difficult channel-crossing.
She is thinking of you; he is thinking of Arnold –
the *Scholar Gipsy* – and how much to leave in tips.
It is there in black and white. On scraps of pasteboard
dying in cupboards lurk views full of faces –
the lovers, the banker, the man selling bread –
nobody posed for, no one will ever identify
while the photographer, intent on a somewhere
watches for sunlight to sharpen his view of the sea

and all the forgettable people go briskly on,
or pause while a match is struck, a glance taken
at something mildly important, and, like the dodo,
dead. Is it you, there, propped in the shadow,
aiming your poem into the sunlight, under the notice
'Please do not shoot the photographer – he is only
doing his best?' For you, your parents, a view of the sea,
two cake-walking sentries outside the Palais de Justice,
the marsupials pouched in the zoological gardens

must be drawn deep, deeper, more deeply yet
into that swell of glass whose fanciful tremblings
of light mirror those on that view of the sea
framed in a Kodak entre deux guerres,
with its bob of girls in stripes and bathing-caps
growing ever more hungry for metempsychosis,
where click, each fluttering thing – *animula vagula blandula* –
must lose its name, become small, flat, so very still,
yet born again, having seen the light, and been saved.

The Old Home

It is Happy Hour in the Cavalier Hotel.
Executives bark and clink at the Long Bar,
laughing the dusk down into its wishing-well.
While Harold fetches the bags in from the car
Doris looks at the window-catch. From where she is sitting
its bobble brass-hat looks back like French knitting

And she thinks 'Is it happy?', watches Mary come through
to make up the fire, collect the tea-things.
Such stuff in her head making such a to-do.
There's Dads and Mr Errold by the till, confabulating,
as Harold used to say, about Tuesday's auction
and how something must be done about old Mrs Jackson.

And are they happy? The ghost of a tennis-ball
slams into the car-park over half-standard roses.
Behind the door marked 'Dames' in the Long Bar wall
a convulsion of water. The Doulton font
disposes of things. The flush-pull, that porcelain
cold as a skull. Is it happy, does it complain?

And Dads is saying 'She never says much, our Doris',
while Mr Errold walks right through her table, slow,
wheezing a little, trimming the yellow gas,
as if there was a little light it could throw
on Death by Chocolate, Rombout's coffee, Pevsner,
the fairy packets of low-calorie sweetener

which might make things happy. Harold looks like trouble.
'I'd best see to the room.' Upstairs, in Number 4,
Alice must be sitting with a Gideon Bible.
She has sleepy sickness. Everyone has a cross to bear.
Dads is tugging at the catch, the dratted thing,
which needs mending, and mends nothing.

Lunch Out

is sitting on grass, hardish, with dogs.
Most do nothing ever so slowly,
unleashed for an hour in their odd cool hats,
dazed out. Jazz clears its throat, sun
buffs the works up in silver and gold,
boats

Clamber about in the cut. Ground,
somewhat downtrodden, perks up enough
for a colourable view of enormous legs,
swatches of bosom and buttock
becalmed over canvas, riding a stiff
sargasso

which will not pull to their foundering
old age with a hatful of ribbons,
the blue man trapped in his tuba,
the singer who sings his invisible toes
to the sunny side of the street,
the girl

strutting again with some barbecue
through children, hatchings of shade,
the processional rise and fall
of glasses always half-full, never half-empty.
Two ancient girls promenade, sashay,
parasols

dipped to the wind off the horn, twirled
in a flutter of gaudy. Out there
soundless and congruent triangles
part the water, as if to be white and happy
were in itself an excuse for not being
dead.

The Letter

I

Twin curtains, trussed against outside,
and stiff as Tudor grave-clothes with ruched topknots:
the room's in hibernation, closed on its fog-smell,
a dead-spice cabinet dreaming of quickened voices,
but only the clock lives for the moments

which rock themselves to sleep in cradles of dust.
A swollen light-bulb with its airy keening
pores over boxes, gives a cluttered table
the spit and polish of pure definition,
picks up a letter you could almost see through,

while stone-washed linen holds an unused day,
glass, following its water-course,
ripples, thickens at the pane's foot.
Something holds its breath; the weeping eye
brightens a little, darkens a little,

as the room starts up and stops. A mirror
plays back the fluster of these tips and wrinkles:
those throbbing filaments, that dying nerve
which sings its tiny love-song to the dark,
and though it tricks with habits of command,

knows that its spell of opening must fail
to stir this clouded concourse: doors and curtains
closed in the compass of a walnut-shell.
Now, only the hands of time, grown luminous,
the unanswered letter, asking to be addressed.

II

The clock, scribbling in longhand, shorthand,
never finds time to reconsider its message,
but says it all in a chattering class of wheels
and a cold heart sleeved under a bell-jar.
Dirt plays with dirt, is written off and away.
For keeps. There's a long chain-letter somewhere,
and only one promise made. Nobody reads it;

the promise will keep till kept. More news
throws its light on nothing heading for nowhere:
the cat sicks up, a rose fingers the window,
there's a fall of soot. It is the clock's office
to note these little deaths, and unrecord them.
Roman hours grow quainter by the minute;
feathers drift into the Grand Canyon

and someone comes into the room: a shadow,
a frown crossing the air, as if in this puzzle
something might be put straight, the bulb changed,
curtains drawn, dead flowers wreathed
in a basket of currency no longer current.
The clock pretends it has stopped. In silence,
the byway of sound, a hand looks for the letter.

III

It is there, where you dropped it. The words
float off the page, as eyes get used
to the passage of time. A marquetry box
dissolves its inlay into a cluster of shades;
they worry themselves to the back of beyond,

the clock comes apart in its hands,
and breaks a shower of meteors over a table
tipping and sliding away as the spirit moves it.
There is only the letter, ready to unfold
its questioning answers: 'Dear one,

You ask for news? Well, I must chronicle
such small beer as our life is made of.
Pascal's been sick again. It comes
of eating mouse on a full stomach. The Albertine
needs pruning – we can hardly see into the garden.

You can't imagine the mess the room's in.
A bird must have got caught in the chimney.
Soot everywhere …' Things grow garrulous.
A pinch of air sniffs at the curtains,
locks the sunlight up in a field of glass

where the rose wanders, and goes still.
The clock looks for the time; clicking its teeth,
finds it. On the letter primed with invisible ink,
a responsive hand draws words into a circle
as up on the high wire, light sings to the dark.

Trevail: Four Children & Summer

A little further. Now you have put yourself
in the picture, look at the children
as they prop out flat on a huge boulder,
facing the space you have walked away from.
Feel their flesh, slabbed cold and wet
and red with the impress of ground-up shell.
There is noise in the air, that familiar blend
of gulls with childhood's animal cry,
a ribboned pleasure-boat snoring into the wind.
There is a place here for you, but no welcome

from those four faces: only a mobile sea
tearing off strips of itself to lay on the sand.
Walk past them – you might try
to find the towels, the cooling thermos,
the camera, safely lost in your empty hands,
the paperback in the raffia basket
whose words have washed quite through,
and possibly over, your head,
Call to them. The words die in your throat
as if, sleep-sticky, you called to wake them,

and yourself, from the drops and edges of things,
to cry with the voice of the wind
an alarm for each fizzing cauldron,
each hole where the Atlantic slams its door
on the dark, or salutes the dying of time
with a dull processional gun. It's late,
so trudge back to the unturned heads,
salt-licked skin, still and quivering limbs,
and, as you pass them, pick them up, and watch
the sun strike home against their unblinking eyes.

Kippford: A View from the Bridge

The transparency
of a transparency:
the sky that day
something borrowed,
something blue.

Three on a plank bridge,
brothers and sister,
sprawl over water:
the slight burn brackish
and moving slowly,

their whispering hair
with its bleached look
spread like twitch
the wind rubs down
in the Traffords' field.

The projector's fan
winnows light;
with a soft whirr:
something winged
might take its flight.

to hover, sing,
over the children's
view from a bridge,
where ageing faces
rise to greet them.

Lea Valley: My Son, My Father

Half-deep in flowers, not thinking of time
as it quietly thinks of them, they are, it seems,
two of the happiest prisoners of summer,
closed in greens and blues and the forest of names
it is second nature for the older one to know.
Nothing is happening Nothing is likely to happen.
Somebody must have said that morning
'Shall we go to …?' So, a little fuss, and here they are.
Parked by this photo, its bonnet juggling the air,
a neat car fills with heat, the road-map lies open,
a cluster of sweets joins hands in the glove compartment.

She rests the camera, walks into the wood,
and leaves this day which is hard to forget, or remember –
an insistent pleat of light in the family album.
The two of them stand easily, and to attention
under a pile of yesterday's papers and knitting
shifting its weight over thickets of grass
which do not droop, but fill the room with a dry
fragrance plucked from damp and darkness.
They look to the cleft of a stream, lost at their feet,
their ears tripped on its clean runnels of sound
while the keys to it all hang dead still from the fascia.

Epithalamion

for Roger Scupham and Jennifer Cassels

New foliage grows to a head on familial trees,
and a thousand hieroglyphs cut by time's leaf-borers
print out their message for the millennial wind.
Though the air grows cold with prognostication,
somewhere, someone is picking a leaf, and reading
'I love you', however runic the language.

Thunder and lightning bounce below the horizon.
Under that ledge of cloud or nightfall, the Schwarzwald
lurks on the marches of the Märchen; there misfortunes
weave thickets of bat-skin, huts grow dark with cloaks
pledged by ogres and witches who curse nightly,
but cannot say 'I love you' in any language,

and are put to flight by the simplest of white magics,
a ring danced on a finger, an exchange of glances.
Let harpies harp away on their one-string fiddles;
in your sunlit Cirque d'Hiver, as the black and white horses
step out in their keyboard tandem, let music say
'I love you' in a language which pays no duty,

and, unpoliced by savage hats and holsters,
is at home in a polis whose frontiers are always open,
whose sunlight mints to silver those flyaway wings
which stitch the Old World and the New together,
and whispers down snow-cold slopes of air
a constant green-world promise to earth: 'I love you,

your trees which dance, die, dance: andante, allegro,
which tell each other that something is always for ever,
though branches thrust and fall, the clung mould thickens.'
What can the green leaves say in the face of winter,
except that, however dead the language, the words
'I love you' are never lost in the new translation.

Song for Sophie

A Granddaughter, born 1998

The world is full of wishes
that sparkle up in fountains,
ride the blackest cats.
They steal a flock of crosses
and blow them into kisses,
pull flowers out of mountains,
rabbits out of hats.

On a far-off yesterday
the first wish hid in darkness
till someone wished it true,
wished lions, cars and postmen,
daisies, mice and milkmen,
and liking all that likeness,
wished, of course, for you.

When you read these verses,
guess by words and spaces
what their wish might be,
thinking hard of postmen
daisies, mice and milkmen –
packed tight with wishes
and saying just like me

each is special, singular,
together in their dancing,
in out, up down, sun, moon, star.
In a packet or a pocket
keep your wish a secret
and tell it just by being
exactly who you are.

The Christmas Owl

I

Christmas Eve: the lilt,
the syllable. Ice
puckers the roadside:
snow on the wind.
The cats will not talk tonight
but weather dances
on the point of a needle
which sets north-east.
Let it sleep if it will
the house in the village
with its riding-lights
bobbing the air-waves,
the tumbril of beet

at the field's groyne.
Let it all sleep:
robes cling like bats
in the vestry cupboard,
Donner and Blitzen
sledge through nowhere.
What can unwrap
the ribboned room?

II

Bees do not sing
in their crowded hive,
no cocks crow
to the numb moon,
but somebody shakes
four hundred years
down the chimney flue:
a Lord of Misrule
with doll-glass eyes
and a wand of wings
to cut and shuffle
the cooling air.
A house of cards
flakes from the mantel;
in high bat-voice
a nest of baubles
chinks from the tree.
Its plump doublet
basted with soot,
Strix Aluco,
the Tawny Owl.

III

Christmas Day.
No shepherds cried
'Ut hoy, ut hoy.'
Nipped blood, foul ways,
we sit like mice
in a dim tree-house
whose hollow trunk

breathes out our breath,
sleepy-eyed
for a little pitcher
with hidden ears.
Whatever is born
to this clouded light
must come to the hooks
beneath the plush.
The murderers too
will need such patience:
wings locked on
and seeking heat
from more than cold
that cuts to the bone.

Riches Heures du Duc de Berry

Seeing, but mostly through, past filmy blueness
patching at star-creep up against the window,
past leaves and branches blotted on free evenings
which rocked the house-glow in their oily cradles,
you looked for something that might be a token.
When all they said was 'Seeing is believing',
what then was seeing but a loose lantern
swung in the night, blindly-starred, and waiting
for light to clean its gates of horn and ivory,
then jump through tiny hoops cut in blue paper
on bedroom darkness rising like a fountain.

The choirstall mullions were infilled by stars
pinned over saints in blood and emerald,
and fierce in judgement when the sun came out
suspended by a press of waxen clouds.
A saint should have stars fountained over him,
a jovial shower of light for each dull nimbus.
Chained at my wrist, a moon-face watch recycles
one simple blue, a splutter of gold ink
as childish, jostled out of constellation,
as the night-sky on my sudden screen-save
or heaven daubed about a wizard's cloak.

Calendar pages, where the so-rich hours,
those cloaks betrothed to blues and silences,
lie weightless to the grass as Disney towers
lie weightless to the hill, your pale, jimp faces
are not inclined to hear our conversations,
but turn to where the sky-beasts penned in azure
perch level-headed among equal stars
dancing a touch, grown fey and tremulous
as coins which have learned to live in fountains:
clusters of spent wishes wished by some
too young or old for seeing and believing.

Kilvert's Winter: 1871

I

Light lords it over Draycot Water,
a whole chinoiserie of lanterns
papering over fire in blue, green, crimson.
They keep delightful station
as Harriet Awdry jumps over a punt,
Arthur Law jumps over a chair,
the cow jumps over the moon
and all the magnesium ribands cry 'Bravo!'
to fire boxed in a roaring pen at the lakeside.
The ice is in splendid order,

sliders and slitherers roped away
from the fancy dancers, heirs and Graces,
the Sydneys, Pagets, Roystons,
and a Mr Calcroft they call 'The Hangman'.
To the strains of a quadrille band
the starlight dances the Lancers,
Snow falls. Men beat the bounds.
To a whisk of brooms, the Gentry
cut their finest figures,
wheel in a circuit of torches.

II

In a room pungent with lime chloride.
Maria Kilvert, a white sheet drawn over,
lies lapped in lead, lapped in oak
lined with white satin.
Authority melts from the face
frozen down into silence.
He steals a silver seal.

On Christmas Day, such cold:
brush and sponge stiff and stark.
Breaking the sheet-ice,
he bathes in broken chandeliers,
his loins jousting with sherds,
cries hosanna through the burning,
the split prisms, the bells.

Mary Price stares at an angel
perched on her arm in grave-clothes
and a child's coffin-cap.
Young Meredith's jaw is locked.
They wrench it open with a screw,
can do nothing for him.
Catherine's skin falls away like scurf.

III

A thinnish crowd skates at Draycot:
such antics from a German lady's maid
as you would expect. Lord Royston sulks.
'Those abominable Miss Awdrys
have contradicted me about the Lancers.'
Lord Cowley, struck by a fiery torch
bangs it about, roaring in fury,
Mr Calcroft takes a heavy tumble.
'Where did you lie last, Hangman?'
A little laughter shines in the bushes.

Tonight there are children calling,
their voices everywhere, so many,
and men are out beating the holly,
beating for blackbirds with a clap-net.
On the Bowood ice, Mr Greenwood's son,
breaks his head on a stone,
dies in an hour by the lakeside.
Children call from the hills
in a great frost and a cloudless sky.
They must be sliding on moonlight.

The Chairs

'She takes away the confidence one should have in
her chair if she were once out of it.'

Dr Johnson

Beat that, poor mouse.
There's so much brilliance going on it hurts.
'Pray, sir, let me help you to another slice of wisdom,
but none of your sauce.' How can silence,
which, as he knows, propagates itself,
be refuted, except by kicking it
and setting the poor bruised table on a roar.

In drab, in mouse,
no heart to heave her heart into her mouth,
no spark to fan with lesser lights and lustres
who congregate about this luminary,
she'd blush to find herself in his concordance,
her table place reserved
to feed the grossness of his humour.

And there she sits,
her chair drawn up into that conversation
where Coleridge rabbits on to someone's button,
Goethe chats up a stone, hedge-philosophers
apostrophize the trees they cannot see
for woods that they are lost in.
A chair is true enlightenment,

feet on the ground
four-square, at ease, taking a social polish,
perfectly in control of legs and arms.
'I say a chair has a bottom of good sense.
A chair is fundamentally sensible.'
It can accommodate John Wilkes
without embracing Whiggish notions

and will absorb
the long weariness of cumbered flesh,
a mind unsettled by the Bench, the Woolsack.
'No more of that, sir!' His veins throb,
and Lady Macdonald lurks in the Hebrides,
mouth open, hands propping her cheeks:
'insipidity on a monument',

as growling, ticking,
he swims against a tide of well-bred faces
to take tea-chat with dead, neglected Tetty,
be alone for just one evening with Molly Aston,
'not happiness, but rapture'.
How they would talk their chairs invisible,
quite out of countenance.

In dark Bolt Court
language lies locked up in folio.
'Confidence' cannot be taken away
and 'Chair ' sleeps easy with its definition:
no slow dissolve in tears and supplications
under that weight of silence. He turns to her:
'Madam, may I assist you – a little tongue?'

A. C. Benson Has a Restless Night

for Noel Lloyd and Geoffrey Palmer

Will such pomps and ceremonies never end,
this cavalcade of small pink bricks, and dons
who toss and dip in a cloud of bibbons and ribbons,
those Heads of Houses and their appalling wives
corpulent in fox-furs, bombazine?

'I confess the sight of men in scarlet vexes me
because of the mad and timid joy that flickers in their eyes.'

Broad-beamed faces, settled in their declension,
and a 'Pomeranian dog with its head stuffed with offal,
strange, large flies – grey and tufted,
a sawn-off face dangling from a tree
dropping a horrid, yellow, viscous substance.'

Oh, and those pretty boys with their family airs,
so eager to please m'tutor: Lyttelton, de Grey,
sauntering by, the world, the ball at their feet,
with their cutaway coats, white-collars, centre-partings
and unformed faces stiffening into command.

'Good, earnest, pure, willing –
and I give nearly nothing of myself to them.'

Young men in blood-stained battledress
'and a small, deformed hairy child,
with a curious lower jaw, very shallow:
over the face it had a kind of horny carapace,
made of some material resembling *pottery*'.

Then love's elect, those quick, ingenuous ones
who understand, careless of explanation,
an old man shaken, 'a seal playing with kittens',
our friendships 'flying sun on a bright morning',
Walpole, Mallory, Lubbock, Rylands.

My father the Archbishop, cassocked in purple,
'a grave, commanding, exacting, loving presence'.

And whose pulse beats to this Marche au Supplice?
'I could see his face twitch and grow suddenly pale …
he got up and ran to the scaffold, as if glad to be gone.
He was pulled in at one of the swing-doors – a silence.
Then a thing like a black semaphore went down.'

Augustus Hare Considers Another Ghost Story

The plush of these huge trees sags with heat
that weighs more than their tonnage of water;
through the small tremblings of a pianoforte
servants move as easily as their shadows.
Ladies and gentlemen talk in the flocked light,
make fresh acquaintance with their solitary lives.

It was his mother who was buried alive
and lived for many years afterwards.
It was known she had been put into her coffin
with a very valuable ring upon her finger,

Ah, these old country palaces are choked with mother,
the furious rustling of aunts, adopted, unadopted,
their close-print faces torn from family bibles.
The child who skitters up steps as fast as the flowers
and is whipped for it, talks of the value of rings,
the Taylors, Abruzzo, his work at the Athenaeum.

and the sexton went in after the funeral,
when the coffin was put into the vault, to get it off.
He opened the coffin, but the ring was hard to move,
and he had to rub the dead finger up and down.

Thripps from the harvest-fields creep under glass,
stain clerical uncles crossed in Oxford frames.
Her necklace molten, Lady Campbell tells Madame du Quaire
'I always wear a live snake round my throat in hot weather:
it keeps one's neck so cool.' A little laughter,
a little sheet-lightning: frocks paler, greens darkening.

This brought Lady Edgecombe to life, and she sat up.
The sexton fled, leaving the doors of the vault and church open.
Lady Mount Edgecombe walked home in her shroud,
and appeared in front of the windows.

The house at dusk is adrift with beautiful women,
their voices climbing up and down the octave.
A propped head in a carriage bobs by in the Via San Claudio:
that Sicilian Marquis, inhabitant of loss, the Family Spy,
a slim frequenter of tarnished moonlight
looking in from out, watching; once only, speaking.

Those within thought it was a ghost.
Then she walked in at the front door.
When she saw her husband she fainted away in his arms.
This gave her family time to decide what should be done,

In great cool rooms heavy with lilies, he watches
each intransigent face melt into death's brief afterglow.
Insistent, insistent – 'What? Where? Whither?
These questions sometimes hold me breathless.'
Does the creator demand the sacrifice of his creature?
Because he loves his cat, Selma, Aunt Edith hangs it.

and they settled to persuade her
it had been a terrible delirium.
When she recovered from her faint, she was in her own bed,
and she ever after believed it had been a dream.

His mother, 'beyond measure disgusted', gives him away;
as the house fills with the chirping of thousands of crickets
his adopted mother, his darling, dies in his arms
with camellias, her bronze wolf, hymn books, little gold tray.
The only words his father ever speaks to him are
'Good little Wolf: good little Wolf.'

The Healer of Sick Pearls

Kipling's Kim refuses to be hypnotised by Lurgan Sahib.

In the House of The Healer of Sick Pearls
devil-masks in frowst and slashed vermilion
peer through bolt on bolt of clothy stuff
scribbled with maze and golden indirection,
while voices nesting in his phonograph
make tuneless plaint of distance, dust and wax.
He floats a jug of water from his hand
which comes to rest on uncreased napery
white as that innocence once claimed for you
by tracts of garden green and crooked wigwams
for noble savages. Look at it closely.
The fired earth curves about the well of self
through which an oil lamp crazy paves the water
with tiny hieroglyphs and half-built faces.
'Now, throw it back!'

        Take it in both hands,
that dark skull throbbing over sick lightning,
and toss it aimlessly. Look, from the lip
and lazy gape, they all come sprawling:
a Palladian bridge breaks to its reflection,
scabbed urinals in a barrack block
gather their sluicing, hissing act together,
the child's toboggan shrieks into a drift
and all goes falling, falling in slow motion
while the room sobs, and all the pictures tousle.
The spectrum dies to nothing but the stain
of some slight threadbare murder on the carpet,
and little bits of gone, and gone for ever
conglobulate and rock in sparkling potsherds,
an unprovisioned fleet which lies at anchor,
scuttled by sun-glow.

                    His fingers crawl
warm at your nape. 'Look carefully,
nothing is lost, the form will not be lost,
watch how it grows, makes itself whole again.
From dust, the drowsy tilt and sway of things,
the pieces move in their attraction,
kiss and click and climb into a jigsaw
which holds the children in their cosy duffles
hauling the sled back up the snowing hill.
The lovers link their fingers on the bridge
and watch their shaken faces gazing back
from clustered black and silver, soldiers wheel
in sunlight bounced away from badge and buckle:
the old light new, and laddering the deep
unsteady, steady flux, the potter's clay
spun on a shining wheel till both are one,
the bright container and the thing contained.
See how the last piece slides into its place,
and all completed, as it was …'

                        You wrench away.
But it is smashed, smashed. Twice three is six,
and one is seven. Slates pile up arithmetic
in all the humming classrooms of the world;
the dead you loved are cleanly gone to ash
and have become the chanciness of wind,
an unremarked addition to the sea.
The bridge is down, the lovers lost in rain,
the armouries are locked and Rosebud burns,
the radiant singulars lie banked in cloud.
Why are you here, encased in sliding velvets,
pestered by faces dragging skin from shadow?
The phonograph spills out its cornucopia
of bird-brained voices into greedy moments
which die as darkly as the new ones dapple
a broken tear-flask.

                        It lies as it was thrown.
The glistening clay confirms its fracture;
that voice is yours and yet that voice is his,
the Healer of Sick Pearls who stands behind you,
his test passed and the Great Game begun.

Now that no flaw was found to fault the jewel
it is time to enter the thousands of disguise,
stretch in your skin, feral, and clean-eyed
to distinguish without impediment
the brief, distinct hexameters of snow,
count the paces between bridge and bridge,
rehearse the chosen password, slip the sentries
lounging in unfamiliar uniforms by gates
where children scuff in flimsy anoraks,
note, attentive, but incurious,
how the girl lights her lover's cigarette
then glances down the street with unlit eyes;
how, on the café table, a carafe,
jiggling the light upon your own reflections
holds water pure as a perfected absence.

Name and Nature

One of those things is out there in the wind.
It must be a cry for help,
the help you want to give when the short hairs
shiver, as Housman said,
and you're in hot water, and shaving

much too close to the wind for comfort,
gravelled for words,
the whole divine afflatus
cooling the neck's nape.
Eyes, prickle – but do not cry. For help is at hand,

O cry-for-help, caught between wind and water,
thing that would rather be said than be,
would like to die happy
out in the spell-bound garden,
covered all over in strawberry leaves

by an alphabet whirled in a puzzle of wind
which will not settle for anything less
than a cry for help
answered, as twenty-six letters
change each body terrestrial to one celestial,

though your going, as wind carries you off and away
over the syllable grass
to the syllable loss
is nothing to cry for. 'Help'
is a one word poem, and writ on water.

This Late Tempest

for Pat Williams

'Then to the elements
Be free, and fare thee well.'

Put down the book. Each syllable,
each small, unwearied fleck of shine
drowned in the long grass, will not rust.
As the island forgets them into music,
the text is lost for words,

becomes ground-bass, ground of being,
bears the burden of that song
sung to the loneliness of it all
by faces darkly horned in leaves,
those chopped ribbons of light

the moon balances on the sea.
Whatever has been abjured
or left here glinting for the wind
to hone in its beachcombing
lies patient for discovery

by hopes whose wreck is yet to come
and tongues that cut wild music
back to thickets, plots and dreams again.
Then you, discarnate, a twist
slipped from traps of cloud,

must gather up such substance
as the words, rising, crying,
can dress your absence in.
There – thunder at the sea's sharp rim.
And all begin again.

'Approach, my Ariel, come!'

Index of First Lines

Index of Titles